ALSO BY LYNN DUMENIL

Freemasonry and American Culture, 1880–1930

THE MODERN TEMPER

THE MODERN
TEMPER

AMERICAN CULTURE AND
SOCIETY IN THE 1920S

LYNN DUMENIL

CONSULTING EDITOR
ERIC FONER

HILL AND WANG • NEW YORK
A division of Farrar, Straus & Giroux

LIBRARY OF CONGRESS CATALOGING-IN-PUBLICATION DATA
Dumenil, Lynn.
The modern temper : American Culture and Society in the 1920s /
Lynn Dumenil.—1st ed.
p. cm.
Includes bibliographical references and index.
1. United States—Civilization—1918-1945.   2. United States—
History—1919-1933.   I. Title.
E169.D912   1995   973.91'5—dc20   94-47198   CIP

973.915
Dume

The lyrics from the song "My Blue Heaven" are reprinted with the permission of the George Whiting Publishing Company, courtesy of Patricia Casali.

"First Fig" by Edna St. Vincent Millay, from *Collected Poems*, HarperCollins. Copyright 1922, 1950, by Edna St. Vincent Millay. Reprinted by permission of Elizabeth Barnett, literary executor.

The lines from "Poem, or Beauty Hurts Mr. Vinal" are reprinted from *Complete Poems, 1904-1962*, by e. e. cummings, edited by George J. Firmage, by permission of Liveright Publishing Corporation. Copyright © 1926, 1954, 1991 by the Trustees for the e. e. cummings Trust. Copyright © 1985 by George James Firmage.

The lines from *The Bridge* are reprinted from *The Bridge* by Hart Crane, with the permission of Liveright Publishing Corporation. Copyright 1933, © 1958, 1970 by Liveright Publishing Corporation.

The lines from "Weary Blues" are from *Selected Poems* by Langston Hughes. Copyright 1926 by Alfred A. Knopf, Inc., and renewed 1954. Reprinted by permission of the publisher and, in the United Kingdom, by Harold Ober Associates Inc.

for Norman

ACKNOWLEDGMENTS

In the seven years it took to write *The Modern Temper*, I have been exceptionally fortunate in the assistance offered by friends, family, colleagues, students, and institutions. Grants from the National Endowment for the Humanities; the Graves Foundation; Claremont McKenna College; the Huntington Library; and the Louis and Hermione Brown Humanities Support Fund of Occidental College have aided the research and writing. I would like to thank individuals at the last three institutions—Robert Middlekauf, Gaines Post, and David L. Axeen—for their faith in and funding of the project.

I have been teaching undergraduate seminars on the 1920s for over twelve years. The questions students asked, especially those at Occidental College, forced me to clarify my ideas, and their own research often inspired me. Two served as excellent research assistants. Joshua Rose, with a fellowship provided by the Ford Foundation, was especially helpful with the chapter on work and consumption, and Jennifer Prine admirably assisted in fine-tuning at the end of the project.

Deborah Smith and Dian J. Teigler at Occidental are both models of what good librarians should be and I'm very appreciative of their efforts to obtain materials in a timely fashion. Librarians at the Huntington Library, the University of Notre

Dame, Catholic University of America, and Hebrew Union College, Los Angeles, also assisted the research.

I have been very fortunate in the people who have read the manuscript. Arthur Wang offered a contract on the basis of one chapter and has been consistently perceptive in his suggestions for revisions. Eric Foner as consulting editor for Hill and Wang made many valuable criticisms. It has been a pleasure and a privilege to work with them. Daniel Horowitz has been an invaluable supporter, offering encouragement and insights that went far beyond his perceptive reading of the manuscript in various stages over the years. Susan Glenn and I have been brainstorming and reading each other's work for many years; her comments on this book were exceptionally shrewd. Paul Boyer read a number of chapters and, as always, managed to combine infectious enthusiasm with acute perceptions. Ellen DuBois has likewise been a source of encouragement and critical insight, especially with her suggestions for the chapter on the New Woman. I benefited from many fruitful conversations with Stuart McConnell and from his thoughtful comments on the introduction. Debbie Martinson quickly and astutely read two chapters and James Halstead came to the rescue several times with advice about economic history. I am immeasurably indebted to Lawrence W. Levine, both for his meticulous reading of this manuscript and for the long-standing intellectual challenge and warm encouragement he has offered since my days as his graduate student. All of these readers embody the very best of scholarly exchange and friendship. I thank them not only for their many contributions to making this a better book, but also for remaining my friends even when at times I obstinately ignored their undoubtedly sound advice.

Many kind friends and family withstood both the gloom and the excitement generated in bringing the book to fruition. The interest and encouragement of my niece, Janet Lynn Chaney, is exceptionally meaningful to me; she is joined by Elinor Accampo, Michael B. Cohen, Nina R. Gelbart, Elliott Gorn, Gayle Green, Sheila Levine, Julia Liss, Barbara Loomis, Margie Proctor, Rita Roberts, Libby Sayre, Helena Wall, and Robert Winter, in helping to make the process more bearable.

Finally, Norman Cohen has worn two hats. As a historian, he brought his considerable expertise and intelligence to his vigorous criticism of the book in all its stages. As a mate, the depth of his love and encouragement—not to mention his outstanding culinary skills—provided a nurturing environment that sustained me at every turn. Part of the joy in finishing the book was the anticipation of dedicating it to him, with love.

CONTENTS

THE MODERN TEMPER

INTRODUCTION

"The world broke in two in 1922 or thereabouts," announced novelist Willa Cather. Journalist Mark Sullivan picked 1914, the beginning of World War I, as the point "of fundamental alteration, from which we would never go back." That these astute observers were joined by many others in offering different dates to mark the watershed of the twentieth century should call into question the historian's penchant for precise periodization. U.S. history covering the last hundred years has tended to fall into neat divisions by decade, a fate especially true of the 1920s. World War I's end in 1918 seemed a natural break, signifying the close of one era and the beginning of a new one that in turn was closed by the stock market crash in 1929. The war's timing encouraged contemporaries and historians to see a sharp break between prewar and postwar America. Moreover, it contributed to a sense that the war had been causal in transforming American cultural and intellectual life by bringing about the alienated, lost generation of intellectuals, creating the new woman, and pushing Americans into hedonism. Recent scholarship has challenged this vision; social historians in particular have made it increasingly clear that many of the changes so evident in the 1920s predated the war. The thrust of social history has been to challenge conventional periodization and to emphasize as well the unevenness of social change and the continuities that characterized the private worlds of individuals.

Why have historians persisted in viewing the period as so distinctive? Is it perhaps that historians cannot escape the fascination for the decade's drama any more than their students can lose their romantic vision of the twenties filtered through the lens of *The Great Gatsby?* In part. It is also because the richness of the newer research—on women, ethnicity, and leisure, for example—makes an attempt at a new synthesis almost irresistible. And it is because an analysis of the decade's events and concerns reveals so clearly the transformation of American culture as it emerged as a "modern" society.

In characterizing the 1920s as modern, I recognize that the essential transformations began in the late nineteenth century, with the triad of rapid industrialization, sprawling urbanization, and massive immigration. Industrial development changed the nature of work and daily life and gave rise to an extensive network of corporations that integrated the country into a national economy. The result, as Robert Wiebe has suggested in *The Search for Order, 1877–1920*, was to erode the isolation of "island communities"—the towns of antebellum America that while part of a market economy had nonetheless maintained a degree of local autonomy and order based on "modesty in women, rectitude in men, and thrift, sobriety, and hard work in both." But the spread of railroads and national corporations after the Civil War transformed American communities. The multiplication of national bureaucratic structures—of voluntary associations, professional organizations, and corporations—led to an organized society in which both individuals and communities found themselves powerfully affected by forces outside their control and increasingly removed from the locus of economic and political power.

The growth of cities added to the complexity of life, as urban dwellers experienced impersonal relationships that replaced the intimate nature of smaller communities. Skyscrapers, elevators, streetcars, and the noise of the metropolis also contributed to a more mechanized, regimented life. And despite the nationalizing trends in the economy that had a certain homogenizing effect, the cities also became bastions of cultural pluralism. A highly visible working class increasingly subjected to the power of corporate employers made urban areas the site of notable episodes of class conflict, such as the Chicago Haymarket Riot of 1886. These tensions invaded the arena of culture as well when working-class saloons, dance halls, and other leisure-time venues became the focus of middle- and upper-class elites' fears about declining morality and disintegrating social order.

These fears were closely associated with the pervasive presence of immigrants in the city. By 1900, "new" immigrants from Southern and Eastern Europe were the target of intense nativism, and in the early twentieth century, two other groups joined the streams of people migrating to American cities. Mexican immigration into the Southwest and Midwest dramatically increased in the teens, and African American migration from the South to the cities of the North accelerated with the beginning of World War I, adding still further diversity to the urban matrix.

The late nineteenth century witnessed other significant transformations. The massacre at Wounded Knee in 1890 signaled the final military conquest of Native Americans. With the displacement of indigenous people and the extension of the railroad, settlement and corporations moved west, leading historian Frederick Jackson Turner to reflect in 1893 on the meaning of the closing of the frontier. At the same time, the trajectory of conquest moved beyond the continent. Through diplomatic negotiations and the Spanish-American War, the United States had acquired an empire and become an international power, a position confirmed by its role in World War I.

Other changes stemmed from the challenges to traditional religious faith embodied in Darwinian science and the new biblical criticism that resulted in denominational upheavals for the churches and spiritual crises for individuals. Assaults on an older order emerged on the gender front as well, as working-class women increasingly entered paid employment and middle-class women began a campaign for women's rights that coalesced in the suffrage amendment of 1919. Both were harbingers of major changes in women's role and the family itself.

Many Americans were of two minds about these transformations. On the one hand, they were fearful about urban poverty, decay, and disorder. The decline in individual and community autonomy and the hardening of class lines prompted anxieties about social mobility and democratic politics. Pluralism threatened the nineteenth-century Victorian worldview that valued hierarchy, order, and a single standard of culture, morality, and values. On the other hand, many people were excited about progress. Breakthroughs in technology, the increase in material wealth, and the beginning of an empire seemingly heralded the upward march of civilization, with America in the forefront. Thus despite prevailing fears about challenges to their ordered world, for the most part Victorians remained optimistic.

In the 1920s, the same broad forces that had so powerfully transformed the nineteenth century continued the process of making America more "modern"—more organized, more bureaucratic, more complex. These continuities will be made evident as most chapters reach back a few years, sometimes a few decades, to set the stage and demonstrate that history resists clear-cut periodization. But despite strong links with the past, we can identify distinctive qualities as well. For example, the sense of unprecedented prosperity—made all the more striking by its dramatic collapse in the stock market crash of 1929—helped to give the decade its singular tone. By 1922 the country had recovered from a debilitating postwar depression and entered a period of stunning industrial productivity, neatly symbolized by auto manufacturer Henry Ford, whose use of mechanization and innovative management helped him to churn out affordable cars at such a spectacular rate that his success earned the label "The Ford Miracle." This productivity, coupled with war-inflicted devastation of European economies, made the United States the dominant world economic power. At home, most Americans enjoyed a higher standard of living. Not everyone shared in the fabled prosperity, however. Many sectors of the economy, especially farming, never truly recovered from the postwar depression, and African Americans and other minorities continued to live in poverty. In general, the aura of wealth obscured a highly skewed distribution of income that placed the bulk of the country's assets in the hands of a few. Nonetheless, the 1920s were marked by a sense of prosperity and a get-rich-quick mentality, evident not only in the stock market but also in giddy land booms in Florida and Los Angeles that reflected prosperous Americans' sense of a new era of unlimited material progress.

The faith in prosperity powerfully shaped the politics of the decade. The Progressive reform era (1900–14) that had preceded World War I gave way in the 1920s to a period of conservatism in which politicians and pundits alike celebrated Big Business as the savior of American democracy and enterprise. The period's Presidents—Warren Harding (1921–23), who died in office, Calvin Coolidge (1923–29), and Herbert Hoover (1929–33) —were Republicans who successfully identified their party with the promise of peace and prosperity. Differing dramatically in temperament and skill, they shared a commitment to promoting strong business/government cooperation that led to almost unbridled corporate power. Their approach to what they called the "New Era" underwrote a sense of complacency and preoccupation with material progress that is one facet of the characteristic tone of the 1920s.

But another key image, and perhaps the most enduring, is that of the roaring twenties—of a fast life, propelled by riches and rapidly changing social values. Dubious get-rich-quick schemes and fads like flagpole sitting contributed to a tone of feverish frivolity. Flappers dancing the Charleston and participating in a sexual revolution, movie stars in already decadent Los Angeles setting the pace for the rest of the country, and speakeasies trafficking in illegal liquor, all suggested a world far removed from Victorian restraint.

One group that contributed to this stereotype was the Lost Generation, a term used to describe the young artists and writers of the decade whose works embodied so much of the spirit of the times. Poets like Edna St. Vincent Millay celebrated the new—and sexually liberated—woman. Novelists like F. Scott

Fitzgerald and Ernest Hemingway depicted a generation's cynicism and disillusionment which seemed to explain the escapism that fueled the excesses of the jazz age. Somewhat older writers like Sinclair Lewis also figured importantly in creating the literary portrait of the twenties. Lewis's *Babbitt* serves as such an enduring critique of middle-class life that "Babbitt" entered dictionaries as a term connoting a businessman caught up in almost ritualistic consumerism and conformity. These writers made a lasting mark, shaping a scenario of the twenties for generations to come. While there is some truth to these images—especially among the urban, white, prosperous middle and upper classes —they overshadow the average Americans who led far more quiet lives and ignore those excluded from the prosperity of the times.

This depiction of the roaring twenties also obscures the complexities lying beneath the surface, especially the considerable social tensions that permeated the culture. After a major period of industrial unrest in 1919–20, in which corporations ruthlessly repressed strikes, labor was for the most part quiescent in the twenties and subject to increased regimentation. But if class conflict for the most part was muted, ethnic and racial tensions came roiling to the surface. Race riots in Chicago and other cities in 1919 signified new dynamics in urban areas that had experienced significant African American migration during the war years. Migration to the North as well as wartime military service helped to create a militant spirit among African Americans. Both the artistic movement termed the Harlem Renaissance and the black nationalism of Marcus Garvey and his Universal Negro Improvement Association symbolized what was popularly called the New Negro. Empowering for African Americans, the new spirit was unsettling to whites who wished to maintain a repressive racial order.

White Anglo-Saxon Protestants also continued to resent the rising influence of immigrants, Catholics, and Jews, and the 1920s were a particularly virulent period of nativism. The decade had been ushered in by the 1919–20 Red Scare, a product of Americans' fears that the 1919 Bolshevik Revolution in Russia might spread to the United States. That fear, coupled with the postwar wave of strikes, unspent wartime nationalism, and long-standing hostility to immigrants, led to a widespread hysteria about radicals and dissenters, with much of the focus on aliens. After a witch hunt marked by massive violations of civil liberties, the extremes of the Red Scare died down, but the animus toward immigrants did not, and Congress passed a series of laws that severely restricted European and Asian immigration. A new Ku Klux Klan modeled after the southern Reconstruction Klan contributed to the nativist furor. Targeting African Americans, immigrants, Catholics, and Jews, it spread its racist and xenophobic ideology and became a potent force in local and national politics until its demise in the mid-twenties. Nativism also figured in another distinctive facet of the 1920s: prohibition. The Eighteenth Amendment outlawing the sale of intoxicating beverages had passed in 1919, but it continued to be a highly contested issue until its repeal in 1933. Supporters viewed prohibition not only as a means of promoting morality and sobriety but as a symbol of the dominance of white Anglo-Saxon Protestant cultural values. Critics assailed it for violating personal liberties while ethnic groups resented its cultural imperialism. Prohibition persisted as a disruptive issue in politics, most notably in the 1928 presidential contest between Hoover and Al Smith, where Smith's immigrant background, Catholicism, and opposition to prohibition figured prominently in the campaign.

Specific events, people, and social movements helped to define the 1920s, but the decade was also distinguished by Americans' growing consciousness of change, a perception that a yawning gulf separated them from the world of only a decade before. World War I set the stage for this shift in tone. Older interpretations of the impact of war centered on the way it crushed the progressive reform movement that had sought to ameliorate problems of industrial, urban society. The war allegedly left in its wake disillusionment and reaction, as indicated by the Red Scare's repression of aliens and radicals. Disillusionment with war and a concomitant search for escape in amusements also suggested an explanation for the nation's retreat from world politics and the Senate's failure to ratify the Covenant of the League of Nations, Woodrow Wilson's cherished plan for an international organization to prevent future wars. In this view, Americans in the 1920s appear to be reactionary, hedonistic, and self-centered, and the stock market crash brings to an end a morality play, with the Great Depression the nation's punishment for its sins of excess and selfishness.

Revisionist historians have long since corrected this image of the jazz age (although it seems quite resilient in popular culture and memory and thus worth addressing here). The 1920s were not a period of unrelieved hedonism, nor did reform completely disappear. Partisan politics, Wilson's intransigence, and the public's ambivalence about internationalism had as much to do with killing the League as did disillusionment. Nor does World War I account for the tremendous social forces transforming American life—industrialization, immigration, urbanization, and changing patterns in work, politics, religion, leisure, and the family were in place well before 1914–18.

Yet, if the impact of the war has been misstated, it was nonetheless a major watershed that is central to understanding the decade. It contributed to the economic boom that made the prosperity of the twenties possible, and also promoted significant population movement—especially the rural-to-urban migration of African Americans, Mexicans, and native whites— thus underscoring the ethnic and racial heterogeneity of the society. Many contemporaries were also convinced that the war, by giving women opportunities in formerly male jobs, had created the liberated woman. Other popular views held that war undermined religious faith and set in motion the secular trends that many observers noted in the 1920s. Although both of these perceptions greatly overstated the impact of the war, nonetheless they point to the way in which the public viewed the war as undermining traditional values, religious faith, and sexual mores.

Indeed, "since the war" emerged as a persistent refrain that people invoked to describe a wide range of changes in daily life and cultural values. Everything from rising divorce rates, "flaming youth," African American militancy, increased standardization and regimentation, and the vogue for fads like crossword puzzles was chalked up to the war. Most commonly, Americans used it to try to pin down a troubling change in mood. From the pages of *Presbyterian Magazine* came the announcement: "The world has been convulsed . . . and every field of thought and action has been disturbed. . . . The most settled principles and laws of society . . . have been attacked." In the popular journal *World's Work*, one author announced that "the World War has accentuated all our differences. It has not created those differences, but it has revealed and emphasized them." The war, in short, became a key metaphor for major changes transforming modern civilization: a marker that helped to explain and thus make more manageable the emergence of a modern society.

A watershed of a different kind was reflected in the U.S. Census Bureau's findings that marked 1920 as the turning point of the country's urbanization: fully one-half of America's 105 million people now lived in cities. To some extent, this was a dubious statistic, since the Census Bureau used a population of 2,500 people as the cutoff for "urban," not a very meaningful measure of urbanization. But the census data formed part of the contemporary assessment of the growth and influence of cities. Observers in the 1920s had a sense—at times oversimplified—that they were witnessing an urban/rural conflict, a battle between the forces of change and the forces of reaction. Prohibition, the Ku Klux Klan, and immigration restriction were just the most well-known manifestations of this tension, and signified native white Protestants' anxious concern that the cities and the culture itself risked being dominated by immigrants and African Americans. For their part, more than ever before, African Americans and other minorities were challenging the status quo, and were demanding a pluralistic vision of American identity that would accord them cultural influence and political power.

In addition to pluralism, the cities also embodied the power of large corporations, their economic influence, and the continued transformation of work. The metropolis was also the home of mass culture—of popular magazines, newspaper syndications, advertising, and the movies. Leisure and consumption provided some of the most visible, modern changes of the 1920s. An urban, cosmopolitan culture, shaped by its pluralism and the agencies of mass culture, spread to the hinterlands and helped to promote new social values. Technology and mass production resulted in a flood of consumer products. Automobiles, electric irons, refrigerators, and radios, a fraction of the goods available to increasingly more Americans, helped to transform daily life dramatically.

The new values and new products signaled the clear emergence of a consumer culture characterized by an emphasis on leisure, purchasing, sociability, expressiveness, and personal pleasure. Changing sexual morality, modified ideas about success and how to achieve it, and mounting secularism merged with the values of consumerism to form a major challenge to the Victorian ethos of restraint, frugality, and order. All of these changes were contested, as some Americans embraced the freedom implied in the new social order while others bemoaned the corruption of the old culture. And for many, both sentiments played a part. As Lawrence W. Levine has suggested, Americans in the twenties harbored feelings of both "progress and nostalgia."

Working with the premise that the decade of the 1920s illuminates fundamental issues of the twentieth century, this book focuses on key aspects of domestic history to explore the coalescence of a modern culture. Ethnic and racial diversity and the tensions it engendered emerge as central motifs. Although there has been a tendency in the historical literature to view the response to modernity in the twenties solely from the point of view of "mainstream" (i.e., native-born, white, Protestant, middle-class) America, the influences changing American society included the increasing heterogeneity of the culture. Thus *The Modern Temper* documents the experiences of African Americans and members of various ethnic groups as they participated in forging a modern culture. Another dominant theme is the erosion of community and personal autonomy in the face of an increasingly nationalized and organized society. The growth of corporate power, the developments reshaping politics, the transformation of work, and the emergence of a mass consumer culture dramatically reshaped American life. And finally, the changing values and behavior in sexual, religious, and other private realms contributed to the shaping of a more pluralistic culture. Together, these themes not only characterize the 1920s but also form the contours of "modernity."

PUBLIC AND PRIVATE POWER

The 1920s have emerged as such a distinctive period in part because it was sandwiched between two major eras of reform, the progressive period and the New Deal. In comparison with what came before and after, the twenties seem an anomaly. Woodrow Wilson and Franklin D. Roosevelt enjoy major reputations as dynamic liberal leaders, while the chief executives of the 1920s fare less well. Noted primarily for the corruption scandals that marred his administration, Warren G. Harding delivered speeches that gave "the impression of an army of pompous phrases moving over the landscape in search of an idea." Calvin Coolidge, whose taciturnity earned him the label "Silent Cal," further contributed to the lackluster tone of politics. History has also been unkind to Herbert Hoover, whose capabilities were overshadowed by his difficulties in coping imaginatively with the Great Depression. Twenties politics seem not just stagnant but reactionary, a period in which many rejected reform and embraced big business and Babbittry.

Although the twenties did witness a reaction against social reform in a spirit of what Harding called the desire for "normalcy," the decade is not as distinct from the reform eras that framed it as might first be supposed. Many of the key political issues of the decade—if not their resolution—were the same ones that permeated the major reform eras. In particular, Americans in the 1920s grappled with a pivotal and persistent question: Given the traditions of localism, democracy, and voluntarism, where should power reside in the complex, industrial, and bureaucratic society that America had become?

This chapter explores the eclipse of reform in the 1920s as part of a broader examination of the political and economic organization of American life. During the progressive era many reformers reacted against the extraordinary power the private sector, especially corporations, had acquired. They struggled with their own ambivalence about a strong state to define a broader role for public—i.e., government—power in protecting the general welfare from being submerged by "special" interests. Despite the persistence of some reformers, in the 1920s the enthusiasm for social justice waned, and the dilemma of the relative influence of the private sector versus the public sector was resolved largely in favor of the former. The decade saw an expansion of private influence which signaled the emergence of interest group politics as a major force in the American polity. At the same time, mounting hostility to federal intervention in the economy and the lives of its citizens reflected a renewed antipathy to government power which continues to shape public discourse in our own time.

THE PROGRESSIVE BACKGROUND

Progressivism has proved a morass for decades of historians trying to delineate its characteristics and supporters. Conflicting interpretations make the complexity and diversity of the movement evident, and at least one historian called into question the utility of the term itself, arguing instead for "an obituary for the progressive movement." Most historians, however, have refused to bury progressivism. The middle-class social reformers, politicians, and intellectuals who were deeply engaged in reform efforts were convinced that they were part of a progressive movement. Its ethos grew out of the disorder that accompanied America's industrialization, urbanization, and immigration.

Swollen cities, with inadequate services and graft-ridden political machines, had resulted in urban chaos. Political corruption seemed to flourish at all levels, from city boss to U.S. senator. The extreme wealth of the new corporate elite contrasted shockingly with widespread poverty. The problems faced by the victims of industrialization—the children of the poor, and working-class men and women—began to attract an outraged middle class. Sympathy and guilt mingled with fear as class conflict in the form of industrial unrest emerged as an unsettling phenomenon. Even more disturbing was the growth of the Socialist Party in the early twentieth century. Alarmed, most of the middle class viewed this as a serious challenge to a social and political order they wanted to improve, not radically transform.

Although progressives offered a variety of analyses of the root of American problems, one of the pivotal themes of the era was the pernicious influence of special interests and private power. The trusts, a vague term that referred to monopolistic corporations, usually headed the list of problems facing the republic. They wielded not only extraordinary economic power but political power too, as muckrakers' exposés of politicians in the pockets of corporations demonstrated. Political machines were another form of inappropriate private power, as were labor unions. At issue here was the belief that private, or special, interests could subvert the general, or public, interest. Above all, progressives envisioned a harmoniously functioning society in which the general interest would triumph.

Another important problem concerned the role of state power in protecting the general interest. Although it is an oversimplification to divide progressives into neat groups, it is possible to discern two major views of government power. One group, probably the largest, identified with Woodrow Wilson's New Freedom, which called upon government action to protect the victims of industrialization, with the ideal of restoring equality and individual autonomy. This group also invoked government power to break down the worst of the trusts and promote competition. These progressives embraced governmental solutions, although they did so with the greatest ambivalence. Drawing upon a long tradition of hostility to government power, they

worried that public power could be just as damaging to individual freedoms as private power.

Another element in progressivism, often associated with the
New Nationalism of Theodore Roosevelt (1901–9), was far more
accepting of the general trend toward organization and the consolidation of federal and state power. The nationalists felt that
the benefits of scale and centralization could be the source of
widespread prosperity. They had a strong belief in efficiency
and experts. As Robert Wiebe has pointed out, many of the new
middle class were themselves turning to more centralized, powerful voluntary associations to rationalize their professions and
give them influence on public policy. As reformers, they sought
to bring order to American society and adjust it to the exigencies
of the modern world by promoting an activist state that would
regulate corporations, direct the economy, and protect the interests of workers and consumers. Unlike the Wilsonians, they
were far more sanguine about state power, viewing it as a necessary antidote to unharnessed private power.

Many progressive reforms indeed resulted in an expansion of
government power and bureaucracy, but they also reflected the
Wilsonian ambivalence toward state, especially federal, power.
Often laws gave government agencies quite limited authority or
inadequate enforcement procedures that considerably weakened their ability to regulate. Nonetheless, at the time progressives viewed their advances optimistically and pointed proudly
to a wide range of legislation. Social justice or humanitarian laws
spanned the range from milk codes, public health laws, workmen's compensation, and child labor laws, including a federal
child labor law. In the cities, good government reformers campaigned to break the power of the machines. Other political
reforms were the direct election of senators, initiative, referendum, and recall, and the use of the secret ballot. Women's suffrage also formed part of progressivism. Reformers touted all of
these political innovations as vehicles for restoring democracy
and limiting the ability of special interests to control politics.
Finally, on the national level, Congress enacted numerous laws
that at the time were promoted as progressive triumphs over
corporate financial interests: in 1906, the Meat Inspection Act,

the Pure Food and Drug Act, and the Hepburn Act, which regulated railroads; in 1913, the Federal Reserve Act to regulate banking, and the Sixteenth Amendment, which provided for a federal income tax. The 1914 Clayton Antitrust Act, which replaced the largely ineffective Sherman Antitrust Act of 1890, was also hailed as a progressive victory. With the exception of the income tax, all these measures set up commissions, staffed by presumably neutral experts who would determine social needs without damaging the basis of prosperity.

For decades, historians took progressivism at its word and depicted the legislation that emerged as part of the effort to restore democracy and control the trusts. Now it is evident that the coalition of groups that supported the era's reforms did not always have the same agenda as self-described progressives. Revisionist historians have made it clear, for example, that much of the corporate legislation had the strong backing of some members of the business community who hoped to use the agency of the federal government for their own purposes. Urban and school reforms provide further evidence that progressivism was far more complex than its leaders' democratic rhetoric would suggest. Business elites often embraced a city manager system and political redistricting as a route to a more efficient city that could serve their needs more adequately. Similarly, they supported the drive to centralize public education. All of these reforms tended to limit the influence of workers, African Americans, immigrants, and the poor, who in the older system had a greater personal identification with their local city government representatives and school board members.

The efforts to minimize the voting influence of ethnic groups and workers in the cities indicate a social control aspect of progressivism that was evident in other reform sentiment as well. Prohibition, which was more controversial among progressives than other measures, nonetheless had strong support from both urban and rural progressives, who viewed it as a means of improving individual lives and industrial productivity. But prohibition, which entailed the coercive use of law to control behavior, also had very strong nativistic underpinnings. Not all progressivism was nativistic, but as both prohibition and the urban political and educational reforms indicate, there was a strong undercurrent throughout the movement to use the law to control and assimilate immigrants to American Protestant morality and standards.

Not surprisingly, ethnic and working-class voters had ambivalent responses to progressive legislation. They tended to oppose the nativistic and elitist trends in the movement, but nonetheless in many cities they comprised an important core of support for reform, especially social justice laws such as factory or tenement legislation. Farmers also sometimes constituted part of the progressive movement, especially in their support for laws limiting corporate power, or those directly affecting their own interests. Thus, undergirding the progressive movement lay an unstable coalition—businessmen, farmers, labor, immigrants, and the middle class—each with a different agenda that reflected its own concerns. The rubric of a general interest that pervaded progressive rhetoric proved elusive.

The contradictory strains within progressivism evident in nativism, elitism, the differing agendas of reforms' supporters, and diverging attitudes about government power also appeared in the way progressives responded to World War I. Many reformers were dismayed by the U.S. entry into the European conflict in 1917, although in the nationalistic climate of the time, relatively few voiced their opposition publicly. Some progressives, suspicious of the trusts, worried that the war would only serve the interests of corporate profiteers, while society paid in lives and money. Wilsonian progressives, always fearful of federal power, correctly anticipated that the war would unleash a nationalistic spirit which would undermine civil liberties and be inimical to reform. But other progressives, many in the Roosevelt New Nationalism camp, were far more optimistic about the potential of war for furthering reform. Seduced by the rhetoric of a war for democracy, they hoped that America's participation in the war effort would be a means of bringing American democracy to the world. On the domestic front, they expected that the wartime emergency would cause the federal government to expand its power in behalf of reform.

In 1918, as the war proceeded, Congress passed a war tax,

which tentatively seemed to point the way to the use of taxation to redistribute income. After a massive transportation breakdown, the government also assumed control over the railroads, which encouraged progressives who viewed this as the entering wedge of government planning of the economy. Railroad workers benefited from federal administration of their industry. Moreover, the government's efforts to maintain price ceilings and control wages and hours of defense employees indicated the possibilities for government protection of working people.

But for the most part, war did not further the domestic reform agenda, in large measure because of the fear of extensive government power. This fear affected the operation of most of the war agencies set up to handle the problems of mobilization. Future President Herbert Hoover, as wartime food administrator, resisted coercing farmers or consumers and relied upon voluntarism to effect conservation and the production of food. The War Industries Board, the major agency charged with coordinating the production and distribution of war matériel, also had little coercive power. Instead, financier Bernard Baruch, its director after March 1918, used his personal influence and the threat of negative publicity to keep corporations in line with government need. This voluntaristic approach of wartime agencies led to a strong sense of government/business cooperation that tended to benefit the corporations. Economist John Kenneth Galbraith accurately described the war years as "massive informal cooperation between government and organized private enterprise."

Thus World War I, whatever hopes progressives had for it, served primarily to promote the organization of corporate power and to link it more closely to cooperation with government. The ideas evident among corporate leaders who had supported some progressive reforms gained substantial ground in the war years. Increasingly, government, as it expanded its influence, served as an instrument to help rationalize businesses and as a mediator between conflicting interest groups. In the process, the progressive idea of the general interest got buried under the weight of special interest power.

THE FATE OF REFORM

The war not only fell far short of progressive expectations; it was also among the factors that extinguished the widespread support for reform. The war disillusioned many progressives. The violation of civil liberties was a serious blow to men and women committed to liberalism, and the coercive nationalistic spirit that encouraged a search for traitors challenged progressives' belief in the rationality of human beings, as did ultimately the total war experience. Moreover, the way in which corporations seemed to benefit from war discouraged reformers who continued to mistrust special interests and insist that their power be curtailed. Finally, disappointment with the Peace of Paris, which did not meet with the lofty aspirations of Wilson's Fourteen Points, made it clear that war had not accomplished any progressive international aims.

But despite the war's undoubtedly negative impact on the reform spirit, when the conflict drew to a close in 1918 optimistic Reconstruction Plans were afloat everywhere, as reformers like Sherwood Eddy looked forward to the postwar period as a "permanent and moral equivalent of the war; in a task infinitely harder and grander, the winning of a new world." The Catholic Church, for example, offered the Bishops' Program of Social Reconstruction, an ambitious document that focused primarily on the protection of workers by promoting "industrial democracy." Many other religious bodies, including the Federal Council of Churches and the Central Conference of American Rabbis, offered similar comprehensive plans for a more just social order. Secular reform organizations, ranging from the Women's Trade Union League and the American Association for Labor Legislation to the National Conference on Social Agencies and Reconstruction, also proposed ambitious agendas that included federal aid to education, conservation, city planning, government loans for home building, insurance and pension plans, civil rights, and laws to establish "industrial standards." Women's peace organizations such as the Women's International League for Peace and Freedom also began what would be a long-standing effort to oppose militarism and promote peace. Thus, despite the discouragements the war brought, many reformers hoped to be able to translate the international victory to a domestic one. The optimism of the immediate postwar period did not last long. The Red Scare, with its insistence that Bolshevism posed serious threats to American institutions, painted most reform with a radical pigment, and reformers knew early on that they would have to struggle against powerful odds to implement their goals. Nonetheless, throughout the 1920s reform efforts persisted. A circle of reformers clustered in a variety of organizations, especially women's groups such as the League of Women Voters, and journals like *The New Republic* and *The Nation* continued at the center of liberal reform thought. For the most part, these advocates for social justice supported moderate, piecemeal reforms, and met with some successes as state legislatures enacted child labor, health, and workmen's compensation laws. Nationally, reformers pushed for a federal child labor amendment after the Supreme Court had invalidated two federal laws. This effort, as well as a campaign for federal aid to education and for the establishment of a federal department of education, failed. The only national success was the Sheppard-Towner Maternity Act, which provided matching federal-state funds for care of dependent mothers and infants until the program was phased out at the end of the decade.

Liberal reformers operated at the periphery of the era, but radicals were even more isolated and marginalized. Severe repression during the war and the Red Scare had crippled many left-wing organizations and periodicals, especially damaging the Socialist Party and the Industrial Workers of the World. Although the Communist Party emerged in 1919, it was tiny for most of the decade. *The New Masses*, founded in 1926, was the major radical vehicle, and constituted an important venue for a small coterie of writers like Michael Gold, Max Eastman, and Genevieve Taggard. Only occasionally did the left and liberals come together in common cause. The trial and dubious conviction of anarchists Nicola Sacco and Bartolomeo Vanzetti for bank robbery and murder in 1921 sparked a wave of protest. Reformers and radicals as well as artists and writers joined forces in an impassioned but futile campaign to halt the two men's execution in 1927.

Early in the decade, many discontented progressives came together, often with more radical elements such as socialists, in a variety of campaigns to bring about a resurgence of progressive political strength. Farmer-labor parties were active in many states. Political efforts gained ground with the establishment in 1922 of the Conference for Progressive Political Action. Started primarily by the railroad unionists, it called for nonpartisan support of progressive candidates, and garnered backing from farmers, consumers, old reformers, socialists, and some elements of organized labor. The 1922 elections saw the defeat of many conservatives and the rise of progressive elements in the states and in Congress. When Robert M. La Follette, a major leader of prewar progressivism, arranged a conference of progressives in 1922, thirteen senators and twenty-three representatives joined other reform leaders to call for a program "to drive special privilege out of the control of the government and restore it to the people." Progressives were too divided a group and too few in number to implement their program in Congress; nonetheless, their swing votes proved critical in blocking some administrative measures that reformers opposed.

The disposition of the Muscle Shoals controversy is a good example of progressives' tiny victories. During the war, the federal government had acquired nitrate and power facilities at Muscle Shoals in the Tennessee River valley. After the war, the Republican administration was more than willing to grant a long-term lease for the Muscle Shoals development to private enterprise, and the first prospective buyer, Henry Ford, negotiated an exceptionally favorable deal. The power industry, worried about Ford's competition, opposed the plan, but a group of enthusiasts for publicly owned power, led by progressive senator George Norris, offered the major congressional opposition. Although the latter group failed in its campaign to establish Muscle Shoals as a site of federally produced power, it did succeed in blocking private development of the area that would later boast the New Deal's Tennessee Valley Authority, which not only produced hydroelectric power but was the Depression decade's most comprehensive effort at government planning. This link between the 1920s and the New Deal suggests that the decade was an important bridge between the two major reform eras.

The progressive bloc of the 1920s, however, foundered quickly. In 1924, La Follette ran for President on the newly established Progressive Party ticket. Although he received the endorsement of the American Federation of Labor, as well as many progressive groups, and garnered five million votes, his candidacy and that of other progressives were buried in a Republican landslide that left the conservatives within the Republican Party in command of Congress. Many congressional Democrats who had been relatively progressive in the first few years of the decade took their party's overwhelming defeat as a rejection of reform and turned more conservative in the post-1924 period. The few progressives who remained in Congress found themselves increasingly isolated.

Although progressives were weak, especially in Congress, it was possible to see in the 1920s the emergence of a new type of reform leader who would later be identified with urban liberalism. One of New York's congressional representatives, Fiorello La Guardia, an immigrant politician of lower-middle-class origins with roots in party machine politics, called for a wide range of reforms that later would comprise elements of the welfare state. Although La Guardia, elected by a primarily immigrant and working-class constituency, was a Republican, more typically it was Democrats who began to make headway in the urban centers, building especially among new immigrant voters. These voters were opposed to immigration restriction and prohibition, both of which they increasingly identified with the Republican Party, especially after the 1928 presidential election that pitted Al Smith against Herbert Hoover. In addition to challenging the nativism of Republicans, many urban Democratic leaders also campaigned as proponents of social reform. As governor of New York, Al Smith, a product of Tammany Hall, and thus anathema to many progressives, nonetheless pursued a variety of reforms while in office during the 1920s. He supported efficiency and economy in government, expansion of workmen's compensation and public health legislation, conservation measures (including state parks), and efforts to use state funds to promote more housing for lower-income families. By the end of the decade, the Democratic Party had not yet emerged as a party of reform, but much of the groundwork had been laid for a new coalition of voters who would support urban liberalism.

Although we can see hints of the coalition of urban liberals that was to characterize the New Deal and the emergence of the welfare state, in the 1920s many progressive leaders had themselves retreated from reform, and much of the public seemed indifferent. The causes for this declining enthusiasm are myriad. One, as we have seen, is the impact of war, in particular the way in which it undercut idealism, deflected energies away from reform, and encouraged at least in some Americans the cynicism so often associated with the postwar generations of youth. Another source for the decline was the splintering of the reform movement: the war exacerbated its fragmentation into a variety of interest groups which pursued their own course. Still another way of understanding the fate of reform in the twenties is to explore what happened to the attitudes toward public and private power that had been such a crucial part of progressivism.

ANTISTATISM

In contrast to the progressive era, the 1920s were characterized by strong hostility to government, especially federal, power. Antistatist sentiment permeated the decade: newspapers, journals, and congressional debates reverberated with stories of the evils of federal government expansion. Critics of federal power emphasized bureaucracy, using the word as shorthand to invoke images of a pervasive and pernicious federal presence that strangled local and individual initiative. These critics linked federal regulatory boards, the Sheppard-Towner Maternity Act, the department of education bill, the proposed child labor amendment, federal highway programs, agricultural extension, women's suffrage, and prohibition as parts of a ubiquitous trend of encroaching federal power. Reflecting both the heritage of war and the Red Scare, they argued that at worst this trend would lead to Prussianism or Bolshevism, at best to bureaucratic paternalism that would standardize American society and rob individuals of their freedom and self-reliance.

What were the sources of this renewed and intense hostility to federal expansion? Most obviously it stemmed from the federal system as well as long-held and deep-seated fears of state power generally, and federal power specifically, that formed an important part of the American political tradition. But the 1920s version of hostility to federal power was not just warmed-over rhetoric about the various states' sovereignty. Responding to an expanded federal government, the new vocabulary focused on the more modern evils of bureaucracy and a paternalistic welfare state. In the post–World War I years the ambivalence toward federal power, always evident in some strands of progressive thought, became pronounced among many former reformers. Senator William E. Borah, a self-professed progressive, vehemently attacked federal bureaucratic power. A well-known opponent of the education bill, he also opposed the suffrage amendment and the proposed child labor amendment, all on the grounds of states' rights and opposition to bureaucracy. The "remorseless urge of centralization, the insatiable maw of bureaucracy," he wrote, "are depriving more and more the people of all voice, all rights touching home and hearthstone, of family and neighbor. There is not a practice, custom, or habit but must soon be censored from Washington." Still other reformers were disillusioned about the wisdom of expanded federal power. Journalist William Hard, for example, complained about "governmentalization," in part because so many federal regulatory agencies were controlled by the interests they had been designed to regulate.

Outside the circle of reformers, predictably enough, the business sector furnished much of the criticism of expanded federal activity and power. For many businessmen the issue was economy in government: the desire to reduce federal expenditures emerged as one of the reasons business groups such as the Chamber of Commerce and the National Association of Manufacturers opposed the education bill. Critics were particularly disturbed about the double tax burden that they claimed matching federal and state funds incurred. They complained that not only did expanded federal services cost money but also legislation such as the Smith-Lever Act for agricultural extension and the education bill was "class" legislation, financial aid for special interests at the taxpayers' expense. In addition to the desire for economizing, other business elites, responding to both progressive reform and wartime federal accretion of power, were anxious to stymie further efforts to expand federal control over the economy.

Leading politicians of both parties also seized upon the issue of recent federal expansion with "states' rights" emerging as a potent political slogan. President Coolidge gave a widely publicized states' rights speech in 1926, but perhaps the most vocal advocate was Maryland's governor, Albert Ritchie, who repeatedly called for resistance to the ubiquitous centralizing tendency, explaining that the call for states' rights is "the call to resist unwarranted encroachment of every kind by the Federal Government upon the sovereign rights of the states and the guaranteed liberties of their people." Surprisingly, Ritchie's advocacy of states' rights did not draw upon the specter of federal intervention in southern patterns of segregation, although other politicians occasionally invoked this theme.

The experiences of the war also profoundly shaped widespread suspicion of federal bureaucratic power. Despite the government's attempt to use voluntaristic methods as much as possible, business, labor, farming, and the general public experienced the long arm of federal regulation of fuel, prices, food, and transportation. Individual liberties were curtailed and dissent repressed, both by the government and by local voluntary associations backed by federal authority. And certainly, young American men felt the weight of federal presence, as they were conscripted, mobilized, and subjected to a battery of psychological and physical tests. While the press and the government's propaganda agency, the Committee on Public Information, represented the country as wholeheartedly behind the government's war effort, there were pockets of resistance and resentment. This was particularly true of the food conservation program and the draft. Thus, given the enlarged federal presence, it is not surprising that critics of the education bill and other reforms would invoke the wartime experience. In opposing the education bill, Senator Charles S. Thomas argued, for example, that the "red tape, multitudinous officials, and inefficiency" in "matters military" had brought the problems of bureaucracy to the attention of the country and made it clear that increasing federal agencies and power proved no solution. And in 1919 a member of the House of Representatives, speaking out against a proposal to extend the war measure of daylight saving time, argued that if the government continued its wartime expansion, "we might soon have laws passed attempting to regulate the volume of air a man should breathe, suspend the law of gravity, or change the colors of the rainbow." Although the encroachment of federal power during the war may have been temporary, by expanding government power and in particular by bringing its bureaucracy into the lives of ordinary Americans, the war brought the issue of federal power to heightened public consciousness. And if the war fueled anxiety about federal power, the subsequent Red Scare stoked the fire. For victims of the 1919 hysteria—dissidents, immigrants, and organized labor—the potential for federal repression was considerable. Conversely, widespread anxiety about Bolshevism and socialism made other Americans particularly susceptible to rhetoric linking social reform to un-American "isms."

Prohibition also fueled diverse groups of Americans' suspicion of federal power. Indeed, it may well have been the pivotal factor that gave federal paternalism and bureaucracy such weight. The leaders of the repeal movement were elite men such as New York senator James Wadsworth and the industrialists Lammot, Pierre S., and Irénée Du Pont, whose concerns centered on social disorder and federal expansionism. Working through the Association Against the Prohibition Amendment, they stressed not only individual rights but states' rights, insisting that the Eighteenth amendment violated the spirit of the Constitution and American traditions. Similarly conservative were the Sentinels of the Republic, a group composed of well-respected elites such as Columbia University president Nicholas

Murray Butler and Solicitor General James Beck, and the fanatical, less respectable, antifeminist Woman Patriots. These groups, along with a variety of lesser-known associations, linked their opposition to prohibition with a wide-ranging list of welfare legislation endorsed by the so-called woman's lobby, including the child labor amendment and the Sheppard-Towner Maternity Act, and the education bill. They criticized all these measures not merely for violating states' rights but for being the precursors of socialism and Bolshevism.

In addition to offending these conservatives, prohibition also brought federal law into the lives of millions, and was the more objectionable because of the perception that a well-organized minority had imposed it upon a hapless majority. Hostility to prohibition shaded into resentment of other attempts to legislate morality, such as movie censorship and laws requiring that places of business stay closed on Sundays. Immigrant, Catholic, and working-class people had for decades been exposed to Protestant middle-class reformers' attempts to legislate morality through local and state laws. Progressivism and nativism had been closely linked. Recognizing some reform agendas as attacks upon their culture, religion, and way of life, immigrants were no strangers to suspicion about state power, but national prohibition, viewed as the ultimate nativist reform, gave their suspicions about government power national focus.

At the other end of the spectrum stood urbane cosmopolitans who chafed against what they viewed as the puritanical streak in 1920s culture. The humor magazine *Life* bristled with articles and cartoons condemning the efforts to legislate morality. The "Moral Life" described the regimented day of a future citizen in 1989 when "the Society for Moral and Efficient Existence" had succeeded in passing its reforms through constitutional amendment. A typical cartoon featuring a gaunt, grim-faced puritan expressed similar sentiments. Wearing a badge reading "film censorship" and holding a volume entitled "Blue Laws," an anti-tobacco sign on his arm and a seltzer bottle labeled prohibition at his feet, he represented "a government of the censor, by the censor, for the censor."

Many Americans, then, Catholic and non-Catholic, immigrant and native, viewed prohibition not as an isolated example, but rather as a way of legislating morality and conformity through federal power. It was the fact of prohibition that made it possible for opponents of other reform legislation to draw in a larger segment of the population and insist on the potential revolutionary impact of expanding federal legislation and agencies.

On a more abstract level, the deep-seated fear of federal bureaucracy with its standardization and conformity, its threat to individual and local control, bespoke a concern for lost community and personal autonomy. With the increased integration of the economy and the decline of "island communities," Americans had every reason to be distraught about lost autonomy. There was a degree of irony in this litany about the baneful effects that federal expansion and bureaucracy would have on individual and local autonomy. Certainly Americans in the 1920s had reason to be suspicious of federal agencies and bureaucrats. What is surprising is not that the public worried about the effect of federal power on American traditions of individualism and democracy, but rather that they worried so little about the implications of private, corporate power for these traditions. The progressive era had been characterized by a pervasive distrust of private power. Perhaps the greatest measure of the collapse of progressivism was this reversal on the issue of private and public power.

PRIVATE POWER AND THE APOTHEOSIS OF BUSINESS

This change from the prewar period's deep suspicion of corporate power was striking. It would have been unthinkable that a progressive era President could say, as Calvin Coolidge did, "The man who builds a factory builds a temple. The man who works there, worships there." Certainly hostility to "the interests" persisted, as the five million people who voted for La Follette suggest, but the overall tone set by leaders in the twenties was one that elevated business and businessmen to an idealized position, almost an apotheosis, captured succinctly in a 1921 *Independent* article: "Thru business properly conceived, managed and conducted, the human race is finally to be redeemed."

The war was one of the sources for the redemption of business. Businessmen and public spokesmen encouraged Americans to view big business as a major partner in the successful war effort: not only had it produced the matériel needed to win the war, but it had done so cooperatively and patriotically. The official historian of the War Industries Board, Grosvenor B. Clarkson, summed it up succinctly: "The Commodity sections were business operating government business for the common good." The Red Scare further enhanced big business's tarnished image. In the midst of widespread hysteria about Bolshevism's threat to American institutions, the business community presented itself as the major bulwark against revolution. Corporations' successful suppression of strikes, which their spokesmen insisted were part of the communist menace, further indicated business loyalty to American institutions and to law and order.

As was evident during the war and the Red Scare, the business sector was highly sensitive to its public image, a concern that stemmed in part from the lessons learned during the progressive era. Business leaders hoped to deflect unwanted regulation by cleaning up their image. They hired public relations firms to flood the media with positive accounts, while their spokesmen lectured incessantly on the new business creed. One of the catchwords of the time was "service," which Joseph Wood Krutch described as a "characteristically American nebulosity." A widely used term, in the business community it meant a devotion to public welfare that gave social responsibility at least an equal role with profits as the raison d'être for private enterprise. It appeared extensively in advertising: meatpacker Armour and Company, for example, announced that it "seeks public good will. Its business is to serve." The slogan also formed part of the vocabulary of small businessmen, associated with clubs like Rotary, who indicated their commitment to service through civic activities. At the same time a movement to establish codes of ethics in various businesses flourished. The

Chamber of Commerce of the United States presented its standards of business conduct to which 750,000 organizations and 300,000 individuals had subscribed by 1925. Corporate executives also jumped on the service bandwagon. Charles Cason, a vice president of Chemical National Bank, exulted: "The best upper class men in business are really genuine in their belief in [service] and are consistent in its practice. Most of them would not consider a policy which enriched them or their company and was at the same time against the public interest." Other corporate spokesmen fine-tuned the idea of service to argue against government regulation and to justify large business enterprises. Thus in *Business in Politics*, Charles N. Fay cautioned against "throwing a governmental monkey-wrench into the complex, powerful, high-speed machinery of trade; whose smooth control alone makes it possible to give that maximum service, at minimum cost, which alone *creates* big business."

The "service" idea could be so persuasive in part because of the rising prosperity of the period. As we will see in the following chapter, many Americans did not participate in the fabled good times of the 1920s, but there was enough money and consumer products around to give the impression of widespread affluence. And who but business could be responsible for it? The mass media, largely accepting of business propaganda, made it abundantly clear that corporations were the source of American well-being. The enjoyment of prosperity by the middle class was particularly important. It helped deflect that group's interest away from the need for social reform and made it more readily convinced of business's beneficence and its contribution to law and order. Thus, many could agree with Boston department store magnate and "business progressive" E. A. Filene that "the modern business system, despised and derided by innumerable reformers, will be both the inspiration and the instrument of the social progress of the future." Enthusiasm even spread to a feisty spokesman of labor. John L. Lewis of the United Mine Workers voted for both Coolidge and Hoover and announced in 1925 that "distrust and hostility toward the business system wanes as it is becoming better understood how the general prosperity and individual and family welfare of modern peoples has been insured by the use of capital in production to multiply the productive power of man's labor, whether of hand or brain."

The idea that prosperity depended upon giving business free rein also appeared in the election of 1924. The Republicans, largely ignoring the Democratic candidate, John W. Davis, used the slogan "Coolidge or Chaos" to warn against the election of La Follette, whose progressivism they pictured as threatening to economic stability. Historian David Thelen argues that many voters—the middle class, farmers, and laborers—influenced by this analysis, gave their votes to Coolidge, "unwilling to risk the 'chaos' that a real threat to large-scale corporations might pose to the economic growth that provided their jobs and markets."

The results of business's restored reputation were significant. Presidential candidate Warren G. Harding's conviction, summed up in the title of a 1920 magazine article, captured the tone for government business relations in the decade: "Less Government in Business and More Business in Government: The Need for a Closer Understanding Between American Government and American Business, and the Economic Benefits That Will Follow It." Under sympathetic Republican administrations that sought to assist business and believed in its beneficence, the idea of using government power to contain corporate power largely faded. The antitrust division of the Justice Department still continued to institute suits, but many of them were against smaller businesses or labor unions. Although 14,000 complaints were filed during the decade, the department investigated fewer than 1,200. Of these, 350 cases were resolved with consent decrees, by which the Justice Department and the company met privately to establish what was acceptable under the law. The company then agreed to uphold the law and received no punishment for its infractions. Another aid to monopolistic practices included the 1918 Webb-Pomerene Act, signed by Wilson and widely used in the 1920s, which explicitly exempted firms in the export trade from antitrust laws by permitting monopolistic combinations. The efforts by trade associations to minimize competition within an industry through price control agreements got support from the Supreme Court in 1925 in the Cement Manufacturers' Protective Association and Maple Flooring Manufacturers' Association cases, which upheld trade associations' practice of sharing price information as long as their explicit goal was not price fixing.

Big corporations also benefited by the way in which Republican Presidents staffed the various regulatory agencies established in the prewar years with members of the business community the agencies were supposed to regulate. One of Coolidge's appointments to the Federal Trade Commission was William Humphrey. A man noted for his hostility to the commission itself, Humphrey announced that he would make it "a bulwark instead of an oppressor." Under Humphrey, the commission worked with trade associations to establish ethical codes, rather than attempt to investigate or police industry. The change in personnel and attitude within the regulatory agencies thus accomplished what business supporters of regulatory legislation had hoped for—government agencies responsive to corporations' effort to rationalize and limit competition. But it was far from what most progressives had anticipated. In an article in *The Nation* (which two other periodicals had refused to publish), Senator George W. Norris argued that the change in regulatory commissions had set the country back twenty-five years. "It is an indirect but positive repeal of Congressional enactments. . . . It is the nullification of federal law by a process of boring from within."

Progressives were also disappointed by revisions in tax law. The Sixteenth Amendment (1913) had held out the promise of an income-distributing tax, and wartime tax laws seemed to point in that direction. During the 1920s, Secretary of the Treasury Andrew Mellon, one of the world's richest men, repeatedly sought to reduce business taxes dramatically. In 1921, Congress repealed an excess profits tax and reduced the maximum surtax to 50 percent, but at the same time increased the corporate profit tax rate from 10 to $12^1/_2$ percent, thus pleasing and displeasing Mellon. In 1925, after the Progressive Party debacle, Mellon obtained more of his tax agenda. Congress reduced the surtax to 40 percent, the estate tax to 20 percent, and repealed the gift tax altogether. In addition, provisions which made income tax returns public were repealed. In 1928, corporate taxes were reduced slightly, to 12 percent. Mellon's policies thus led to a major tax savings for wealthy individuals and corporations.

Other business-inspired legislation included the Fordney-McCumber Tariff of 1922. Business interests were, of course, not monolithic, and international firms did not want high tariff barriers, while domestic firms did. The resulting compromise legislation set the tariff at one of the highest levels in U.S. history, but the bill also included a provision for most-favored-nation status, which extended tariff concessions to those nations which treated U.S. exports favorably. Elsewhere on the international front, the government assisted corporations in expanding their markets and developing sources of raw materials. For example, the government consistently sought to help American corporations break down other countries' monopolistic control of raw materials. In the case of Britain's control of oil in Iraq, the State Department's intervention enabled American firms to purchase 25 percent of the British concession and to form an international cartel, the Iraq Petroleum Company. The government also used diplomatic, economic, and military pressure to protect U.S. interests in Central America. Firms such as United Fruit dominated the economies and often the politics of Guatemala, Haiti, Honduras, Nicaragua, and Santo Domingo. Although in some instances the government used subtle pressure to maintain policies acceptable to U.S. corporations, it also employed troops in Nicaragua, Honduras, Haiti, and Santo Domingo to maintain stability and governments friendly to U.S. corporations.

Thus both domestically and internationally there was exceptionally close government/business cooperation, so close that *The Wall Street Journal* could exult: "Never before, here or anywhere else, has a government been so completely fused with business." One of the major architects of this fusion was Herbert Hoover. Although he did not become President until 1929, he was Secretary of Commerce from 1921 until his election, and from this position he made some of his most important marks on American history. A mining engineer and self-made millionaire, Hoover had extensive public service behind him, including organizing the Belgium relief drive during the war. He brought to his position in the Commerce Department a vision of what Ellis Hawley has called "the associative state." Acutely conscious of the need to bring order and predictability to the business cycle to assure permanent prosperity, Hoover envisioned government-assisted cooperation between businesses which would eliminate wasteful and inefficient competition, and thereby help to provide "freedom from those fluctuations from boom to slump which bring on the one hand the periods of unemployment and bankruptcy and, on the other, speculation and waste."

Hoover believed that the ideal mechanism for this cooperation was the trade association, a voluntary group that could bring order into each segment of industry and commerce by cooperating in such areas as product standardization, accounting methods, wages, and prices. Although Hoover emphasized that the private sector would accomplish this organization of the economy without federal coercion, he nonetheless felt that government had a special role in assisting the process. Assistance took several forms. As Secretary of Commerce, Hoover tried to get advance agreement from the Justice Department that trade associations which exchanged price information would not be liable to prosecution under antitrust laws. He was given no guarantee, but the point became moot when in 1925 the Supreme Court upheld the right of trade associations to publish prices. In sectors of the economy where no association existed, the Commerce Department called conferences and sent out mailings which resulted in new organizations. Although Hoover's department was not responsible for all of them, national associations did expand dramatically under Hoover's approving eye. In 1919, there were 700 in the country; by 1929 when he became President, there were over 2,000.

Hoover also restructured and dramatically expanded the small Commerce Department. The number of employees tripled and its annual expenditures rose from $860,000 to $5 million. It also established fifty international offices, where attachés worked with members of the State Department to collect and distribute information about foreign markets for American firms. Domestically, the department published a vast amount of statistical information, including the Census Bureau's *Survey of Current Business*, to assist firms and trade associations in organizing their industries. The department's Bureau of Standards also encouraged rationalization of products and standardization of industrial measures and tools that had begun during the war. Finally, one of Hoover's most significant innovations was the reorganization of the Bureau of Foreign and Domestic Commerce, which he divided along commodity lines, appointing as chief for each commodity section an official usually selected by the trade association involved. It was this sort of development that led journalist William Hard to note approvingly in 1928 that "Mr. Hoover has evolved the public-private department. He has evoked the private-public citizen." Hard's observation succinctly expressed the heart of Hoover's associative state and its blurring of the lines between the public and the private sector.

Hoover was untroubled by the pseudo-public power the government vested in trade associations, because he so deeply believed in the public-spirited quality of American private enterprise. As he explained in 1928: "Our whole business system would break down in a day if there was not a high sense of moral responsibility in our business world." This faith in business's commitment to service shaped Hoover's sense that coercive control by the government was not necessary. His ideas about limiting government intervention in the economy were also molded by a deep commitment to American individualism, which he defined in his 1922 book of the same title as each individual's "equality of opportunity to take that position in the community to which his intelligence, character, ability, and ambition entitle him." Throughout his career Hoover often expressed hostility to a large, centralized state and to bureaucracy which undermined individualism: "You cannot extend the mastery of the government over the daily working life of a people without at the same time making it the master of the people's souls and thoughts." But despite this rhetoric of antistatism and hostility to bureaucracy, Hoover's efforts in the Department of Commerce were responsible for expanding government bureaucracy and involving the state far more intimately with the economy.

Although there were undoubtedly inconsistencies in Hoover's philosophy, he nonetheless emphatically denied that his programs undermined individualism or democratic ideals. He insisted that the bureaucracy he created was not like others; it was efficient and was responsive to the people it served—e.g., the business community. By promoting industrial self-government it actually limited the expansion of government itself. Moreover, Hoover believed that because the Commerce Department did not use the coercive power of the state, it did not undermine American traditions. According to Hoover, the beauty of trade associations, which were merely assisted, not controlled, by the government, was that they maintained the principle of self-government. Finally, Hoover expected that the activities of the Commerce Department were transitional, and that government could retreat once it accomplished its aims of establishing a mechanism for stabilizing the business cycle. For Hoover, public power was alarming, but private power was not.

Hoover's views were widely shared by America's political and business leaders. Given this favorable climate, it is not surprising that in the 1920s American corporations increased their organization and expanded their economic power. With government indifferent to antitrust laws, consolidations and mergers proceeded unhindered. In manufacturing and mining, over 1,200 mergers took place during the decade, and over 8,000 firms disappeared. Bank mergers also increased dramatically. In 1919 there were 80 mergers; in 1927, over 259; by 1929, 46 percent of the country's banking resources were controlled by 1 percent of the banks. In the same year, 200 corporations owned approximately 20 percent of the nation's wealth. Oligopoly reigned. In the meatpacking industry, for example, four firms controlled 70 percent of the production. The process even extended to the movie industry. In 1912, more than sixty companies made movies, in contrast to the "Big Eight" that produced 90 percent of the films in the early twenties. These firms controlled not only the making of the films but their distribution as well by acquiring theater chains. As movie mogul Marcus Loew put it: "Chain store methods in the movies are just like what you had in railroads, telephones, and automobiles." Internationally, American firms also dominated the world market. General Electric controlled most of the world's major electric manufacturers; American Telephone and Telegraph cornered the telephone equipment market, and the Ford Motor Company had a virtual monopoly on tractors.

Thus American corporations achieved untold economic power in the 1920s, and with it came political power as well. The giant corporations—U.S. Steel, Standard Oil, and the like —were large enough to work independently with government agencies. Others exercised their influence through rapidly growing trade associations. The business sector found numerous channels for shaping public policy and manipulating government for its own advantage.

THE NEW LOBBYING

The possibilities for the exercise of private power so evident in the trade associations were linked to another important development in the twenties—the emergence of what contemporaries called the "new lobbying." Of course, there was nothing new about lobbying itself, but in contrast to the older, informal, and secretive methods of nineteenth-century lobbyists, who primarily represented individual corporations, the new lobbying was institutionalized, public, and conducted by voluntary associations. It first emerged as a significant phenomenon in the early twentieth century and its growth mushroomed during World War I, as hundreds of organizations, including trade associations, labor unions, and reform societies, flocked to Washington to establish permanent lobbies. One observer in the 1920s insisted that "the lobbyists were so thick they were constantly falling over one another." Another reported accurately that the "growth of organizations has proceeded to the point where scarcely a line of activity—industrial, commercial, social, religious, political, patriotic, fraternal, or what not—is not represented by a national association." By the mid-twenties, over 150 groups had offices in the capital, although contemporary assessments suggested that probably only sixty or so were generally effective at winning legislative goals. Undeniably part of the political fabric, the new lobbying met with mixed responses as observers variously viewed it as the savior and nemesis of American democracy.

Various factors encouraged the growth of the new lobbying. The progressive movement was one catalyst. By expanding the role of government in the economy, by establishing commissions, regulatory boards, and the like, reform created a situation in which more groups had reason to wish to influence public policy. "The hand of the government is felt more acutely than ever before," as one lobbying expert, E. Pendleton Herring, put it. "Business is forced to take an active interest in the activities of the powers at the capital." The expansion of government in World War I also promoted the new lobbying. Government agencies worked with the new trade associations as well as with the American Federation of Labor, the Federal Council of Churches, the National Catholic War Council, and a variety of other private associations, as a means of coordinating the war effort. This cooperation helped to legitimate pressure groups, as well as providing experience in negotiating in Washington that would serve lobbyists well in the postwar years.

The task of selling the war to the American people, as it was implemented by the Committee on Public Information set up by advertising specialist George Creel, also contributed to the shape of future efforts to influence public policy. Edward B. Logan, another lobby investigator, credited the committee with extensive influence: "No doubt much of the recent activity in applying high power salesmanship and propaganda methods by groups owes its origin to ideas derived from knowledge of the work of the Bureau of Public Information during the war." Other models came from two of the most successful campaigns ever: the drives for prohibition and women's suffrage. The Anti-Saloon League and the National American Woman Suffrage Association stood as excellent examples of voluntary associations which achieved their political goals through well-organized pressure politics.

The final source of the new lobbying—at its most basic—was the ever-increasing organization of American society. The economic concentration first evidenced in major corporations engendered the drive of other economic groups—for example, small businessmen in the Chamber of Commerce, less powerful corporations in trade associations, and workers in labor unions —to organize for their protection. Moreover, as economic life became more complex and centralized, community autonomy diminished dramatically. For those people whose economic or professional identity gave them a national rather than a local focus, community became less associated with place, and more socially constructed. The result was a multiplicity of communities defined by shared interests based on economic goals, professional status, cultural or religious perspectives, gender, ethnicity, or race. Lobbyists for these diverse communities focused on a wide range of issues—from tariffs to ethnic defense, from social reform to foreign affairs, from prohibition to its repeal. All shared the goal of using their voluntary associations to achieve political power.

They also excelled in the newest techniques of influencing public opinion and officials. Most legislative agents—the term "lobbyist" was rarely used because of its older association with corruption—had a card-file system for keeping detailed records on members of Congress. An important part of the lobbyist's job took place in the increasingly significant congressional committees, whose decisions on bills often determined their success in Congress. For these hearings, legislative agents arranged for distinguished witnesses to present their side of the issue, and assembled masses of "scientific," fact-filled information to persuade committee members of the validity of their stance. This ability to present detailed analyses was a crucial part of their activity, for congressmen inevitably relied upon the reams of material put out by trade associations and other groups in making their decisions. As experts, legislative agents often drew up the bills themselves, and placed them in the hands of friendly legislators. Finally, lobbyists pushed beyond Capitol Hill in putting pressure on legislators as they became adept at distributing propaganda in support of their measures. By giving the appearance of a groundswell of grass-roots support—often achieved through a well-orchestrated letter-writing campaign—lobbyists could subtly or not so subtly threaten retaliation at the polls.

Not surprisingly, lobbies designed to promote the economic interests of their members were the most numerous and powerful. Workers' associations, which ranged from the American Federation of Labor to the National Federation of Federal Employees, had relatively little impact in this period. In contrast, a variety of powerful institutions looked after the concerns of business groups. In addition to the growing presence of trade associations, business interests were represented by the National Association of Manufacturers and the Chamber of Commerce. The latter, which brought together relatively small businesses compared to the industrial giants, in 1928 represented 876,152 companies, and gave as its purpose, "to obtain the matured judgment of business on national questions and to present and interpret those views to the agencies of government and to the public." The national chamber put out a monthly journal, *The Nation's Business*, conducted referenda on important issues, and had a research division which investigated legislative issues in great depth and distributed to its members a bulletin "which contains 'up-to-the-minute' information as to the activities of governmental departments, bureaus, and commissions of concern to business." Because the national chamber consisted of thousands of local chambers of commerce, it could present itself as a representative body of American businessmen, and used its significant voice of authority to influence congressional action.

Of the powerful business interests represented by the new lobbying, perhaps the most tenacious was the public utilities industry. Public utilities almost by definition were monopolies, and were increasingly knit into an oligopolistic industry by mergers and combinations. Highly organized lobbies on both state and national levels were determined to protect the industry's profits and resist publicly owned power schemes. The campaign to develop Muscle Shoals as a federally owned power plant and a similar plan for the Colorado River brought the power companies out in full force. A 1928–29 congressional investigation of the power trust, as it was called, revealed an extraordinarily well-organized campaign against publicly owned power. The National Electric Light Association coordinated state associations of power companies, which spent more than a million dollars a

year and distributed thousands of pamphlets and other literature. As one observer put it: "Information flowed out through
the press, through schools, the pulpit, the lecture platform, the
radio, the motion picture, agents, books, and other methods.
The plans were in one way or another to reach every man,
woman and child." Newspapers, often owned by power companies, or beholden to them because of massive advertising
budgets, ran favorable stories and editorials written by power
company spokesmen whose authorship was not acknowledged.
Well-known speakers were subsidized privately to speak or write
against public ownership of utilities. Colleges were given large
grants to promote the sympathetic study of power: Harvard's
Graduate School of Business Administration received an annual
subsidy of $30,000; Northwestern received $25,000. And in some
schools, individual professors were subsidized as well. Finally, in
the public schools, power companies conducted an even more
energetic propaganda campaign in which they insinuated their
viewpoint into classrooms and textbooks.

Contemporary observers, noting the public outcry against the
power trust, argued that it had overshot its mark, that their excesses had put it in disfavor. While it is true that the power trust
received unfavorable publicity, the major criticism of its actions
seemed to be its secrecy, not its extraordinary influence per se.
The power trust ultimately lost its campaign to control Muscle
Shoals and the Colorado dam, both of which were publicly developed in the 1930s. However, in the long run the extensive
propaganda campaign, which distributed material touting the
inefficiency of public ownership, undoubtedly had a significant
impact on ideas about public and private ownership, and helped
to create an environment which praised private industry and
was suspicious of government power.

The American Farm Bureau Federation (AFBF), the national
association of farmers which the federal government had assisted in organizing during World War I, was yet another powerful presence in the capital. By 1928, it represented forty-five
state bureaus which claimed between one and one and a half
million American farmers. Just as the Chamber of Commerce
insisted that it represented American business, the AFBF

claimed to be the voice of all American farmers, and used similar methods to influence legislators. In its early years (1920–23), under the direction of its Washington agent, Gary Silver, the AFBF was exceptionally effective. As one observer put it: "The power [Silver] has is an enormous one, and the pressure he can bring to bear upon Senators and Representatives from the 'folks back home' . . . is almost irresistible." In 1921, Silver helped to organize the congressional farm bloc, an informal group which included over twenty senators from farming regions, who sought to have government aid agriculture in ways comparable to its assistance in industry. Although the farm bloc was of short duration—the 1924 elections ended its cohesion—it passed a significant number of acts that Silver and other farm spokesmen promoted. In 1922, Congress enacted the Capper-Volstead Act, which legalized farm cooperatives. In 1923, in response to the dire need of farmers for more flexible credit, it passed the Agricultural Credits Act, which set up twelve farm credit banks under the control of the Federal Farm Loan Board, which could make loans to farm cooperatives. Other legislation included regulation of packers and stockyards, a futures trading law to help curb speculation in farm commodities, and concessions to farmers in the Fordney-McCumber Tariff.

Although the farm bloc itself lost steam, the AFBF persisted throughout the decade and beyond in agitating for farm relief. By 1925, its major legislative agenda was a plan for price parity, which was eventually termed McNary-Haugenism after the senator and congressman who introduced the plan to Congress in 1924. The plan was proposed by farmers of major commodities such as wheat and corn to contend with the high production that exacerbated the problem of glutted internal and domestic markets and resulted in declining prices. While most of the country had pulled out of the postwar depression, the agricultural sector lagged behind, and only gradually improved after 1923. For the rest of the decade, farm conditions varied throughout the country and among the different classes of farmers. Significant poverty characterized the lives of many farmers. For others, low prices and indebtedness made it difficult to share in the higher standard of living that much of the country so conspicuously enjoyed. The perception that farmers were the backbone of the nation, a survival of Jeffersonian ideology, gave added impetus to farmers' outrage and their insistence on government intervention.

The McNary-Haugen solution to the problem of low prices and high volume was a plan to raise farm prices to the point where they were equivalent to farmers' purchasing power in the prosperous prewar period. The initial idea was that whenever prices of any of the eight major commodities fell below that prewar level, the Secretary of Agriculture could set in motion a plan whereby surplus products would be dumped abroad at the world (presumably low) price. The losses entailed would be made up by an equalization tax on domestic sales, which with the removal of the surplus could be sold at a high price. It was in effect a device for the federal government to guarantee farm prices.

Midwestern and southern cotton farmers strongly supported the bill, arguing that this government cooperation in price fixing was nothing more than what government already did for major businesses through tariffs and other forms of assistance. McNary-Haugenism represented for them "Equity for Agriculture." By 1927, they had generated a significant amount of support and Congress passed a slightly revised McNary-Haugen bill, which was vetoed by President Coolidge. The process was repeated in 1928. Although the AFBF had managed to develop significant clout in Congress, it had not gained as much ground with the Republican Party leadership. The AFBF was not as powerful as many of its critics—usually representatives of business interests—claimed, but it certainly laid the groundwork for the massive assistance given agriculture by the New Deal. By that time, the AFBF was as powerful as its detractors had claimed it was in the 1920s, and one could speak of the AFBF as the representative of big agriculture.

Professional associations also sought government assistance for their goals. The American Medical Association and the American Bar Association were among the most important. The National Education Association (NEA), another significant group, had engaged in sporadic and halfhearted lobbying in the late nineteenth century, but did not wholeheartedly embark on the new lobbying until 1918, when, like many other groups, it established a new national headquarters in Washington, D.C. After the war, the NEA's major legislative focus was on getting Congress to pass the Smith-Towner education bill. Although an important part of the goal was indeed to improve education, enthusiasm for the bill also stemmed from the benefits it would give to teachers—in improved salaries and even in improved status for teachers.

The NEA efforts throughout the 1920s in behalf of the education bill provides an excellent example of the new lobbying. Charl Williams, its major lobbyist in these years, conducted an extensive publicity campaign that included mass mailings as well as exhaustive speaking tours. She maintained a card file on congressmen and kept in close contact with sympathetic members in Congress, who in turn advised the NEA on strategy. Williams and other NEA officials also coordinated the support of other groups, soliciting resolutions, publicity, and appearances at committee hearings on the bill.

Part of the organizational support the NEA brought in was from the Women's Joint Congressional Committee, which was popularly called the women's lobby. At its peak, the committee encompassed twenty-one component institutions. Among the charter members were the League of Women Voters, the General Federation of Women's Clubs, the Women's Christian Temperance Union, and the Women's Trade Union League. At the behest of five member organizations, the WJCC would set up a lobbying committee for specific legislation and then coordinate efforts. Throughout the decade it supported legislation to protect women as well as a wide variety of social reforms.

In the first half of the decade, women activists were highly optimistic about the power of organization to achieve their goals. Spokeswomen referred proudly to themselves as having made lobbying respectable. They worked in the open and insisted that their efforts were not selfish, but rather in the general interest. Maud Wood Park, the leading female lobbyist of the period, argued that senators and representatives "rather pride themselves on having it known that they are voting in the way the women want them to vote," and furthermore insisted:

> The women's lobby is a "front-door" lobby. It works in the open and is effective by reason of the millions of women behind it. Seventeen national organizations of women have representatives who work for legislation of interest to women generally regardless of political affiliation. They make no secret of it, for publicity is one of their three tremendous assets. The millions of voters behind them and the inherent common sense of the bills they push are the other two.

Despite their optimism, after some initial successes in the beginning of the decade, women lobbyists found their programs blocked and their influence diminished. Reforms they had supported, including the education bill, failed to pass. But despite its short-lived power, the women's lobby was extremely significant as part of the process by which the new lobbying emerged and eventually became legitimated.

The list of voluntary associations eager to make their influence felt on issues other than economic ones was a long one. The Anti-Saloon League continued its campaign for prohibition by lobbying to strengthen the enforcement of prohibition and in resisting the efforts of groups like the Association Against the Prohibition Amendment to end "the noble experiment." The American Legion campaigned in behalf of its version of super-patriotic nationalism, but also attempted to further the economic interests of its members by lobbying for a soldier's bonus. A variety of national ethnic and religious organizations fought against the restriction of immigration. The National Catholic Welfare Council opposed the federal department of education out of fear that it was designed to restrict Catholic education. The NAACP lobbied for an antilynching bill. Outspoken militancy was common as leaders of these associations strongly insisted on their right to organize, usually on the ground that self-defense required it. But, unlike the women's lobby, most were uneasy about being identified with lobbying. For example, in private correspondence, Father John Ryan urged that Catholics establish a lobbying group and hire a legislative agent, but that they do so discreetly since "the American public opinion would not take very kindly to a Catholic legislative bureau." Catholics' caution reveals both their vulnerability and the perception that pressure group politics were still far from legitimate, especially when conducted by minorities who had yet to establish their "Americanness."

Contemporary assessments reveal this ambivalence about the expansion of pressure groups. Some observers invoked familiar progressive ideology about the evils of private power. *The Nation*, a journal closely associated with progressivism, was the most outspoken in this regard. In a 1929 article entitled "Lobbying Good and Bad," the editors made a distinction between lobbying in the public and the private interests, arguing that "Washington ought to be full of lobbies, only they ought to represent genuine public interests, not mere private and personal ones, and they ought to do their work honestly and openly." In the opposite ideological camp were critics of lobbying who reserved some of their strongest criticism for the lobbyists who had implemented "paternalistic" reforms. An outspoken female critic of the women's lobby harshly criticized women for "so gayly [sic] doing what we can to destroy our own and our fellow citizens' constitutional freedom; doing all that we can, through the multiplying of bureaus and the strengthening of bureaucracy, to change our government into a democratic autocracy." In a similar vein, critics complained that organized minorities—prohibitionists, representatives of ethnic and religious groups—used unfair and un-American organized pressure to implement their goals. For the most part, criticism sparked by the various congressional hearings into lobbying activity in the 1920s concentrated on the issue of secrecy. There was relatively little overt complaint about the power per se that organized groups were able to acquire. Rather, the objections concentrated on the methods that lobbyists used to achieve political influence.

Although some observers criticized the new lobbying, others approved, viewing it as an inevitable part of modern society.

Not surprisingly, business representatives most stridently defended the new process of influencing public policy. Defenders repeatedly emphasized the idea that lobbies served the public interest. In particular, the expert knowledge that legislative agents provided lawmakers was essential in responding to the complexity of modern legislation. In a 1929 *North American Review* article, Oliver McKee, Jr., a prominent supporter of the new trend, praised the public service that group representation made possible, arguing that "the great lobbies, time and again, have helped Congress frame necessary and beneficial legislation," and that these groups were "the clearing house for the views of the 'best minds' in the particular group concerned." McKee further argued that the new lobbying ultimately promoted democracy. "Lobbies give these economic groups a representation in the National Capitol, and thus help to broaden the bases of our democracy."

But it was not just business spokesmen who viewed the possibilities of lobbying so positively. In *Politics: The Citizen's Business* (1924), progressive journalist William Allen White insisted that lobbying should be regulated, but was optimistic about its democratic potential. Arguing that "this new government is easily accessible. One has but to reach out his hand to become effective in it," White believed that "Democracy never was so near the people as it is in the United States of America" today. Political scientists also held a brief for the new lobbying, although they were not as uncritical as more popular enthusiasts were. E. Pendleton Herring worried about the way in which the general interest could be lost in the groups' struggle for their own aims. Nonetheless, he felt that the complicated nature of society meant that group representation was necessary. By the end of the decade, as historian Daniel Rodgers has noted, many political scientists were beginning to reject the notion of a general interest that had so shaped progressive era thought, and were insisting that government's essential function was in essence the working out of conflicting group interests.

This conception of the role of government was to be implemented in the New Deal. Although neither Franklin D. Roosevelt nor his advisers consciously planned it that way, by the end of the New Deal observers were describing the federal government as a broker state, mediating between the interests of the country's major economic groups: business, agriculture, and labor. The post–World War II years saw the continuation of the legitimation of interest groups, with many political scientists celebrating "interest group liberalism." In an analysis that evoked some of the defenses of the new lobbyists in the 1920s, political scientists like Robert Dahl insisted that interest groups served democracy by offering new forms of representation. Noting that the majority of organized groups were voluntary associations, which observers assumed had mechanisms for democratic representations, some political scientists claimed that individuals obtained their political voice through their associations. Furthermore, the fact that so many organized special interests existed helped to prevent any one group from becoming too influential, thus providing an important check on power. Even with this analysis of the value of interest groups, complaints about the existence of private power—especially its ability to corrupt legislators—surfaced periodically. But as Grant McConnell has pointed out in his seminal work *Private Power in American Democracy* (1966), the critique was never very persistent, for it was undercut by Americans' deep-rooted suspicion of government. While nervous about the influence pressure groups and corporations could have, Americans were far more anxious about "big government." Thus they could view the proliferation of private power groups—presumably voluntaristic and democratic—as a check on public power, rather than an abuse of government power for private ends. Here, then, was a means of governing a complex nation that seemed far less alarming than expanded government power.

In the 1920s, this legitimation of private power groups had just begun. There was still enough residue from the progressive era's complaint about the "interests" to create concern about "class" legislation, as it was so often called. Observers were particularly critical of the "organized minorities" represented by ethnic groups and prohibition associations. Both types of organizations were described as asserting an "un-American" pressure which undermined majority rule. There was less criticism of business lobbying in the 1920s, undoubtedly because of the beneficent reputation big business maintained for most of the decade. Moreover, it had defenders like Herbert Hoover, who constantly praised the associative state and insisted that business organization was in the general interest.

Whether Americans welcomed the new lobbying or not, it was a political fact of life. The 1920s saw the systematizing of lobbying that caused a permanent change in the political process. Congressmen, especially those serving on important committees, were subjected to an intense barrage by legislative agents, as were administrators on various regulatory commissions. In a position to present "expert" facts, legislative agents drafted or heavily influenced legislation and commission decisions; they changed the face of lawmaking. The intensive indirect lobbying—through well-orchestrated propaganda campaigns in local, state, and national media—also represented a significant development, and provided those with enough money and influence to reach the public with a means of obtaining exceptional political leverage.

It is undoubtedly true that the new lobbying did provide greater representation to voices other than big business, which had so dominated the late-nineteenth-century polity. In varying degrees, farmers, ethnic groups, workers, among others, were eventually to use pressure politics to their advantage. But it would be a mistake to accept the assumptions of those political scientists who argued that interest groups promoted a new form of democracy. Organizations that allegedly represented their constituents democratically were usually in fact highly oligarchic, and decisions were made by small numbers of people at the top of the hierarchy. There is little basis for viewing them as an extension of democracy. Moreover, enthusiasts for interest group liberalism overlooked those who were not organized. Thoughtful commentators in the 1920s were aware that the vast majority of Americans were not part of the associative state, and in particular the poor and working classes were the least likely to have influence in the new "democracy."

A related problem was the impact new-lobbying groups had

on political participation. In the late nineteenth century, voter participation had been high: 79 percent of the electorate had voted in 1896, but after that election participation steadily declined. By 1904, observers began to note a falling-off in voting (65 percent), which continued in the 1920s, with national elections at around 49 percent, except for the 1928 election (57 percent), which pitted Smith against Hoover over the highly volatile issues of religion, ethnicity, and prohibition. Michael E. McGerr has characterized the 1920s as a "massive political withdrawal." This was especially true in the South, where the turnout was as low as 20 percent, but the North also witnessed a decline to 58 percent in presidential elections. The nonvoters tended to be the poor and new voters—women, African Americans, and naturalized immigrants.

The major reason for voter apathy was the decline in party identification, which had been intense until the 1890s but had begun to erode by the turn of the century. The intensity of popular politics, which included torchlight parades and public theater, had served to socialize young men into political partisanship and voting, and, moreover, had been an expression of local community. But such popular politics were discouraged by reformers in the late nineteenth and the early twentieth centuries who insisted that parties were corrupt and failed to address significant issues. Progressives who wished to unseat city bosses and to restore government to "the people" often concentrated it in the hands of the "best citizens," and brought about a new political style which discouraged the rank and file by putting a distance between them and their representatives. Moreover, progressive innovations such as the referendum and recall and direct election of senators undercut political party organizations. The rise of independent journalism, made possible by technological innovations in printing, also spelled an end to party-controlled newspapers which had helped to maintain political party identification.

Many other factors eroded partisan identification. As elites organized in professional and kindred associations based on economic and other shared concerns, they weakened localism. Moreover, finding political parties based on geographical representation unsuited to their needs, they turned to interest groups as a means affecting public policy. In doing so, they diminished the importance of the political parties. The relationship between interest groups and parties was dialectic: the decline of parties also created a void into which pressure groups quickly stepped. Daniel Rodgers has argued that "as the intense partisanship which had drawn nineteenth-century Americans to the polls in massive numbers began to erode, swamped in a bombardment of new stimuli and appeals, the political arena was thrown open to extraparty pressure groups of all sorts."

Pressure groups had another impact on political parties and voting. As they grew in strength in the twentieth century, they encouraged a sense of the individual voter's political powerlessness. Numerous observers of lobbying discussed this phenomenon. Donald Wilhelm, in a highly critical 1925 article, "The Washington Soviets," argued that lobbying "operates to disfranchise the individual citizen so unfortunate as to be unrepresented by any one of them," and concluded: "It is probably because the average citizen has half-consciously sensed his individual impotence that less than sixty per cent of us take the trouble to cast our votes." The increasing dominance of government by special interests was one of the factors that alienated twentieth-century Americans from the political process.

The 1920s, then, bring into sharp relief many key issues of twentieth-century American politics—the decline in partisan voting, the mechanisms of lobbying, and the shift from localism to a more national orientation. In the development and legitimation of interest group politics, the decade pointed the way to future political dynamics. The decade's reaction against reform, and more importantly its intense hostility to federal power, also shaped political discourse. The reform ethos has ebbed and flowed, but antistatism, solidified by the debates of the 1920s, has remained a constant, acting as a constraint on public policy even during periods of social reform. Moreover, the specter of encroaching federal power and bureaucracy continues to be an extraordinarily potent political symbol. As in the 1920s, its constant invocation deflects serious consideration of the power of the private sector, while serving as a convenient rhetorical device for tapping anxieties about individual and local power in a modern, organized society.

WORK AND CONSUMPTION

In an early scene in King Vidor's 1928 film *The Crowd*, the camera dramatically pans up a New York City skyscraper, then takes the viewer through a window into an office full of men, each at identical desks performing identical tasks. The camera stops at John, the protagonist, who had vowed when he was orphaned at twelve that *"I'm going to be somebody big."* But John is simply part of the crowd, a disappointed white-collar slave, lost in a bureaucratic mass society. At one point, in frustration, he quits his job and nearly destroys his marriage. A caption concludes: "We do not know how big the crowd is, and what opposition it is . . . until we get out of step with it." Vidor not only sketches the grimness of low-level white-collar work; he also portrays its compensations. Throughout the movie, John and his wife, Mary, participate in a consumer culture. Their first date is a delightfully filmed romp through an amusement park, where they enjoy themselves immensely on rides, in a hall of mirrors, and in the tunnel of love. On their honeymoon trip, they flip through a magazine and study the advertisements, fantasizing about a home they hope to own in the future. When John wins a prize for composing an advertisement slogan, he brings home presents for his family, and together John and Mary dance around the drab apartment, gleefully holding John's purchases above their heads. Finally, the film ends with John's determination to get new work, however lowly, and win back his family. Together, they go to a vaudeville theater. We see them laughing uproariously, then the camera slowly moves back and exposes the entire audience, a mass of people all laughing just like John and Mary.

The Crowd provides excellent testimony to the emergence of America as a consumer culture. It not only highlights the way in which people turned to leisure and consumption to find satisfaction in life, but also suggests one important causal factor: the degradation of work and the erosion of individual autonomy in a mass, corporate culture. The twenties are a critical period for these transformations, for the decade embodies much of what constitutes consumer culture: the cornucopia of material goods; an occupational and corporate structure that limits individual autonomy; and a shift in behavior and values away from the Victorian "production" ethos of work, restraint, and order, toward one that embraces leisure, consumption, and self-expression as vehicles for individual satisfaction.

Complex patterns underlay the solidification of the consumer culture in the 1920s. First of all, to analyze its appeal, we need to go beyond standard explanations that emphasize disillusionment with war and reform, and beyond the fact that more products existed and that Americans had more money and leisure in that decade. We must follow King Vidor's path and look at the flip side of consumption and leisure: work. And not just work in and of itself, but its relationship to America's increasingly powerful corporations, and in the context of the nationalization of the American economy. Since the majority of women still did not labor outside the home, the problem of work and alienation was still primarily a male dilemma. But more women were working in the 1920s (see Chapter III) and, moreover, they shared with men participation in an urban-dominated society powerfully shaped by mass culture and the corporate structure. For both men and women, issues related to the place of the individual in a transformed society had resonance. A second key factor is that Americans experienced the consumer culture filtered through the lens of class, ethnicity, and race. Not everyone was on the consumer bandwagon; not everyone experienced it in an identical fashion. Blue-collar and white-collar workers' worlds diverged in significant ways. In varying degrees, however, both groups found in the consumer culture an antidote to the loss of power in the modern world, to the problem of hierarchy, routinization, and standardization.

THE BLUE-COLLAR WORLD OF WORK

The experiences of blue-collar workers, especially those employed in manufacturing, provide the clearest example of the processes leading to the consumer culture. The 1920s bring out in sharp relief the extent to which work became regimented and alienating, as innovations like the assembly line and scientific management spread and contributed to the deskilling of labor. In addition, especially in contrast with the gains of organized labor in the preceding decade, the 1920s marked a period in which union strength declined and corporations extended their control over the shop floor and workers themselves. Finally, although generally limited in the amount of consumption they could engage in, blue-collar workers produced the goods that fueled the general prosperity of the decade.

The flowering of the consumer culture was made possible by exceptional industrial productivity. A few numbers tell the tale. In the period 1910–20, industrial production rose 12 percent, but for 1920–30, the rate was 64 percent. A variety of industries led this boom, most notably the automobile: the number of cars produced annually rose between 1919 and 1929 from 1.5 to 4.8 million. That industry in turn stimulated the production of steel, glass, gasoline, and rubber. The chemical industry, boosted by World War I, flourished in its aftermath. New home construction, including suburban tract dwellings, further stimulated the economy, as did the extensive road construction which accompanied the nation's burgeoning love affair with the car.

This enhanced productivity resulted in part from technological developments. By 1929, 70 percent of industries had been electrified, compared with only 30 percent in 1919, a growth that transformed the factory floor and made production far more efficient. Many of the devices that electric motors ran were the ubiquitous new machines that cut production time and labor costs. In textiles, a warp-tying device eliminated ten to fifteen workers per machine, and in the automobile industry, a new machine that painted the decorative stripe around the chassis replaced ten men. Electrification and mechanization were crucial to the decade's 72 percent increase in the amount of production per worker, a process that allowed manufacturers to produce substantially more with a workforce that remained constant. In addition, technology decreased the need for skilled workers, as the machine substituted its precision and power for the worker's craft, a process most pronounced in the great mass production industries—autos, rubber, steel, textiles, and electrical products.

For many observers, the moving assembly line, first introduced by Henry Ford in 1914, was the epitome of mass production's transformation of the nature of work. Prior to 1914, a team of men worked on one car and finished it; with the innovation in place, men remained stationary and the car itself moved. For the company this meant tremendous productivity: by 1928 the Ford factory turned out 6,400 Model A's a day. For the workers, the moving assembly line made work simplified and repetitive. Hugh Grant Adams, an Australian who was one of many foreign observers who trekked to America to witness firsthand the miracle of mass production, was appalled at the dehumanization of what he called the chain gang:

> At 8 a.m. the worker takes his place at the side of a narrow platform down the centre of which runs a great chain moving at the rate of a foot a minute. His tool is an electrically-driven riveter. As he stands, riveter poised, the half-built framework of the car passes slowly in front of him. . . . Once, twice, he plunges the riveter down upon the hot metal . . . once, twice . . . once, twice . . . and so on for six, eight or ten hours, whatever the rule of the factory may be, day after day, year after year. . . . There is not a job on the

mass-production chain more complicated technically than that. The chain never stops. The pace never varies. The man is part of the chain, the feeder and the slave of it.

The assembly line represented not so much technological innovation as it did organizational development—i.e., the more systematic management of machines and their tenders. The drive for system, for efficiency, was encapsulated in Frederick W. Taylor's term "scientific management." In the prewar years, Taylor had been the major proponent of bringing system to the factory. Convinced that efficiency was possible only if management could expand its control over the shop floor and the work process, he insisted that decision making, planning, and implementation be removed from foremen and workers and shifted to professional engineers who could effect "the deliberate gathering in on the part of those on the management's side of all of the great mass of traditional knowledge, which in the past has been in the hands of workmen." Although there were many components of Taylor's system, among the most important was the time-motion study in which the engineer, stopwatch in hand, would time a work process to determine its maximum speed and procedure. Management then gave workers explicit instructions as to method and speed. Relatively few firms followed the Taylor system exactly, but the general ideas of specialization, systemization, and managerial control did spread and were commonplace by the 1920s. The process was not yet complete, but throughout factories and sometimes even offices and department stores, managers in the 1920s were encroaching on worker skill and autonomy.

The drive for efficiency also invariably seemed to result in the speedup, which forced workers, paced by a machine, to labor at a faster pace for the same amount of money. In textile mills, for example, the "stretch-out," as workers called it, which became commonplace in the twenties, required workers to operate more looms and other machinery than ever before. In 1929, resentful workers in a Gastonia, North Carolina, textile mill used public theater to express their displeasure with both their superintendent and the stretch-out. They held a parade featuring a coffin with an effigy of the unpopular superintendent. As historian Liston Pope described it: "At intervals. . . . the effigy would sit up and shout: 'How many are carrying this thing?' The marchers roared: 'Eight.' To which the effigy answered: 'Lay off two; six can do the work.' "

Technology, organization, and scientific management, then, coalesced to create a workforce that was not only less skilled but more vulnerable and subject to greater control and authority. Of course, not all workers experienced the extremes of mass production routinization. Agriculture continued to be transformed by technology, but in crops resistant to mechanical innovation, like cotton and vegetables, a significant percentage of farm laborers, especially African Americans and Chicanos, continued in older patterns of backbreaking hand labor, combined with oppressive labor management. Although mechanization had touched coal mining and construction, in the 1920s workers in these sectors overwhelmingly still labored by hand. Their work was arduous and dangerous, but their environment was less subject to the control of machines, supervisors, and stopwatches.

Even workers who were machine tenders did not share identical experiences. Skilled craftsman in industries that no longer needed their specific skill suffered the most in terms of a decline in skill, autonomy, and status. Unskilled newcomers to industry—rural migrants and immigrants, for example—had few factory skills to lose, but nonetheless must have found the new routinized environment and long supervised hours harsh. With little control over the process, it is doubtful that they found much satisfaction in their work. Contemporary accounts of the period often elaborated on the alienation of the machine tender. Economist Sumner Slichter reported that an old lathe hand revealed that at the end of the day "you don't feel as if you'd accomplished anything. And you haven't. You've just made a horse of yourself so someone else can take things easy. You ought to be put in a stable and fed just like a horse."

Some workers attempted to fight back. There are sporadic accounts of spontaneous work stoppages in the face of the speedup or wage cuts. Workers also often resisted time-motion studies. One of the informants in *Like a Family: The Making of a Southern Cotton Mill World,* a study of mill workers in North Carolina, recounted: "Twice, when a time study man showed up at Arwin Mills in Durham, workers insisted that 'they did not want to be studied' and pushed him out a window." Perhaps more common was the deliberate effort to fool the engineer by surreptitiously slowing the pace of production. Stanley Mathewson, an unsympathetic observer who in 1931 examined workers' techniques to restrict output, concluded that "the efforts of managers to speed up working people have been offset by the ingenuity of the workers in developing restrictive practices." Mathewson probably exaggerated how successful workers were in their struggle to retain some power on the shop floor, but it was true that the battle for control was far from over. However, their position had been undercut. Behind the managers stood increased corporate power, a pro-business climate, and technological and managerial innovation. This relegated workers to what David Montgomery has aptly characterized as guerrilla warfare, their various efforts at sabotage constituting "a submerged, impenetrable obstacle to management's sovereignty."

Most workers did not turn to unions, one obvious means of fighting managerial sovereignty. The decade was a bleak time for organized labor, especially compared with what came before and after. World War I had followed years of industrial strife and union agitation, with significant success for the house of labor, and with war's end labor unions continued to grow, so that by 1920 they had doubled their prewar numbers. The widespread strikes of 1919 grew out of inflation and war-generated expectations. They fought for increased worker control, union recognition, and improvements in wages and hours. Although most of these strikes were unsuccessful, organized labor entered 1920 militant, with membership at its high point of 5 million, or 18.6 percent of the labor force. From that point decline set in, and by 1923 there were only 3.6 million unionized workers, a downward trend not significantly reversed until the early 1930s. This weakness was underscored by the fact that the majority of these members were concentrated in five main sectors: printing, public service, transportation, building, and theaters.

Most mass production industries—automobiles, food packaging, steel, textiles, electricity, and rubber—remained impenetrable.

Yet another set of statistics indicates the weakness of the labor movement: the number of strikes steadily declined during the decade. For the period 1916–21, they averaged approximately one hundred per year; in 1920–25, the number was thirty-four; and in 1926–30, eighteen. Although fewer strikes erupted, some industries and areas experienced persistent labor unrest. Strikes punctuated the troubled coal industry. For example, in 1924, Pittsburgh Coal broke its contract with the United Mine Workers, who then struck. The company evicted workers from company housing and brought in strikebreakers and armed guards. Many observers decried the brutality and terrorism of the owners, but their tactics were successful: the union was broken, as it was in other coal strikes during the decade. In California, a 1928 strike by unionized Chicano farmworkers against melon growers was one of many that was suppressed by the increasingly powerful agribusiness sector. In the South, textile workers were relatively quiet until the end of the decade, when workers in Elizabethton, North Carolina, the vast majority of them women, rebelled in a spontaneous strike. At that point the United Textile Workers came in, and although the strike was lost, the incident contributed to a "Piedmont revolt" of union organizing and bitter, unsuccessful strikes that helped to lay the groundwork for Depression era militancy and unionization. Although it is important to note workers' efforts to try to wrest power from their employers in the 1920s, it is still the case that these were the exception. For the most part the decade was characterized, in historian Irving Bernstein's words, by "a calm seldom if ever matched in American industrial history."

Unions were not only weak in strength but conservative in tone. The Red Scare was in part to blame for this. The repression of communists, socialists, and syndicalists that grew out of the 1919–20 hysteria not only undermined radical institutions like the Industrial Workers of the World (IWW) but also created a climate that did not welcome radicals. Communists, for example, were defeated in struggles for influence in the Interna-

tional Ladies' Garment Workers' Union (ILGWU) and the
United Mine Workers. Some leftist organizers hoped for political solutions in the early 1920s. Railroad workers, for example,
backed the Plumb plan, which called for the federal government
to buy the railroads from their owners and set up a corporation
to run them, with labor having a significant share in decisions.
Labor activists had also been an important part of the Congress
for Progressive Political Action, and others envisioned a third
party comparable to the British Labour Party, but the hopes of
both groups quickly evaporated. The recently founded Communist Party was quite weak in this period. It worked, with
minimal success, through the Trade Union Education League
to "bore from within" the established unions. In Detroit, for
example, communists eventually dominated the tiny Auto
Workers Union. Although their numbers never grew beyond
300, they established shop nuclei at most of the city's auto
plants and worked through immigrant benevolent and social associations to spread their critique of industrial capitalism. Although the communists had little concrete impact in the 1920s,
they helped pave the way for industrial unions in mass production and would be an important component of militant labor in
the 1930s.

With radicals marginalized, conservative leaders within the
American Federation of Labor (AFL) increasingly headed the
labor movement. Industrial unions—organized by industry and
including a wide range of skills—had made some headway in
the prewar years within the AFL. The United Mine Workers
and the ILGWU tended to be more militant than the craft-based
unions, but both of them were weakened in the 1920s. The AFL
was thus dominated by craft unions that spoke primarily for
skilled workers, a group increasingly less representative of American workers as technology and management undermined skill.
The AFL leadership concentrated on maintaining benefits for
its own skilled group, and evinced little interest in organizing
mass production industries. Moreover, the racism and sexism
that characterized most AFL unions was a major factor contributing to their failure to expand unions to underrepresented
groups—Mexicans, African Americans, Asians, and women.

The AFL's conservatism was also expressed in a tendency toward "business unionism": the unions themselves began to replicate corporate hierarchy, with the leadership consolidating its position through bureaucracy at the expense of the rank and file. In addition, business unionism entailed a willingness to cooperate with management, a tendency widespread in the 1920s, as many unions sought to compensate for their weakness vis-à-vis management by accepting scientific management and participating in the drive for efficiency.

Destructive, internecine jurisdictional conflicts that weakened a number of major unions compounded the AFL's problems. But while unions themselves, with their conservatism and their infighting, were a part of the problem organized labor faced, far more important was the political and economic climate that strangled union and worker initiative. The considerable power of corporations, as we have seen, gave employers a sympathetic government and public. Another aspect of that inhospitable climate was the intensity of ethnic and racial conflict. The American workforce had always been diverse, but in the 1920s it was exceptionally so. European immigrants were restricted by the 1924 immigration act, but they and their children remained an important part of the labor pool, and they were joined increasingly by Mexican immigrants in both southwestern agriculture and in the factories of the Midwest. White and black rural Americans and women were other new components of the industrial labor force. These groups would have been difficult to organize, even if unions had sought them out. White rural dwellers, for example, possessed a strong ethos of independence and individualism that made them suspicious of unions' demands for a collective identity, and African Americans were dubious about white-dominated unions that had so often discriminated against them. More important, it was difficult for this diverse group of workers to see common interest in the context of a decade in which the Klan, the Red Scare, immigration restriction, race riots, and Henry Ford greatly exacerbated the differences between workers.

The state of the economy also hampered unionization. Despite the fabled prosperity of the 1920s, the decade began with a serious depression characterized by a severe drop in prices and over 100,000 bankruptcies. Workers and their unions were hard hit by wage cuts and a 19.5 percent rate of unemployment. The bulk of the economy recovered by 1922, but the fortunes of organized labor did not, especially in so-called sick industries such as coal and textiles. In search of cost reduction, corporations in both these sectors moved their operations to the South, where the labor supply was cheaper and far less accustomed to unions.

Another, related problem that faced workers in many industries was a labor surplus which undercut their bargaining power. The AFL had lobbied for a reduction in immigration, with the expectation that restriction of Asians and Europeans would create a favorable market for domestic labor, but the influx of Mexicans, ruralites, and women helped to offset the numbers lost. The surplus was also promoted by technology. Management's drive to cut labor costs with mechanization had not only created unemployment but also eliminated the need for skills, making workers more easily replaceable. In some southern textile mills, managers kept a roster of "spare hands," as *Like a Family* reported: "These 'extras' were available at a moment's notice to fill the job of any employee who dared complain, effectively undermining millhands' bargaining power on the shop floor." The situation was not always as obvious as the "spare hand" list in southern mill towns, but the reality of the labor surplus undoubtedly shaped workers' perception of the need to safeguard their jobs.

The decision to implement technology or move to the South was not the result of some abstract or inevitable industrial process, but rather was part of corporate strategy to maximize profit by controlling labor costs and the activities of the workers. Just as management's use of technology made individual workers more vulnerable, the open-shop drive undermined their collective strength. The campaign began in earnest in 1919 in the aftermath of labor's World War I gains and postwar militancy, and by the fall of 1920, there were open-shop associations in 240 cities, which promoted, as they put it, the American Plan. The National Association of Manufacturers and the Chamber of Commerce helped to give national focus to the ubiquitous drive to assure an open shop—which by their definition was a shop closed to unions. Blacklisting kept radicals and union sympathizers out of plants and mines. The "yellow dog" contract, which required that workers sign a contract agreeing not to join a union as a condition of employment, gave workers little choice—to work or to reserve the right to join the union. Open-shop companies also engaged in extensive industrial spying, and many large firms had their own private police force to maintain industrial peace, by force if necessary. They were determined to eliminate unions from their industrial equation. As one textile mill worker told an interviewer: "The boss don't want any union because he ain't so much the boss then."

Managers kept out unions by a system of intimidation and repression that was assisted at every turn by the state in the probusiness climate of the 1920s. The Clayton Antitrust Act of 1914 had held out the promise that labor unions would be exempt from antitrust prosecution. But in the 1920s the courts thought otherwise and, with the Supreme Court's endorsement, issued injunctions against union officials in record numbers. The Supreme Court also outlawed sympathy strikes, placed severe limitations on picketing, upheld the yellow dog contract, and ruled that unions could be held liable for damages. In this light, the weakness and the conservatism of unions can be better understood. Unions were outflanked by the power of the corporation—not just on the shop floor but in the cultural, economic, and political arena as well.

In addition to coercive measures, managers tried to achieve corporate hegemony through welfare capitalism. A broad term for a wide range of programs designed to instill worker loyalty and to promote efficiency, welfare capitalism emerged well before World War I but flourished in the early years of the 1920s. These programs ran the gamut from company unions to profit sharing, life insurance, and company softball teams. For the most part, welfare capitalism was confined to the largest, most prosperous firms, such as Bethlehem Steel, Goodyear, General Electric, and International Harvester. At its height, in the mid-1920s, estimates suggest that four million workers experienced some form of welfare capitalism. Its most vocal supporters were self-styled business progressives who offered a new approach to managing the labor problem. Instead of the conflict of the past, they argued, the new watchword should be cooperation.

Many companies sought to instill a sense of loyalty by offering practical incentives. Stock-purchase and profit-sharing plans, company-built housing for sale or rent, group life insurance, health and dental care for employees and their families, and improved wages and working conditions were widely publicized components of welfare capitalism. These programs undoubtedly benefited workers, but relatively few companies offered these programs and the scope of those that did was often limited. Despite the outpouring of publicity for these forms of welfare capitalism, their practical effect fell far short of managerial rhetoric proclaiming a new era in protection and security for the worker.

The most common form of welfare capitalism was "employee representation" or company unions. These plans varied from firm to firm, but most provided for election of representatives and a formalized grievance system. The high point of employee representation was reached in the mid-1920s; a 1926 survey found 432 plants, mostly large corporations, with employee representation plans. Although managers touted them as industrial democracy, company unions gave lie to the rhetoric. Unlike unions, they had no professional organizers experienced at negotiation or knowledgeable about circumstances in other plants and firms. The issues that they could address were circumscribed: wages and hours often were not within their purview, for example. Certainly some workers appreciated the procedures company unions gave them. African Americans and women, groups largely ignored by most unions, may have found employee representation, despite its limits, a welcome innovation.

Although some workers may have responded favorably, there is little question that company unions offered merely the appearance of power. Rather than fostering democracy, they were a means of manipulating workers. Not surprisingly, many employers instituted company unions shortly before announcing a pay cut, and used the representation plan to deflect dissent before it could be effectively mobilized. And although enthusiasts pictured employee representation as a means of communication, a "recognition of a natural human desire in every one of us to express his own individuality, to have something to say in the business which he is making his life work," it boiled down to an effective means of management-controlled communication.

Managers used other methods in their drive to mold employees in their image of the ideal citizen of the factory. One ubiquitous type of worker education was the Americanization program, which inculcated the values of good worker citizenship by teaching English with texts that celebrated punctuality and loyalty. Another vehicle for worker education was the company magazine, which documented employees' social activities and provided a medium for managers to communicate specific information about production and profits and to spread the ideal of company loyalty. As Gerald Zahavi found in his study of the shoe manufacturing firm of Endicott Johnson, the *E-J Workers' Review* was filled with exhortations such as: "Every worker should do his best. Let us look for the leaks and avoid all mistakes and waste of material. An interest taken for the E.J. Corporation is an interest for us all." The company also used the magazine, as well as bulletin boards and local newspapers, to develop the idea of the company as "The Happy Family," an image often used by welfare capitalists who hoped to instill in their workers a family loyalty to their firm. Family ideology was also evident in the concern some managers had for workers' home life. Worried that part of industrial unrest stemmed from disruptions in family life, many firms, with Ford leading the way, tied welfare capitalism benefits to evidence of a "decent" home life and sent welfare workers to employees' homes to investigate and educate.

Another widely popular version of welfare capitalism, practiced by both large and small firms, was to provide recreational respite—chorales, music, and films were featured during lunchtime at many factories. Even more common were team sports such as bowling and softball, with the link to work underlined by uniforms with company logos. The idea was to promote physical well-being as well as "school"—corporate—spirit. An important aspect of the emphasis placed on leisure time was captured in the illustrations of the General Electric house organ, *Work News*. David E. Nye found that the cover generally featured a photograph of an individual worker performing some highly skilled operation, an anomaly in a mass production factory. Work was rarely depicted between the covers. Instead, photographs highlighted personal stories and documented work-linked leisure activities, revealing a tacit understanding of the implications of the changing nature of work. As it became more routinized and meaningless, workers sought satisfaction outside the job in leisure. Many employers facilitated and institutionalized this substitution. Corporate-sponsored leisure was part of the process by which companies tried to mold workers' values, to direct them toward productive leisure that would make them loyal and efficient workers. And this, indeed, was the major thrust of all welfare capitalism. As historian Stuart Brandes summed it up: "The ultimate goal of welfare capitalism was no less than the propagation of an improved American working man: thrifty, clean, temperate, intelligent, and especially, industrious and loyal."

America's large corporations embarked on a variety of tactics to bind workers to firms, to encourage efficient production and undermine the appeal of unions. Did these strategies create loyal workers, seduced by the rhetoric of cooperation and benefits to reject protest and unionization? Union officials were adamant in their protest against all forms of welfare capitalism, but what about workers themselves? Strikes declined in the twenties, as did union membership. But welfare capitalism was not widespread enough to account for labor quiescence. Moreover, the only systematic effort to survey workers at the time concluded that they were not fooled by programs and rhetoric. J. David Houser's survey of one corporation indicated that workers' appreciation of their working conditions and facilities "is offset by the low esteem in which they hold their opportunities for participation and expression." Studies of company unions indicate widespread apathy, with low turnouts in elections for representatives, surely an indication that workers recognized that company unions were virtually powerless. Zahavi's study of the Endicott Johnson shoe corporation concludes that welfare capitalism did work to an extent. Labor disturbances were low in comparison with elsewhere in the industry, and workers in oral history interviews recalled a degree of satisfaction and loyalty. But they also revealed that workers used managers' rhetoric to their own ends. Once having instituted various forms of welfare capitalism, managers found that workers considered benefits to be "what they were owed," not what they were given, and consistently put pressure on their employers to measure up to their promises of consideration for workers' opinions and needs. The Endicott Johnson experience suggests that workers were not so easily manipulated as managers expected, and that their accommodation to welfare capitalism had its limits.

Welfare capitalism was a short-lived experiment. Corporations continued programs throughout the decade, but the movement peaked by the mid-twenties: there were fewer new programs and some older ones were discontinued. With union strength already reduced and labor turnover well under control, managers were under less pressure to consider "the human element." The Depression put an end to all but a handful of programs. When benefits once again became part of a worker's packet, they were no longer provided primarily by the corporation, but came through the agency of unions and the federal government. But however brief or limited, welfare capitalism is important for understanding workers' experience in the 1920s. By itself, it was just one device used to undermine unions and maintain labor stability. Taken together with the drive for the open shop and the spread of scientific management and technology, it represents the largely successful corporate assault on workers' power and autonomy in the postwar years.

THE WHITE-COLLAR WORLD OF WORK

Just as working people's lives were transformed by developments within the corporation, so too the expanding middle class felt the impact of corporate consolidation, technology, and power. For several decades, the nature of the middle class had been shifting from an older one of entrepreneurs and self-employed professionals to a new one of salaried white-collar workers needed to staff increasingly complicated businesses. By 1920, 20.4 percent of the total workforce were from the new category, while 8.1 percent were from the old middle class. Old or new, middle-class work and leisure were shaped by the growing organization of American society that contributed to the emergence of the consumer culture.

Although the old middle class was clearly becoming overshadowed by the growth of the new, it nonetheless persisted as an important part of the economy. Small stores still dominated the retail market, for example, and offered opportunity to a wide range of entrepreneurs, including immigrant and African American proprietors who formed the core of the small ethnic middle class in their communities. These small entrepreneurs' control over their enterprise was increasingly circumscribed by their relationship to the large national firms that produced or shipped their merchandise. The popularity of brand-name products with national advertising placed limits on the small business's ability to determine its stock and prices. Equally significant, chain stores, such as the A & P for groceries, Woolworth's for variety goods, and United Cigar Stores for smoking products, expanded dramatically in the 1920s, so that by 1930 there were over 7,000 chains with close to 160,000 stores. At the beginning of the decade, they had accounted for 4 percent of the total retail trade; at its end, 20 percent. Their lower prices, quick turnover, and extensive advertising, combined with the ability that automobiles gave shoppers to venture from their own neighborhoods and small towns, made it possible for chain stores to mount an alarming incursion into the retail market of small businesses.

Yet another example of the way in which national firms threatened the autonomy of smaller businesses was the transformation in the content and format of small-town newspapers. In the 1920s, because of developments in technology and distribution, they increasingly consisted of syndicated news information and photographs. According to Sally Griffith, for example, Kansan William Allen White's *Emporia Gazette* regularly featured a page of "The Day's News in Pictures," supplied by the Central Press Agency. In addition, "photographs and features about the latest celebrities were now distributed in mats with stylish layout and headlines already provided." Preprepared manufacturer's advertising tied to local retailers also became common, as did bold and glamorous movie ads. As newspapers featured national news, celebrities, and advertisements, local news, which had been central to small newspapers before the war, was segregated—and marginalized—into special columns. For readers, as Griffith points out, "increased advertising and greater access to syndicated materials was to diminish the very centrality of its community." For the owners, the innovations, especially the advertisements, meant increased profits. But in exchange, their control over their enterprise was limited by their dependency on outside agencies to supply news and generate income.

Small entrepreneurs faced a dilemma. Like other middle-class Americans in the 1920s, they took pride in their country's productivity and progress, and undoubtedly believed that prosperity was linked to big business. As the preceding chapter has shown, the decade witnessed no sustained attack on the trusts that had characterized the prewar years. But small retailers did attempt to focus attention on the spread of chain stores, the most obvious threat to their profits and local control. Throughout the twenties, there were campaigns, almost all unsuccessful, to enact state legislation designed to cripple the chains' ability to undermine their competition. By the end of the decade, a national drive for federal legislation had begun. The plight of the small retailer became a potent political symbol of the economic powerlessness of middling Americans when in the thirties the Depression brought their vulnerability into sharp relief.

White-collar employees were less ambiguously part of the new scheme of things. A diverse group, they ranged from lowly clerks to relatively powerful managers. The income of most clerical workers, many of whom were women, was not generally sufficient to support middle-class standards of living; nonetheless, the President's Research Committee on Recent Social Trends believed that low-level white-collar workers "are commonly jealous of their status as a part of the middle class." More than perception set them apart from the working class. Better educated than blue-collar workers, they were also more likely to be white and either old stock or the children of European immigrants. Exposure to the public schools and the office undoubtedly familiarized them as well with middle-class aspirations of mobility and consumption. Above this group were the more solidly middle-class—the army of accountants, advertising agents, salesmen, engineers, and managers who constituted the modern corporation hierarchy.

As the workforce changed, education became the central requirement for the white-collar employee. A 1926 survey of office employees in the lower and middle ranks indicated that 86 percent had some high school and 64 percent had some sort of commercial education. Only 9.5 percent had attended college. For the higher range of employees—engineers and managers—specialized college education was increasingly expected and obtained. Public school attendance also expanded dramatically in the teens and twenties, so that by 1930, over 40 percent of seventeen-year-olds were in school. Curriculum changes accompanied expansion as schools offered a variety of vocational classes to prepare students for trade and business. In their sociological study of Muncie, Indiana, *Middletown* (1929), Robert and Helen Lynd noted a blending of traditional and newer trends, but thought that the main thrust in the high schools was toward a program "to train for specific tool and skill activities in factory, office, and home."

Colleges and universities also emphasized specialized education. Engineering training had become more formalized and increasingly undertaken in universities and graduate programs that were closely allied with manufacturers. Business education also flourished. The Harvard Business School had been established in 1905, and other private and public institutions followed, so that by the 1920s it was becoming accepted that managers needed professional, specialized training. Professionalization was further indicated by the appearance of management organizations and journals such as the *Harvard Business*

Review and the American Management Association's *Management Review*. Schools such as the International Correspondence School or La Salle Extension University also flourished by offering techniques of accounting, salesmanship, and other skills for the lower-level corporate hierarchy. These institutions stressed that it was no longer possible to "pick up" the necessary skills for a career in business: "These days a man must study the theory and practice of business just as earnestly as another man studies law or medicine or engineering."

The correspondence school ads were revealing in another way. They suggest that not only the means to success was changing, but also the meaning of success. Clearly targeting the new middle class or aspiring middle class, their promises included more money—but also a means of working one's way up a corporate ladder. In an ad directed to "clerks, bookkeepers, and other routine workers," the Walton School of Commerce provided a graphic picture of a young man at a desk poring over papers. The picture was framed by a huge glass bottle surrounding the young man: "Don't Stay Bottled Up." Other correspondence school ads featured a man with a private office, polished desk, and other accoutrements of corporate success looking out from his office over a sea of indistinguishable men perched on stools hard at work over ledgers. The end product of correspondence courses was not just more money but also individuation: a private office—and authority—over those below you.

At the time some critics worried about the implications of all those bottled-up men—not just those at the very bottom but also those who achieved middling success as they struggled up the corporate ladder. Observers equated routinization, standardization, and bureaucracy with a decline in individuality and autonomy. King Vidor's *The Crowd* clearly offered a searing critique of the grimness and marginality of white-collar men's and women's lives. Elmer Rice's play *The Adding Machine* (1923) was another striking indictment. Its protagonist, Mr. Zero, is a bookkeeper who enters figures all day long "upon a large square sheet of ruled paper," and plans finally to approach his boss for a promotion into the front office: "I'll say, 'I ain't quite satisfied. I been on the job twenty-five years now and if I'm gonna stay I gotta see a future ahead of me.' " Emboldened when he learns that he is to be replaced by an adding machine, he kills his boss, and is executed for his crime. The play ends with his afterlife discovery that he is to be reincarnated in yet another soulless job, this time as an operator of a "super-adding machine." As the introduction to the book version summed it up, Rice "has studied the rich barrenness and the ridiculous unbeauty of these 'white-collar' slaves." Thus the vulnerability and alienation of white-collar workers—already so evident in the working class— was also becoming apparent to at least some observers in the 1920s, as more individuals became subject to the bureaucracy and work became less meaningful.

CONSUMER CULTURE

In the early pages of *Babbitt*, Sinclair Lewis painstakingly de-scribes the material objects that formed such a crucial part of George F. Babbitt's sense of identity and well-being. His alarm clock was "the best of nationally advertised and quantitatively produced" clocks, "with cathedral chime, intermittent alarm, and a phosphorescent dial." The bathroom boasted "a sensa-tional exhibit of tooth-brush holder, shaving-brush holder, soap-dish, sponge-dish, and medicine-cabinet, so glittering and so ingenious that they resembled an electrical instrument-board." And as George drove to his real estate office and engaged in an interior dialogue about his income and the things he owned or desired to own, he surrendered to his profound longing for a genuine nickel-plated lighter for his car, and made a detour to buy the "dandy little refinement, lending the last touch of class to a gentleman's auto."

As *Babbitt* suggests, one of the most enduring clichés of the jazz age features the hedonistic spending spree that was part of what F. Scott Fitzgerald called the world's most expensive orgy. This vision conjures up flappers and jazzhounds engaged in a relentless pursuit of pleasure, as well as the Babbitt family's love affair with consumer goods and gadgets. Although these stereo-types are vastly overdrawn, nonetheless the decade did witness a plethora of material goods: cosmetics, books, phonographs, radios, and household appliances and furnishings were more plentiful and more readily affordable to a wide range of people who eagerly purchased them. Central to the decade's sense of material abundance and progress was the automobile. Between 1913 and 1931, the number of automobiles in the country had grown twentyfold, and by the end of the twenties, more than 20 percent of Americans owned a car, with its promise of freedom, status, and mobility.

In addition to products, the consumer culture also enshrined leisure and commercialized it. Americans' expenditures on recreation increased by a remarkable 300 percent during the decade. The mass-produced, cheaper car, in conjunction with the spread of paid vacations for a great many workers, produced the modern vacation and helped to spawn the ubiquitous tourist camps, precursors to modern motels, that were multiplying throughout the country. And for weekends and evenings, a wide range of commercial entertainment beckoned. Nightclubs and amusement parks, although not new to the twenties, flourished, capturing the quick-paced style of urban amusements, and allowing their patrons to let down their hair, relax, and participate in the dance craze of the day. And the twenties established the movies as a central American icon, as a wide range of people— an estimated twenty to thirty million weekly—flocked to the increasingly glamorous movie palace.

And this was the golden age of sports. Boxing, baseball, and college football proved highly popular and immensely profitable to its organizers. Participatory sports spread as well, especially with the middle-class fads of golf and tennis, which in turn helped create a demand for country clubs and civic recreation parks, not to mention golf clubs and tennis rackets. Sports embodied leisure, and offered an escape from the workaday world; in addition it helped to enshrine commercialized youth and vitality as central parts of the consumer culture. The attention to sports also spawned the sport hero—women like swimmer Gertrude Ederle and tennis star Helen Wills and men like football icons Red Grange and Knute Rockne, boxers Jack Dempsey and Gene Tunney, baseball players Babe Ruth and Lou Gehrig, and golfer Bobby Jones. Although sports idols embodied the new culture, they also seemed to reaffirm older ideas about success. They represented a path to attainment outside the bureaucracy and regimentation of the corporation, and they also held out the reassuring prospect that success was linked not just to hard work and individual discipline but also to following the clear-cut rules of the individual sport and of sportsmanship.

Sports heroes took their place alongside movie idols Clara Bow, Charlie Chaplin, Rudolph Valentino, Douglas Fairbanks, and Mary Pickford; they were part of a panoply of national heroes and heroines celebrated in the mass media. They hawked goods in advertisements, hired publicity agents, and became the subject of intense media scrutiny aimed at feeding a seemingly insatiable public curiosity. The vehicles for promoting these heroes—movies, magazines, newspapers, and advertising— pointed to the nationalization of American culture, its dominance by large corporations, which, although not complete, was well in place by the 1920s. In addition, the emphasis on the personal lives of consumption idols, as Leo Lowenthal called them, represented not merely the emergence of an ethos of leisure and spending but one that placed private, individual, commodity-based self-realization at its center.

BLUE-COLLAR CONSUMPTION AND LEISURE

Although there is significant evidence both for the nationalization of culture and for the emergence of this consumption ethos in the 1920s, it would be a mistake to picture all Americans equally engaged by these modern trends. Certainly, for the working class, hardly a homogeneous group, the culture of consumption held out the promise of compensations for the alienating nature of work, the power of employers, and the harshness of life. But family income, race, and ethnicity mediated between working-class people and consumer culture and made their participation in it ambiguous and complex.

Contemporary observers rarely pretended that blue-collar

workers found satisfaction in their labor, but many assumed that alienating work had its compensations: a share in the new era of prosperity and an ability to participate in the burgeoning consumer culture. Some historians have agreed and suggested that workers' indifference to unions stemmed from a complacence encouraged by their participation in the fruits of prosperity. On the surface, this seems valid. Although the five-day week remained elusive for all but a handful of workers, and in some industries like textiles the ten-hour day was common, most production workers experienced a decline in hours from an average of 46.3 per week in 1919 to 44.2 in 1929 that gave them slightly more leisure time after work. Moreover, various contemporary surveys of worker income indicate gains in real wages in the 1920s, although not as dramatic or as evenly distributed as some observers and historians have thought. Frank Stricker, in an appropriately titled article, "Affluence for Whom?," has carefully analyzed these surveys and argues persuasively that while production workers' wages advanced 14.5 percent for the period 1919–29, between 1923 and 1929, the most prosperous period of the postwar years, the gain slowed to a far more modest 4.7 percent. Furthermore, this aggregate figure does not take into account the significant wage differentials between skilled, semi-skilled, and unskilled workers. This disparity also points to another inequality, for the latter were invariably new immigrants and African Americans. Both could expect to be paid less than native white workers and to spend more on rent. And finally, women's wages remained constant during the decade and in a sex-segregated job market their pay was significantly less than men's. African American women in particular were disadvantaged. In some cities, their most common occupation, domestic service, paid around a dollar a day. Thus, it was mostly skilled workers—autoworkers, railroad operators, workers in the building trades, hosiery workers, and printers—who participated fully in the much-vaunted prosperity of the twenties.

The tenuous economic status of most working-class families stemmed primarily from insecurity of employment or underemployment. Systematic government statistics of unemployment were not yet collected in this period, but social scientist

Paul Douglas's survey during the twenties indicated that at its lowest, unemployment for manufacturing, mining, transportation, and building was 8.1 percent. Most workers simply could not count on steady work. John Bodnar's oral history interview with Rose Popovich, the wife of a Pennsylvania steelworker, captured the implications of unsteady work: "You couldn't save very much because my husband was more out of work than working." They went into debt when he was out of work: "By the time he started back to work I owed so much. By the time I paid what I owed, he stopped work again. The only time that he worked good was during the war. He worked steady for two years without stopping. There were times when he worked just one day a month. It was just awful."

People like the Popoviches had few resources; they might have some savings, a commercial life insurance policy, or benefits tied to membership in the ubiquitous fraternal society that could help a little in time of illness, unemployment, and death. All but four states had some form of workmen's compensation for industrial accidents, but the benefits were relatively meager and not enough to keep a family from experiencing hard times in the case of accident to a member of the family economy. Most workers did not have enough of a safety net to protect them from distress at best, disaster at worst.

If these problems were not enough, blue-collar workers invariably had raised expectations about the standard of living to which they could aspire. Flush toilets, gleaming bathrooms and kitchens, electric irons, washing machines, and stoves were all heavily advertised and desirable. Automobiles poured off the assembly lines and were made more affordable by the advent of installment buying. But how accessible were the fruits of prosperity to workers? Some estimates are that 50 percent of all nonfarm households owned cars, but scattered surveys of car ownership indicate that workers were not well represented as owners: in Chicago in 1924, only 3 percent of unskilled workers, and in San Francisco in 1928, 26.5 percent of streetcar workers, had cars. Less expensive items had a wider distribution: by 1930, 97.8 percent of homes with electricity had irons, 44.4 percent vacuum cleaners, and 35.1 percent washing machines. Ready-made fashionable clothing had also become more affordable, even to the young garment workers who made it. Although most workers shared disproportionately in the full fruits of the consumer society their labor helped to produce, many had access to its less expensive manifestations. And they could look to it to find the compensations that their work and income failed to offer.

The working class in addition participated in a variety of leisure-time pursuits. For much of the nineteenth century, workers had resisted industrialists' and Protestant reformers' efforts to induce a more regimented sense of time and more orderly behavior. Working-class leisure tended to be more boisterous than Victorian middle-class Protestant sensibilities would have liked. The popularity of bare-knuckle fighting for working-class men, which to the middle class was scarcely respectable, was just one example of a class-based and often ethnic-based form of recreation. Saloons were another male-oriented symbol of working-class and ethnic culture, and served as a reminder of an important difference between the working class and the middle class over the acceptability of alcoholic consumption. Another bone of contention between the old stock and the new concerned Sabbath observance, with many working-class people valuing Sunday as the day for recreation, not rest. Ethnic institutions—churches and fraternal orders—which often had no objection to alcohol or Sunday events—also contributed to distinctive working-class patterns of leisure.

By the turn of the century, competing attractions emerged that took advantage of the working-class desire for recreation. Amusement parks, nickelodeons, and dime museums attracted a heavily working-class clientele. These commercialized entertainments undoubtedly transformed working-class leisure, ultimately contributing to the decline of ethnic identity. However, the ethnic working class also influenced the new entertainment. Just to offer a few examples, elements of African American music and dance were appropriated by white entertainers and incorporated into mainstream culture. Similarly, Jewish performers were heavily represented in various forms of mass entertainment and Jewish entrepreneurs helped to shape the direction of the movie industry. More broadly, as they swelled the urban population, immigrants and other working-class Americans, with their different ideas about leisure and sociability, helped to erode the cultural hegemony of middle-class Victorians, and with it the restraints associated with the Protestant, producer work ethic.

Working-class Americans were not just passive recipients of the reorientation of culture, but helped to shape it. There is also evidence that many resisted the homogenizing trends of mass, commercialized culture and pursued their leisure within an ethnic or racial context. In many urban neighborhoods, working-class people enjoyed a vibrant street life of visiting and ethnic food and music. African Americans, many of them new migrants to the cities, flocked to jazz clubs and rent parties. Fraternal orders helped to maintain an ethnic sociability by organizing parties and balls and sponsoring festivals and entertainment which evoked traditional leisure activities.

Lizabeth Cohen's study of Chicago also suggests that some immigrant and African American communities maintained their distinctiveness even as vehicles of mass culture invaded them. In the early days of radio, most programs originated locally and offered ethnic nationality hours or were produced by ethnic stations. Churches, labor unions, and fraternal orders were among the most common broadcasters. Homes or shops with a radio became the gathering place for neighbors and friends who shared their entertainment. This local flavor was to change with the rise of national corporations by the end of the decade, but for a brief period radio helped to promote "ethnic, religious, and working-class affiliations."

By the 1920s movies were already part of national corporations, but here, too, there was room for the neighborhood to influence how residents experienced mass culture. In Chicago ethnic working-class neighborhoods, movie houses were not sumptuous palaces, but rather modest, locally owned enterprises. Films might be interspersed with ethnic entertainments, and perhaps even transformed by them. In "race" movie theaters, according to the disapproving black newspaper *The Chicago Defender*, "during a death scene . . . you are likely to hear the orchestra jazzing away on 'Clap Hands, Here Comes Charlie,'" as the accompanists injected their own music into the theater. The existence of "race" theaters also pointed to racial lines that separated the leisure of both African Americans and Mexicans, who were usually excluded from the small white ethnic neighborhood theaters. As with radio, the ability to maintain a local quality in movie houses eroded by the late twenties. Chain theaters began to challenge local independents as movie producers consolidated their control over distribution. The introduction of talkies, which required significant capital investment in equipment, further undermined the ability of small entrepreneurs to compete; local houses increasingly were squeezed out or limited in what they could show.

Other forms of entertainment reinforced ethnic identity. By 1920, the recording industry had discovered the profit potential of foreign and "race" records. African Americans could buy records of blues and jazz and hear such favorites as Mamie Smith, Ida Cox, Bessie Smith, and Ethel Waters. As Kathy Ogren reports in her study of jazz, African Americans flocked to record stores. According to Clarence Williams, who owned a Chicago store: "Colored people would form a line twice around the block when the latest record of Bessie or Ma or Clara or Mamie came in." "Hillbilly" music tapped an audience of southern whites with records such as "The Old Hen Cackled and the Rooster's Going to Crow." Records by Pedro Gonzalez of Los Angeles made him a celebrity figure within the Southern California Mexican American community. European immigrants— from Irish to Albanians—could also find music that spoke to their traditions. While large corporations like Victrola dominated the industry, the relative cheapness of the pressing process made it possible for small entrepreneurs to produce records for their communities, such as the Parsekian (Armenian), Srpske Gusle (Serbian), and Black Swan (African American) labels.

Sports was another leisure arena in which class and ethnicity mattered. While major league baseball was a key forum for sports enthusiasts in the 1920s, working-class Americans were perhaps more likely to attend sandlot games, which were less expensive and more community-oriented. This was especially evident among African Americans, who were excluded from playing major league baseball. Negro professional leagues, which multiplied in the twenties, offered one arena for African Americans to enjoy baseball. Also common were the black sandlot, semiprofessional, semicommercialized teams that flourished in most American cities. Rob Ruck has described black-controlled teams in Pittsburgh as an important part of the African American community. "Clubs like the 19th Ward, the Garfield Eagles, and the Crawfords helped bind their neighborhoods around teams that excelled in one of the few fields equally open to blacks and whites."

Amateur and professional basketball and boxing were other working-class sports that reflected ethnic and racial identity. A list of the leading basketball professional teams of the period provides ample testimony to their ethnic focus: Harlem Renaissance Five, South Philadelphia Hebrew All-Stars, Irish Brooklyn Visitations, and Polish Detroit Pulaskis. Boxing had shed some of its shady reputation by the 1920s and had an expanding audience among the middle and upper classes, but it still maintained its working-class and ethnic associations and was important to immigrant and African American communities.

The ethnic and racial cast of leisure in urban communities did not mean that workers and their families were unaffected by mainstream mass culture. Undoubtedly, Hollywood movies, Tin Pan Alley music, and Madison Avenue advertisements made their way into most working-class lives, immigrant, native white, and African American, and began a process of incorporating a wide spectrum of Americans into a more homogenized consumer culture. But although the 1920s pointed to new developments, race, ethnicity, and class continued to shape leisure and consumption for many workers. This not only indicates the diversity of American culture but also sheds some light on how workers coped with difficult circumstances and the alienation and powerlessness of their work. The Lynds in *Middletown* painted a grim picture of workers who led isolated, bleak existences, with few friends or sociability. Their analysis may have been weakened by their decision to examine a community with no substantial racial or ethnic diversity. In contrast, historians who have examined white Appalachian, African American, and immigrant communities suggest a different, far less bleak scenario. On the one hand, consumption and leisure-time pursuits offered some compensations for the harshness of their lives. On the other hand, ethnicity or race, combined with class, helped to create a strong sense of family and community ties. These bonds defined their lives, helped give them meaning separate from work, and to some extent minimized their dependence on mainstream culture and institutions.

WHITE-COLLAR CONSUMPTION AND LEISURE

Clearly, it was the middle class for whom the consumer culture had the most import in the 1920s, an import that went beyond having the income to participate in expanded recreational opportunities and to acquire the material products that rolled off the assembly line. Scholars have identified a behavioral and value shift embodied in the emergence of a new social type. In *The Lonely Crowd* (1950), David Riesman contrasted the nineteenth-century middle-class character type, "inner-directed," with the twentieth-century "other-directed" individual whose life was organized by keeping tuned in to the impressions and opinions of others. Leo Lowenthal posited a shift from individuals geared to the Horatio Alger values of the nineteenth century that emphasized "production" to people attuned to the consumer values of the twentieth. Warren Susman characterized the shift as linked to changing perceptions of the self, with the nineteenth-century emphasis on character giving way to a twentieth-century obsession with personality. "The vision of self-sacrifice began to yield to that of self-realization." Jackson Lears has identified this concern with personality as part of a therapeutic ethos, a widespread trend in twentieth-century middle-class culture that pervaded religion, social sciences, success ideology, and advertising, and concentrated on self-expression and self-realization through consumption and leisure.

Although there are significant differences between these schemas, they all point to a fundamental cultural change arising from the emergence of a modern, organized society. For many of the new middle class, especially men, because they were the ones who expected to remain in the workforce permanently, work was becoming intrinsically less meaningful, while at the same time rising prosperity, consumer goods, and increased leisure time offered new venues for meaning: one could seek satisfaction and definition in the personal realm of leisure and consumption. Other factors influenced both men and women. As already noted, the increasing pluralism of America's cities helped to challenge Victorian cultural hegemony and promote alternative visions of leisure and sociability. The expansion of the corporate national economy eroded local ties and propagated bureaucracy, specialization, and routinization, helping to undermine the individual's sense of community and autonomy. Similarly, urban mass society underlined the individual's fragile status in an anonymous society and compounded a sense of fragmentation. Although many Americans sought to root themselves in religion, mounting secularization further contributed to a search for secular forms of salvation.

All of these factors were in place before the 1920s, of course, but that decade helped to cement the trends. The decline in voting and the widespread indifference to reform, outlined in the previous chapter, signaled a rejection of civic responsibility and a shift to the private and the personal. Although prosperity was not universal, the flood of consumer goods, made more accessible by installment buying, did provide more Americans than ever with the delights and perils of conspicuous consumption. Moreover, the continued expansion of the mass media and commercial entertainment, most notably the increased importance of advertising and movies, reflected and reinforced the thrust of the consumer culture toward leisure and consumption.

While consumption and participation in leisure-time pursuits constituted the basic conditions of a consumer society, equally important was a shift in values, in the ways in which Americans interpreted their society and circumstances. These values were scarcely universal or uncontested, for here as in many other arenas where Americans faced the new modern culture, individuals diverged in their response to social changes. One clear and important pattern emerges in the messages of the purveyors of mass culture—advertising agents, moviemakers, popular writers, and the like—who articulated the therapeutic ethos. They offered consumption and leisure as partial antidotes to the dilemmas of the modern world and promoted the cultivation of personality and other-direction as the key to the individual's success and satisfaction in a mass society.

Many observers in the 1920s were insistent in their denial that success or even individuality must be sacrificed in the new white-collar business world. This was particularly evident in success books and schemes of the decade that modified the older tradition of success ideology identified with Horatio Alger. Nineteenth-century success stories posited hard work, sobriety, thrift, and restraint as the keys to personal and business good fortune. And invariably the success in mind was that of the old middle class—material rewards, civic virtue, and personal autonomy. By the 1920s, there was a subtle shift. Reflecting in part the popularization of Freudian thought, an important theme became the subconscious, which one writer described as "an infinite storehouse of intelligence and power" that man could draw upon to "supply his needs and wants." This idea of being able to marshal one's innate ability through exercise of will emerged in articles and books and was also popularized by agencies such as the Pelman Institute of America, whose advertisements in popular magazines offered "Scientific Mind Training." Pelmanism promised that it "awakens the giant, the superman, within you; it enables you to *realize your true self*, to become the man or woman you have dimly felt all along that you ought to be." Similarly, Frenchman Emile Coué took the country by storm by urging the daily invocation of a simple mantra: "Day by day, in every way, I am getting better and better." These approaches reaffirmed the possibilities for success, even in the modern corporate structure, by offering up-to-date techniques for realizing individual potential.

Perhaps the most famous success guru was Dale Carnegie. In the twenties, Carnegie was well known in business circles, and toured the country giving speeches and teaching businessmen how to speak, to present themselves, and to manage people. His best-seller *How to Win Friends and Influence People* was not published until 1936, but its ideas had already gained currency in the 1920s. The chapter titles are themselves revealing: "Fundamental Techniques in Handling People," "Six Ways to Make People Like You," "Twelve Ways to Win People to Your Way of Life." The key to success as it emerged in Carnegie's work was the manipulation of others, presentation of self, and an acute consciousness of impressions.

Although these proponents of success certainly directed themselves toward men and occupational mobility, they also promised a more fulfilling personal life as well. This blurring of the lines between qualities needed for work and those needed for leisure meant that, unlike the Horatio Alger tradition, the more modernized success formulas encompassed women as well as men. The question behind them was not just how to live in the business world but how to live in the modern world.

Many other forms of popular culture addressed the same questions and pointed to the same reorientation of the culture. The managers and editors of the Book-of-the-Month Club, founded in 1926, offered a complex message. On the one hand, as Joan Shelley Rubin argues, the books the editors chose to feature were often those in keeping with the traditional genteel culture's emphasis on "character," such as Marjorie Kinnan Rawlings' *The Yearling* or Clarence Day's *Life With Father*. But the BOMC's promotion techniques—its advertisements and newsletters—decidedly reflected the newer emphasis on the self and personality and assured the book buyer that he could be "completely informed about *all the interesting new books*. He knows about them and can talk about them." The BOMC, in Rubin's words, "promised to cure the floundering self's social distress by enabling subscribers to convey the instant and favorable impression required for success in a bureaucratic, anonymous society."

The message that one could purchase what one needed for personal growth and success permeated the advertising industry. Advertising itself mushroomed in the twenties. Estimates are that in 1914 the volume of advertising stood at $682 million; by 1929 it had grown to $2,987 million. Although radio would become important toward the end of the decade, the most significant advertising medium was the mass magazines, whose circulation had exploded in the early twentieth century, so that by 1929 they were selling 202 million copies. Even the most cursory examination reveals the consumer culture orientation of magazine advertising: large and, as the decade progressed, colorful photographs of products and, increasingly, of individuals enjoying the products. As a car manufacturer summed it up, in a lushly colored scene of the countryside: "You find *a Road of Happiness* the day you buy a Buick." Advertisements like these repeatedly depicted the satisfactions of leisure and the products that created or enhanced leisure.

Beyond a mere glorification of consumption and leisure, advertising agents were often self-consciously "apostles of modernism," as Roland Marchand puts it. In hawking their various products, they sought to associate their clients' goods with the modern era, with fashion, style, and progress. But on a different level, admen—and the majority were men—revealed a darker side of modernity and sought to sell their products by addressing consumers' anxieties occasioned by the modern world, and in particular sought to soothe the embattled self: "Adopting a therapeutic mission, advertising provided comforting reassurances to those who anxiously watched the institutions of their society assume a larger, more complex, and more impersonal scale."

The advertisements of products for jangled nerves were the most obvious example of the therapeutic model in advertising. Post Bran Flakes' picture of a harassed businessman was captioned: "Too Busy to Keep Well!" The text began: "We Americans, what a hurly-burly race we are! Getting up by the alarm clock; racing through our meals; hurrying from this appointment to that as though our lives depended on it." The resulting poor health and constipation, however, happily could be cured by eating Post Bran Flakes regularly. Examples concerning poor energy, health, and nerves could be repeated endlessly. And other products, not directly related to health, also played on the same theme of the stress accompanying the modern world.

On a relatively subtle note, an advertisement for tourist tents celebrated outdoor leisure, and announced: "A Million Brain Workers Will Soon Want Tents" because "auto camping is the fastest-growing sport in the world, because it is based on freedom, economy and common sense." Hammermill Bond was more explicit. A color ad featured two businessmen on a busy street, with one declining an invitation because "I'd get fired." The text bemoaned that it was "the same old story of the nose on the grindstone. No time for play. No time for anything but work. And no time then to make a success of himself. Always too busy grinding—grinding. A slave to routine work." The imaginative solution to this grind was simple: preprinted office forms that would relieve men of "details and free themselves for advancement."

Another advertising theme that seemed directed at the plight of the individual in modern mass society was the personal approach, the tendency to include "you" in the text. As Roland Marchand has argued, advertisements, inspired by tabloid journalism's and movie matinees' phenomenal success, created mini-dramas of the consumer's life and solved them with products ranging from face creams to batteries. Other techniques of personalizing consumption included the celebrity endorsement, which linked movie stars and sports figures to ordinary Americans in shared consumption, and the advent of company spokespersons such as Betty Crocker, who humanized the corporate image. All of these techniques aimed at reassuring consumers that they had connections to their purchases, that they could exercise some control even in a mass society.

Perhaps the clearest indication of advertising's concern with the fragile self was the extraordinary emphasis ads placed on the opinions of others as vehicles for personal and business success, a theme especially evident in ads for toiletries. Mouthwash, deodorants, cosmetics, and perfumes were scarce products at the turn of the century, but by the 1920s they had become a major industry, with large advertising campaigns that accounted for the second most advertised range of products, next to food. Deodorant manufacturers took their small discreet advertisements off the back pages and used full-page ads to address "The Most

Humiliating Moment in My Life." Cosmetics manufacturers surrounded women with mirrors and underlined the centrality of fashionable and youthful appearance in striving for personal fulfillment. Listerine publicized and more or less invented the fear of halitosis, "the unforgivable social offense," and promised to keep its users on "the safe and polite side." The Listerine campaign was especially revealing of the other-directed sense of the self conveyed in advertising, because, as Vincent Vinikas has noted, the users of mouthwash "had to be so attuned to appeasing others that they would routinely engage in a practice, the results of which were, from the user's perspective, virtually imperceptible." Certainly not all ads played on consumers' anxieties and insecurities, or promised antidotes to the various ills of modern society, but these themes were pervasive and point to the importance of advertising in shaping the contours of the personality-oriented consumer culture.

Equally significant were the movies. Modern films began to emerge shortly before World War I. As movies shifted from nickelodeons, with primarily a working-class audience, to photoplays, they became more sophisticated and also began to attract the middle class. As they moved into middle-class districts, their numbers expanded, with the twenties witnessing significant growth. As theaters became part of the chain-store phenomenon, firms like Loew's and First National Exhibitors' Circuit started the process of consolidating movie distribution. Theater architecture was also transformed: movie houses became palaces, large buildings, seating up to several thousand, sometimes air-conditioned, and increasingly luxurious. In the teens the firm of Balaban and Katz of Chicago started the trend that would culminate in such flights of fancy as Los Angeles' Grauman's Chinese "palace" and the Egyptian "temple." The decor was often geared to specific movies. A review in *The New York Times* reported that for the premier of *The Thief of Bagdad* (1924), the theater had assumed "a thoroughly Oriental atmosphere, with drums, ululating vocal offerings, odiferous incense, perfume from Bagdad, magic carpets and ushers in Arabian attire, who during the intermission made a brave effort to bear cups of Turkish coffee to the women in the audience." The exotic, glamorous settings for the films underlined their appeal: they were not merely entertainment, but an escape from the mundane, workaday world.

If movies as recreation represented an antidote to the modern world, their content further offered a variety of messages appropriate to the consumer culture. Some films (most noticeably those of Douglas Fairbanks in the late teens) directly addressed the issue of the degradation of work. As Lary May has pointed out, many of these movies featured a white-collar worker frustrated by the confines of meaningless work. Thus, one caption described the hero: "his boundless energy is trapped at a desk in a button factory." The solution to the dilemma was never to change work itself—but to find meaning in leisure. "The heroes in Fairbanks' films," May notes, "discover new energy through boxing, tumbling, fencing, or gymnastics." Fairbanks was one of the first major stars whose personal life became the subject of intense public interest. As an "idol of consumption," Fairbanks promoted the new leisure not only in films but also in real life. In articles, speeches, and books, he propounded a new leisure ethic: "We read so much of work and success that someone needs to preach the glory of play."

In the 1920s, Fairbanks' films shifted to another way of challenging the older Victorian traditions of restraint associated with the work ethic and "character." He often played foreigners, tanned, robust, vibrant. These roles emphasized not only physicality but escape into an exotic world. A poster for *The Thief of Bagdad* that did justice to the tone of the movie portrayed him astride a magnificent winged horse, his sword upheld, as he streaked across the sky, with the minarets and mosques of Bagdad in the background. Fairbanks' physical grace and vibrancy evoked sexuality, but kept eroticism in check; far more explicit was the sensation of the decade, Rudolph Valentino. Valentino became synonymous with the role he played in *The Sheik*, a character of aggressive physicality and smoldering passion, unfettered by the restraints of "civilization." Appropriately, "Ben-Allah," in his biography, *Rudolph Valentino: His Romantic Life and Death* (1926), repeatedly insisted that the key to the box office idol's success was personality: "With nothing but his personality to sell, Valentino sold it and at a price that but few have done in the history of the world." Both in their films and personally, stars like Fairbanks and Valentino emphasized charm, youth, and physical expressiveness, thus helping to set the tone for an updated version of masculinity, as well as for the new cultural emphasis on self-expression, leisure, and personality.

At the opposite end of the spectrum, away from daring exploits and desert romances, were the vastly popular comedies featuring stars like Charlie Chaplin, Harold Lloyd, and Buster Keaton. But they, too, with their ironic humor and visual gags, offered challenges to older notions of order, restraint, and propriety. In some cases, the characters that screen comics played came up against machines or the bureaucratic world and made wry comments on the individual's plight in urban mass society. Harold Lloyd in *Safety Last* (1923) played a not too successful clerk in a department store. In an effort to achieve a promotion and impress a young woman, he devises an advertising stunt: a human fly to climb up the side of the store's building. The stuntman is delayed by a run-in with a policeman and Lloyd's character must go up—hindered by a variety of hair-raising obstacles, including being caught by an appropriate symbol of modern times, a huge clock. He finally succeeds and wins the girl. As Robert Sklar has commented: "One could hardly ask for a more graphic satire on the theme of 'upward mobility.'"

Another movie addressed upward mobility in modern times more directly, and is a perfect exemplar of the confluence of consumption, personality, and success. In *Skinner's Dress Suit* (1925), a white-collar husband is ground down by his monotonous job. He punches a clock and commutes to suburbia to a wife who spends above her means and buys on the installment plan. One of her purchases was dance lessons. The film's denouement is an office party, staged at an Arabian-theme nightclub, where the Skinners' skill at the new dances brings the husband to the attention of his boss. As Lary May concludes: "Now his employer promotes Skinner away from his desk, for they realize he has a personality that can sell goods. . . . In the age of cooperation, personality is a commodity that will advance one up the ladder."

The films of Cecil B. De Mille further illustrate the linkage between consumption, personality, and success. In contrast to D. W. Griffith, a leading director of the prewar years whose films aimed at shoring up Victorian values, De Mille embraced new values. Many of his films depicted modern marriage. His characters remake themselves into more modern individuals in order to find ultimate happiness in updated marriages. Films such as *Foolish Wives* and *Male and Female* are particularly striking in the way in which they portray women's identity as inseparable from the clothes and cosmetics that adorn them, an issue that will be analyzed in the following chapter. De Mille's films further suggest the trend toward privatization, with individuals looking for satisfaction increasingly in the personal sphere, and achieving it through consumption, leisure, and self-expression.

Finally, the first talkie, *The Jazz Singer*, suggests the way in which movies reflected and reinforced the consumer culture. The film centers on the character Jack Robin, played by Al Jolson. He is a second-generation New York Jew whose father, a cantor wedded to Jewish orthodoxy, wants his son to follow in his footsteps. Jack wants to use his voice in a more secular way; he is a jazz singer. He rejects the old world for the new and embarks on his entertainment career, in the process becoming estranged from his parents. When he returns to New York and is about to be featured in a major show at the Winter Garden, he discovers that his father is dying and that the synagogue will have no cantor for Yom Kippur, the day of atonement, a central Jewish holiday. On his deathbed, the old cantor urges his son to sing Kaddish. But if Jack fulfills his Jewish and filial duty, he will miss the opening of the show, and his big chance. In the play the movie was based upon, Jack sings Kaddish for the synagogue and the play ends. Family, ethnicity, and religion triumph together. In the movie, Jack fulfills his familial obligation. He sings Kaddish, but he returns to the Winter Garden the next night, where he has his big chance and sings "Mammy" to an approving audience that includes his mother.

The film offers many messages. One clearly is a story of assimilation. Jews can be Americans and pursue their individual goals but still be loyal children. But the film is also an unintentional reminder of the various threads that went into the fabric of the emerging consumer culture. Jack is a Jewish entertainer, albeit an Americanized one, who sings in blackface. As many scholars have noted, one of the functions of blackface was to offer whites a mask that allowed them to be more expressive than the Victorian norm permitted whites. The meaning of Jews, another outsider group, donning blackface is beyond our story here, but *The Jazz Singer* does suggest that both African American and immigrant performers helped influence the contours of the new culture. More overtly, the film's message is significant in that Jack's career choice was one that put him at the center of consumer culture: he is an entertainer, a *jazz* singer. Jack's character is exuberant; when he sings, he emotes, he dances, he has personality, he is an exemplar of the reorientation of culture, toward the new, the modern that Hollywood so often celebrated.

Despite the clear messages about consumption, leisure, and identity that emerge in various forms of the mass media, we should not assume that middle-class Americans willy-nilly accepted the messages, that they were hapless victims of the manipulation of admen, movie moguls, and other agents of mass culture. Just as ethnic, working-class consumers could interpret media messages in ways that made sense to them, so too could the middle class. Moreover, the purveyors of mass culture, after all, had products to sell; their success depended upon constructing a message that appealed to their audience. They undeniably constituted a powerful force in formulating the contours of the new culture, but consumers were crucial as well. As Lawrence W. Levine has argued, "Choices were being made; in every popular genre, audiences distinguished between what they found meaningful, appealing, and functional and what they did not." Their choices reflected their needs and desires as they sought new ways to define success and achieve satisfaction in the complex terrain of modern life.

And as pervasive as the reorientation of culture and leisure was, it would be a mistake to overstate it, for there is also evidence of Americans' ambivalence to the changes transforming culture and society. In 1927, Charles A. Lindbergh became the first person to fly the Atlantic alone and was an instant celebrity of extraordinary proportions. Americans feted him and turned out reams of prose demonstrating how Lindbergh personified their culture. In "The Meaning of Lindbergh's Flight," John William Ward discovered two seemingly contradictory interpretations of Lindbergh's feat. On the one hand, writers lionized the flyer for representing the American past of the frontier and the rugged individual. The fact that he flew alone was central to this celebration. According to the *New York Sun*: ". . . no kingly plane for him; / No endless data, comrades, moneyed chums; / No bards, no councils, no directors grim— / He plans ALONE . . . and takes luck as it comes." Lindbergh represented in part the democratic individual of the past triumphing over the modern bureaucratic, corporate environment that hemmed in most Americans.

But conversely, writers celebrated Lindbergh for embodying American progress, for symbolizing the machine age. *The New York Times* exulted that Lindbergh "is, indeed, the Icarus of the twentieth century; not himself an inventor of his own wings, but a son of that omnipotent Daedalus whose ingenuity has created the modern world." President Calvin Coolidge more explicitly stated that Lindbergh "represented American industry." What are we to make of these two contradictory interpretations of Lindbergh's symbolic meaning? Ward suggested that Americans were of two minds about progress: they wanted the fruits of the corporation and its technology and organization, but still worried about their implications for individuals' freedom and autonomy.

In a study of the intensely publicized boxing matches between Gene Tunney and Jack Dempsey, Elliott Gorn also discovered in the celebration of heroes a complex pattern of cultural dilemmas. Newspaper coverage of the two fighters revealed the middle-class Tunney as an exemplar of the hope that old and new values were not incompatible, "that virtue and self-reliance could still thrive in a technocratic environment." In contrast, Dempsey's public persona, reflective of his rough-and-tumble working-class background, "represented the secret impulse to smash through the restrictions imposed on men by bourgeois, bureaucratic society," to resist "the social subordination which channelled individuals into narrow roles and tasks."

The Tunney-Dempsey clash highlights some of the complexities underlying America's social and cultural transformations. The difference between the two men was rooted partially in class and serves as a reminder that not all Americans embraced these changes in identical fashion. Ethnicity, race, and class were especially strong mediating factors. Clearly, middle-class Americans were much more engaged in the emerging consumer culture. They had the income and the time to participate most fully in new patterns of consumption and leisure. With a greater stake in society, they had more incentives to make at least an uneasy peace with the urban, industrial, corporate order by embracing the therapeutic ethos.

Dempsey and Tunney are also important because their considerable celebrity stemmed from their being products of the commercialization of leisure. Boxing, although not corporate, was big business. Moreover, the two men's fame, like Lindbergh's, was spread through the mass media—newspapers, radio, and even movies. There is a heavy irony here. Purveyors of mass culture articulated antidotes to the stress and alienation of modern life and work. But much of what they proposed, such as consumption and commercialized leisure, was made possible by mass production, mass advertising, and massive corporations. However much the consumer culture might glorify individual self-expression and freedom, Americans were tied symbiotically to the constraints of the modern corporate order.

THE NEW WOMAN

III

Women's lives, like those of men's, were profoundly affected by the increasingly organized nature of society, the emergence of the mass media and a consumer culture, and the changes in work and politics. And, like men, women constituted a heterogeneous group divided by race, class, ethnicity, and cultural values, whose very diversity testified to the increasingly pluralistic nature of society. Similarities in what men and women encountered in the 1920s are important, but gender was crucial in determining experience. Contemporary observers recognized this implicitly by characterizing the "new woman," as she was called, as a telling marker, a symbol, of modernity itself. They were right in their assessment that women's lives had changed dramatically since the late nineteenth century. Their entry into the public arena through participation in politics and an expanded presence in the workplace challenged older assumptions about women's proper sphere. Changing sexual mores also set the stage for a new conception of womanhood. This chapter explores the contours of the new womanhood by examining politics, work, and the personal arena. While documenting the complex changes which transformed and in many ways modernized women's lives, it demonstrates that for most women the modern goals of equality and personal autonomy were often elusive.

THE NEW WOMAN AND POLITICS

Perceptions of a new woman emerged as early as the 1890s. The term itself referred to women's increased college attendance and modest entry into the professions, and to their new athleticism and rejection of bulky, restrictive Victorian garments. It also encompassed the way in which late-nineteenth-century middle-class women had begun to shed traditional notions that their place was exclusively in the home. They were pushing out the boundaries of their traditional sphere and entering the political arena. Through their voluntary associations, these women had become political actors, lobbying for progressive reform legislation such as factory and child labor laws, prohibition, and urban reforms.

Women also continued the battle for full political rights through suffrage. A significant number of twentieth-century suffragists argued that women's superior morality would place them above the corruption of politics and they would bring their moral influence into the political scene and effect wide-ranging reforms. The practical uses of the vote attracted both upper- and middle-class reformers as well as working-class women to the campaign. Black women in their communities, although generally rebuffed by white women's organizations, also campaigned for suffrage, which they viewed as one step toward racial progress.

The long battle for suffrage heated up in 1910 when the state of Washington approved a suffrage referendum and brought renewed enthusiasm to the campaign. At about the same time, more radical voices were heard within the movement. Although elite and middle-class women were in the forefront of the fight, working-class and socialist women were a growing presence and helped to strengthen the Congressional Union, later called the National Woman's Party (NWP). The Congressional Union was founded in 1913, and a year later, led by Alice Paul, it broke with the more conservative National American Woman Suffrage Association (NAWSA), directed by Carrie Chapman Catt, and launched a campaign for a national amendment. Influenced both by British "suffragettes" and by the experiences of American working-class women with industrial strikes, Congressional

Union members picketed the White House during World War I to protest that while the country fought a war for democracy abroad it denied women their democratic rights at home. Distressed by such militant tactics, NAWSA leaders continued their more moderate campaigns in which they emphasized women's wartime service to the country. This uneasy alliance of a wide variety of women, using different tactics, finally overcame determined opposition, and in 1920 the federal amendment passed, enfranchising women throughout the nation. Having won the vote, women's leaders entered the new decade with optimism about their newly enlarged public responsibilities. They expected women voters to make a difference on a variety of fronts. They would pursue equality through legislation to expand their legal rights. Through organizations like the Women's International League for Peace and Freedom and the Women's Committee for World Disarmament, they would bring about disarmament and set the framework for a lasting peace, and domestically, they would implement a wide range of social reforms.

Women activists were not alone in their expectations about the potential power of female voters. Male politicians, many of whom had resisted suffrage and the disruption it threatened to the political equilibrium, took suffragists at their word that women would be a force to reckon with. The Democratic National Convention of 1920 incorporated twelve of twenty recommendations of the newly founded League of Women Voters; the Republican Party adopted five. Women became active as cadre in the political parties, and through their voluntary associations they lobbied for a variety of reforms.

Given the enthusiasm, energy, and commitment of these activists, and the susceptibility of politicians to claims about women's political power, one of the crucial questions of twentieth-century women's history has been why they accomplished relatively little with their votes. By the end of the 1920s, social reform had stalled, and the women's movement itself was in the doldrums. The new woman had clearly not fulfilled the great political expectations that her supporters had prophesied. The explanation is complex. External circumstances, particularly the conservative political climate of the 1920s, were important factors in setting limits to women's gains. In addition, weaknesses within the movement played a part. Before suffrage, diverse women could unite behind the single issue of the vote, but the women's movement, like progressivism itself, had been a fragile coalition and it fissured in the 1920s. Once the vote was achieved, differences and special interests surfaced. As activist Frances Kellor put it in 1923: "The American woman's movement, and her interest in great moral and social questions, is splintered into a hundred fragments under as many warring leaders."

The many splinters suggest an increasing awareness on women's part of the significance of categories other than gender that defined them. Certainly this was the case with African American women. Like their white counterparts, middle-class black women were well organized in the late nineteenth century. Through groups such as the National Association of Colored Women, founded in 1893, they sought to "uplift" their race through a variety of reforms. In addition, many women leaders had a strong feminist sense as well, and were eager to raise women's position. Black women, in at least twenty suffrage organizations, were strong supporters of the campaign for the vote, especially after 1910. Black suffragists sought the vote in part as a means of protecting their sisters, but they also viewed it as a way of addressing racial issues such as Jim Crow, male disenfranchisement, and economic discrimination, goals that underlined their view that the elevation of black women was inseparable from racial progress.

With few exceptions, black women were excluded from the white-dominated suffrage groups. Racism, as well as a fear that black participation in the movement would confirm southern perceptions that the amendment would disrupt well-established black disenfranchisement in that region, led white suffragists to rebuff black women's overtures at cooperation. Undeterred, even before the amendment passed, black women's organizations had embarked on voter registration campaigns in states that had adopted the suffrage. It was not coincidental that New York State sent its first black legislator to Albany and Chicago elected its first black alderman shortly after women gained the vote in New York and Illinois. After the amendment was ratified, black women redoubled their efforts, focusing especially on the South, where the majority of blacks, male and female, were disenfranchised. For example, spurred on by the Nineteenth Amendment, Florida black women outregistered white women, who responded by forming the white supremacist Duval County League of Democratic Women voters, which vowed to register white women voters. More typically, white Southerners resisted black female registration through official channels that had long been used to deny suffrage to black men—tax qualifications, educational tests, grandfather clauses, and harassment. Black women, through the National Association of Colored Women, assisted by the NAACP, fought back. They assembled evidence, which the NAACP presented to Congress, along with a call to pass the Tinkham bill, designed to reduce congressional representation of states which restricted women's suffrage. When this tactic failed, black women approached white women's organizations to elicit some support for enforcing the Nineteenth Amendment.

But neither the League of Women Voters, the successor to NAWSA, nor the Woman's Party was willing to support the reform efforts of black women voters in the South. The Woman's Party's indifference was typical of what black women encountered. At its 1921 convention, the National Association of Colored Women worked persistently to get the party to establish a committee to "bring pressure to bear on Congress for the appointment of a Special Congressional Committee to investigate the violation of the intent and purposes of the Nineteenth Amendment." Alice Paul, arguing that this was a racial rather than a woman's issue, refused to give the women specific convention time, even after a delegation of sixty black women called upon her. In the end, the frustrated black women presented the resolution from the floor, reminding the convention that "five million women in the United States cannot be denied their rights without all the women of the United States feeling the effect of that denial. No women are free until all women are free." The resolution failed to pass.

It is not surprising, then, that black women pulled away from addressing specifically women's issues that concerned white women and concentrated more on racial ones that they viewed as part of black women's agenda for improving the lives of all African Americans. One outspoken woman who explicitly criticized organizations like the Woman's Party and the League of Women Voters was Amy Jacques Garvey, Marcus Garvey's wife and a leader of the Universal Negro Improvement Association in her own right. Garvey, a strong believer in women's capabilities, shared the black nationalism of the UNIA, but she did not let her racial agenda obscure her interest in advancing the cause of black women. She called for equality with men within the organization and argued that women should be at the forefront of the struggle for black liberation.

Other African American women in the 1920s increasingly worked within male-dominated black organizations to pursue their common racial interests. Black women's organizations had been leaders in the anti-lynching campaign of the late nineteenth century. In 1922, Mary B. Talbert established the Anti-Lynching Women Crusaders as a division of the NAACP, and organized over 700 state workers, who compiled statistics about lynching and conducted research. As they concentrated on lynching and economic improvement, black women backed away from white women's organizations, as well as from their own campaign to obtain the vote for blacks in the South. In 1928, the National Association of Colored Women's official program did not include the suffrage issue as one of its priorities. In a 1925 article published in *The Crisis* ("The Double Task: The Struggle of Negro Women for Race and Sex Emancipation"), Elsie J. MacDonald summed up the disaffection concisely by explaining that black "feminist efforts are directed chiefly toward the realization of the equality of the races, the sex struggle assuming a subordinate place." The white/black division among women was striking and it points to the tremendous difficulty facing women pursuing feminist goals. In emphasizing a common ground of shared gender, white women tended to have a more narrow sense of women's issues than did black women. Moreover, they did not agree among themselves on the appropriate agenda for newly enfranchised citizens.

The best-known division was the split among white activists

over the question of a federal Equal Rights Amendment (ERA). The Woman's Party, still dominated in the twenties by Alice Paul, was the key proponent of the ERA, which its members viewed as a means of achieving complete equality. In opposition were a variety of women's reform organizations, which feared that an ERA would damage long-standing efforts to secure or maintain sex-based labor legislation governing wages, hours, and conditions of women workers that had been designed to protect working women from exploitation. Although not the only point of dispute among women activists, the issue is especially important because not only did it create ill feeling but it also exposed conflicting opinions about women's nature and the meaning of equality, problems that hampered the maintenance of a strong women's movement in the 1920s.

The Woman's Party based its support of the ERA on the realization that although suffrage represented a major breakthrough for political equality, many limitations persisted, including women's representation on juries; their ability to execute contracts and deeds and to be executors and trustees; inequities in married women's property rights; and discrimination in wages. While the Women's Party initially promoted laws redressing specific inequities, eventually it focused on the idea of winning a comprehensive constitutional amendment. Following its tactics in the suffrage campaign, the party devoted most of its energies to a federal Equal Rights Amendment ("Men and women shall have equal rights throughout the United States and every place subject to its jurisdiction"), which it first introduced in Congress in 1923. The party viewed the ERA as a quicker solution to women's disabilities and the only way to produce change in states in which legislators still resisted women's legal equality. As it pushed for an ERA on the national level, it also hardened its resistance to sex-based or, as it was often called, "protective" labor legislation for women. Its spokeswomen argued that these laws treated women as invalids and set up the possibility for limiting their economic opportunity. "Labor laws for women only are vertical," as Lavinia Dock, a Woman's Party leader, put it in 1926, "and like a wall, may be so built as to shut out as many as they shut in."

The rhetoric of Woman's Party leaders emphasized the bond between women, but their activities and tactics tended to drive women apart. The elite-run organization did not build up a grass-roots following. It made relatively little educational effort to bring in young women, who in the 1920s were increasingly indifferent to the feminist movement. The decision to pursue the ERA exclusively also shut down broader possibilities for promoting female solidarity. The 1921 Woman's Party convention was a turning point. Alice Paul organized it ostensibly as a forum for discussing the direction of the movement, but she structured the convention's agenda so as to suppress advocates of birth control and black women's call for suffrage rights. The convention also voted down a disarmament plank and overwhelmingly defeated socialist Crystal Eastman's proposal for a broad-ranging program that encompassed birth control and aid to dependent mothers, thus disaffecting radical feminists who had been attracted to the party before the war and who had offered the most far-ranging definition of feminism, addressing issues of sexual, economic, and political freedom. By the midtwenties, the term "feminism" had been appropriated by the Woman's Party, which insisted that its meaning was synonymous with the pursuit of equality through the ERA.

The Woman's Party also alienated the great majority of activists in a variety of women's organizations such as the National Consumers League, the Women's Trade Union League, and the League of Women Voters, which supported sex-based labor legislation. These social reformers, who had a broader agenda than ensuring women's equality, felt that the NWP abandoned poor and working-class women to their own devices. The NWP's stance on protective legislation reflects in part the class interests of its leaders. The same narrowness that figured in the party's rebuff of black women's request for commitment to black women voters in the South shaped its belief that women's issues did not include the specific problems of working-class women. The focus of the party's struggle—legal discrimination—addressed primarily the interests of white, middle-class, propertied women. For example, they often assumed that the married woman worker whom they championed had adequate child care and servants. Moreover, they did not really address the problems of women who combined work and responsibilities at home. In response to the difficulties faced by industrial women workers, the NWP was sympathetic, but insisted that their problems were due not to gender but to class and suggested unionization and industrial legislation for all workers. They denied that these issues were appropriate for an organization devoted to women's rights. Thus despite rhetoric about the bond between women, the NWP's narrow vision contributed to the splintering of the women's movement in the 1920s.

Ironically, regardless of the deep differences between the two groups, the women who supported sex-based labor legislation were in many ways similar to their adversaries in the Women's Party. They, too, were upper and middle class and had been active in the suffrage movement. They, too, addressed the problem of women's legal disabilities and lobbied for corrective legislation. However, unlike the NWP leaders, whose rhetoric tended to underplay the differences between men and women in the pursuit of equal rights, women social reformers like Julia Lathrop and Frances Perkins stressed the distinctiveness of women. They stressed the biological differences that required protective legislation. Moreover, their sense of women's moral superiority and special maternal qualities, a remnant of the nineteenth-century ideology of separate spheres, shaped their commitment to social reform. Their notion of women's special sensitivity as mothers and of their superior moral nature that elevated them above politics informed many women's deep involvement in the peace movement in the interwar years. They fought against universal military training and for arms limitation, a naval treaty, and the Kellogg-Briand Pact, which pledged nations to renounce war. They also supported a gamut of domestic reforms that included, in addition to protective legislation for women and children workers, a variety of good government reforms, especially city management, for which women claimed a special affinity because they viewed themselves as above partisan politics. Early in the decade, most women reformers were also strong supporters of prohibition. Although these women worked through a number of diverse institutions, one of the most significant was a new one, the League of Women Voters, which emerged out of NAWSA when suffrage was achieved. The League was never as numerically strong as its parent. In 1920 NAWSA had 2 million members, but in 1930, after a decade of building, the League's rolls consisted of only 100,000 women. The League's leaders debated what role women should play now that they were enfranchised. Rejecting partisan politics, including the idea of a separate women's party, with the argument that the appearance of a women's voting bloc would alienate public opinion and produce a backlash, they concluded that women should maintain a position above party politics and planned to pursue women's goals through civic education and lobbying.

Get-out-the-vote campaigns formed an important part of the League's efforts to improve political life. The low turnout during the 1920 election (53 percent), which some observers attributed to the disinterest of new women voters rather than realizing that it was part of a broad trend toward political apathy, prompted the League to set up citizenship classes and establish local campaigns to get women to the polls. Ironically, after its exhaustive efforts, the percentage of voters in 1924 continued to decline, although there were some spectacular local successes after League campaigns. Voting records by sex are unavailable, but scattered statistics suggest that although women's voting increased during the decade, women probably still did not vote in as high a proportion as men. Nor is there much evidence for discernible bloc voting among women. By mid-decade contemporary assessments assumed that most women were indifferent to the franchise.

On the state level, the League supported much of the same type of equalitarian legislation, with the exclusion of the ERAs, as the Women's Party. But unlike the Women's Party, the League also pursued a wide variety of reform legislation not specific to women. As part of their program to clean up politics, state leagues were especially active in municipal reform and were one of the major forces behind the city manager movement, which was viewed as a means to enhanced efficiency and the elimination of the power of urban machines. Child welfare laws, touching on work, school attendance, and child custody, were another important arena for social reform. The League also lobbied for women's protective labor legislation, while at the same time it vigorously fought the state and national ERAs that the Women's Party supported. On the national level, the League worked primarily through an organization it had been instrumental in establishing in 1920, the Women's Joint Congressional Committee. It counted as one of its major successes the Sheppard-Towner Maternity Act of 1921, which provided matching federal funds for states to provide health care and other services for mothers and children. Women not only were instrumental in passing the bill but also were crucial in assuring its implementation in the states by agitating for the state appropriations required.

Although women reformers had important early successes on both the state and the national level, there were sobering defeats as well. Throughout the decade, devoted lobbyists failed to achieve a national department of education, with matching state funds to tackle illiteracy and other educational deficiencies. The drive to eliminate the exploitation of child labor also failed. In 1921, the Supreme Court found Congress's second national child labor law to be unconstitutional. In response, Florence Kelley, working through the National Consumers' League and the Women's Joint Congressional Committee, succeeded in pushing Congress to pass the Child Labor Amendment in 1924, which would have authorized Congress to pass legislation regulating the labor of children under eighteen. But despite the exhaustive efforts of the Organizations Associated for Ratification of the Child Labor Amendment, composed primarily of women's groups, the amendment received little support in the states. By 1930, a mere six states had ratified.

Other disappointments followed. In 1929, federal appropriations for the Maternity Act ceased and the program was phased out. Failures on the federal level were mirrored in the states. Both social reform and women's rights legislation had foundered by the late 1920s. Moreover, women had made relatively few inroads into the power structure of the political parties. Women formed an important part of the party cadres, especially in the

Democratic camp, but relatively few were rewarded with power. As an article in *Current History* put it: "Where there is dignity of office but little else, or where there is routine work, little glory, and low pay, men prove willing to admit women to an equal share in the spoils of office." In addition, many of the women who did achieve positions of prestige within the parties were party loyalists, who did not have any background in the women's movement and were not interested in social reform.

Thus, after the auspicious beginning in the first years after suffrage, women had not been able to translate their voting power into meaningful, sustained political power. What were the sources of this failure? One important factor was the oppressive political climate of the 1920s. Despite women activists' persistent efforts, the decade was increasingly characterized by hostility to reform. Young college women, once the mainstay of women reformers, were largely indifferent to social reform or women's rights. Their lack of interest in politics stemmed in part from their enthusiasm for their personal pursuits of courtship and consumerism. Their indifference to politics and reform was, of course, shared by many men. Resentment of federal power, increased by the resistance to prohibition, was a widespread sentiment that politicians and business interests, eager to keep private enterprise unfettered, manipulated to oppose specific reform legislation. The lingering of the Red Scare also made it relatively easy to portray measures such as the Sheppard-Towner Maternity Act and the Child Labor Amendment as the beginnings of socialism. Pacifism and efforts to promote disarmament and to oppose military spending and universal military training were similarly branded as part of an international Bolshevik plot. Not surprisingly, given women's sympathies with reform and the peace movement, critics of reform explicitly linked women's organizations to the Bolshevik threat.

The Red Scare hurt women's efforts at reform, and it also helped to widen divisions among women. Red baiting caused some women's groups to disassociate themselves from the Women's Joint Congressional Committee. Pacifist organizations tended to moderate their stance out of self-defense, and become more conservative. Support for the peace movement, one of the few arenas where women were united in the early part of the decade, became controversial. Red baiting points to another division as well. Preeminent among the opponents of reform were right-wing women's organizations. The Women Sentinels of the Republic was a small but vocal group that opposed social reform as the forerunner of Bolshevism. The Daughters of the American Revolution, initially interested in women's social reform efforts, had by mid-decade also taken up the red-baiting hysteria.

The polar opposition of the Women Sentinels and the Women's Joint Congressional Committee suggests another source for the rout of the women's movement. Both supporters of the ERA and women who backed a wide range of social reforms had believed that women's moral sensibilities linked all women, both in a sense of sisterhood and in programs for improving the public arena and expanding their rights. But by mid-decade it became clear that women leaders in the major organizations had not been successful in galvanizing the mass of women voters to rally behind their cause. Moreover, the activists themselves were not politically united. The Women Sentinels and the Women's Joint Congressional Committee; the National Woman's Party, and the League of Women Voters; African American women and southern white women; party regulars and bipartisan women; prohibitionists and antiprohibitionists—all suggest the diversity of public women's agenda.

The ideas of the leaders who had assumed a bond between women based on shared gender identity had been forged by the existence of a distinct women's political culture in the nineteenth century that grew out of the idea of separate spheres that had posited rigid roles for men and women and had relegated the latter exclusively to the private arena. Women's exclusion from the public sphere, especially the arena of politics, had helped to define their unity. This unity was to some extent, of course, fictive. Class, race, and ethnicity were largely insurmountable barriers in the nineteenth century. But as historian Estelle Freedman has argued, within the upper and middle classes there was a separate political culture that gave an apparent cohesion to women activists. In the 1920s both the cohesion and the separatism began to erode. Both the vote and, as we will see, changes in the workplace and the personal realm narrowed the great gap between male and female experience. With more access to the public arena, with more options to choose from in their personal lives, other distinctions that divided women came more obviously to the fore. There was not a new woman, but many new women. In the political sphere, women achieved more rights and became more integrated into the mainstream political culture. But women's widely varying agendas made it difficult for them to translate political enfranchisement into political power.

THE NEW WOMAN AND WORK

Since it was popularly believed that suffrage had led to a new equality and freedom for women, it was assumed that women were becoming economically independent in the early twentieth century, especially after World War I. As Frederick Lewis Allen put it in the popular history *Only Yesterday* (1931), women "poured out of schools and colleges into all manner of occupations." Allen assumed that these new jobs brought the financial independence that led to the "slackening of husbandly and parental authority," which in turn had set in motion a moral revolution that encouraged both divorce and women's "headlong pursuit of freedom."

This view of women, work, and liberation is distorted and inaccurate. To begin with, the war had little permanent impact on female employment—only a small percentage of women working during the war were new workers. And although during the war women could be found working in traditionally male occupations such as mail carriers, streetcar conductors, skilled factory workers, and government-employed physicians, after the war most women lost these more desirable jobs. As one contemporary observer, Constance Green, commented: "The brief interlude . . . which some enthusiasts heralded as launching a new era for women in industry . . . came and went with astonishingly little permanent effect upon women's opportunities." Although

there were significant differences in the experiences of working women in the 1920s that centered on marital status, race, ethnicity, and class, they shared a narrow and highly sex-segregated labor market which classified their jobs as "women's work," and thereby devalued them.

Although the war itself was not necessarily a transforming experience for most women, nonetheless in the first decades of the twentieth century there were important changes that permanently affected American women's working lives. Beginning with 1900, the percentage of females over sixteen who worked rose, from 20.6 to 25.3 percent, in 1930. The increase in women's employment signaled the erosion of the traditional women's sphere in the home, but it did not necessarily mean that women enjoyed enhanced equality or liberation. In 1930, almost a third of working women were employed in the decidedly unglamorous field of domestic service, and more than half were either black or foreign-born whites, whose need was greatest and whose job opportunities were the most limited. In the 1920s, 86 percent of women were clustered in ten occupations, in jobs in which they made less money and had lower status and lower levels of skills than men.

More startling to contemporaries than the increase in the number of women working was the change in wives' participation in the workforce. In 1900, 15 percent of working women were married; in 1930, the percentage was 29. The jobs of most working wives and single mothers tended to be among the least desirable. Only a fraction of married workers were in professional or semiprofessional work; the vast majority of those not in agriculture were in manufacturing, retail trade, and domestic and personal service. A significant proportion of working wives were African Americans whose poverty pushed them into the workforce. Some remained at home, taking in boarders, but most of the jobs available to black women were in the most devalued field, that of domestic service.

Although not quite as limited, European immigrant married women workers' occupational horizons were also circumscribed. In the nineteenth century, because of the paternalistic nature of their cultures, relatively few wives had worked outside the home for wages. They contributed to the family income by taking in boarders and by doing piecework. In the 1920s, few married immigrant women worked outside the home, although there was a small increase during the decade. By mid-decade, immigration restriction had reduced the number of new immigrants seeking lodging, and changes in the structure of mass production industries had begun to shrink the demand for piecework. Moreover, compulsory school attendance and child labor laws forced some children out of the workforce, and their mothers took jobs in their stead. Despite the increased visibility of working wives, only 10 percent of all wives worked in the 1920s. The vast majority of employed women were single, and although there was a rise in the age of women workers in this period, the female workforce was preponderantly young. Some lived alone. Statistics are hard to come by, but surveys for the period 1900–30 give estimates of "women adrift" ranging from 10 to 25 percent of working women. While some of these single women had no choice, others sought out an independent existence that gave them freedom from family restraints and obligations. Although many may have achieved some personal autonomy, their poor pay compelled most lone women to live under harsh conditions, barely making ends meet.

Most working-class daughters, like their brothers, were expected to contribute to the family income. In 1923, a study of poverty-level families revealed that while almost all fathers, sons, and daughters worked for wages, only around 25 percent of wives or mothers did. The types of jobs available to young women varied according to race and ethnicity. Not surprisingly, the white working class had the most options. In the twenties most European immigrant daughters continued patterns set in the late nineteenth century. Family need forced them to leave school at a young age to contribute to the family income. In the 1920s, young women stayed in school longer, but by age sixteen they were likely to be in the labor force, and remained in it until marriage. Daughters, unlike their brothers, turned over their entire pay packet to their mothers and then received a small expense allowance, a practice that became a source of contention in many families by the 1920s. Eager to participate in the consumer culture, and encouraged by the rising prosperity of their families, working-class daughters demanded more of the fruits of their labor. The possibilities of consumption, as well as congenial work groups consisting of other adolescent women, made tedious work tolerable.

In the late nineteenth century, immigrant women had worked primarily in factories, performing unskilled or semiskilled "light" labor such as assembling, packing, and garment sewing. This continued into the twentieth century, although there were changes. The hours declined to an average of forty-eight a week; technology and social reform had made the labor somewhat less arduous; and wages improved, although they remained on average a bit more than half of what men earned. In addition, by the 1910s the daughters of European immigrants increasingly were able to win white-collar jobs, as increased demand and their improved education level offered new opportunities. But in the white-collar field immigrant daughters had to compete with "old stock" women, who may have had more education and were certainly preferred by employers for their perceived refinement and status. In stores, native-born older women sold the high-priced goods, while immigrants and young women were at the counters selling cheaper items. At the office, too, immigrant daughters clustered at the bottom of the job hierarchy.

The increase in white-collar work was of great importance for white women in the early twentieth century. Nineteenth-century clerical work had been primarily a male preserve and often served as means of advancement up the office ladder, but by the 1920s the lower rungs of the ladder, stenographers and file clerks, had become feminized, and young women poured into America's offices. Clerical work was the second-largest field for female workers: by the end of the decade, 19 percent of working women over sixteen, the vast majority of them single, were in these jobs. Saleswomen and clerks in stores represented around 6 percent of the female labor force in the 1920s. These new jobs not only widened the opportunities of immigrant daughters but also brought in middle-class workers who would have found factory work and domestic service demeaning.

Middle-class young women in white-collar work stood out and contributed to the sense of a new working woman, and undoubtedly prompted the media to glamorize them. They appeared in fiction and advertising, but especially in movies.

In the early part of the decade movies were rarely concerned with the nature of women's work itself. Rather they featured salesgirls and clerks who found in their jobs the environment for meeting desirable husbands. In addition to emphasizing the life of working girls, films also pictured work as a means of acquiring consumer goods and enjoying the new urban pleasures, and a few films linked consumption and marriage by presenting some working women as "gold diggers." By the late 1920s, as historian Mary Ryan has pointed out, the glamorous and unrealistic depiction of young working women became somewhat muted, perhaps because by then the novelty had worn off. Later films began to portray some of the more mundane aspects of white-collar work. In *Ankles Preferred* (1930), actress Madge Bellamy played a bored department store clerk, impatiently awaiting closing time. Superimposed on her face was a large clock, graphically suggesting the routinization of her work.

Later films more accurately reflected reality. For the most part, office workers put in long stretches of monotonous work, typing, filing, and other routine tasks. In some offices, the routine was made more oppressive by the introduction of scientific management techniques designed to measure and increase output. For the most part, office jobs meant specialized work with limited variety and responsibility. Sales work—where skill in interaction with customers was crucial—gave saleswomen a less regimented environment. As Susan Porter Benson has noted, a strong female work culture of sociability and solidarity helped saleswomen resist much of management's efforts to control them. But here, too, work could be arduous, with the combined frustration of pleasing the boss and the customer, while staying on one's feet all day.

As a rule, white-collar work—despite its appeal as a clean job with higher status than most women's work—was not well paid. Clerical workers' average annual wage in the 1920s was less than $1,200 (about $10,000 in 1990's dollars). There was much variation within the retail industry. Most saleswomen earned less than clerical workers, with salaries ranging from $688 in Kentucky to $1,085 in New Jersey, but their salaries were still not high. And there was a large wage differential between men and women: women earned 42 to 63 percent of male salesmen's salaries. In neither sales nor office work could many women expect to support themselves in a comfortable manner.

White-collar work did not lead to major changes in women's power in the workplace. Similar limits are evident in the experiences of the more fortunate women—the small cadre of professionals. The professional woman generated much publicity in the 1920s as an exemplar of the new woman, yet the percentage of women in professions was quite small. In 1910, 9 percent of working women were professionals. There was a steady increase in the next twenty years, so that by 1930 they constituted 14 percent. Enthusiastic about their status and optimistic about the future, these women represented the new women most likely to enjoy autonomy and personal satisfaction from their work. But a closer examination suggests the limited nature of their gains. The vast majority of female professionals were clustered in teaching, nursing, and a relatively new field, social work. Even in these "feminized" fields, women met with discrimination. Throughout the decade, the percentage of working women who were lawyers remained steady and small: 3 percent. Physicians lost ground: in 1920, they represented 5 percent of the female workforce; in 1930, 4.4 percent. Women interested in medicine were thwarted by minute medical school quotas and the widespread refusal of hospitals to accept women doctors as interns. In the 1920s, eight out of ten teachers were women, but women constituted only one in sixty-three superintendents. Thus in an arena which women might hope to achieve a degree of personal and economic autonomy, their numbers and opportunities were limited. Since well-educated white women in both clerical and professional fields had relatively limited options, it is hardly surprising that women of color met with even greater difficulty in earning their living. For African Americans and women of Japanese and Mexican descent, gender and race were powerful determinants that graphically illustrate the limits to the new woman in the workplace.

For African American women, the wartime migration had held out tremendous promise. Like men, they had sought better conditions in the North. They hoped to escape the discrimination and sexual exploitation of the South, where black women had little protection from the demands of white men. Above all, they sought better jobs. In the South, they were limited to agriculture, domestic service, and marginal, poorly paid jobs in factories and industry. Initially, their northern quest met with success, as work in railroads, the garment industry, government munitions, and a variety of other factory jobs became available to them during the war emergency.

But even during the war years, black women's jobs were the least desirable in the industrial sector, usually, as the *New York Age* put it, "doing work which white women will not do." And even these limited gains were not to last. Although some black women did maintain a toehold in industry, again in the worst jobs, after the war they were overwhelmingly concentrated in domestic service, laundry work, and agricultural labor. Domestic and laundry work was hard, debilitating labor for poor pay. Increasingly in the 1920s, black women refused jobs as live-in servants. As Elizabeth Clark-Lewis' oral history of Washington, D.C., domestic workers suggests, this small change, symbolized by their refusal to wear uniforms in day jobs, allowed these women to carve out a small degree of control over their work lives and their private time. But while day work offered an improvement over live-in situations, nonetheless domestic work continued to be highly exploitative.

Those few women who had factory jobs encountered harsh conditions and discrimination. A Women's Bureau investigator, Emma L. Shields, found in 1922 that black tobacco workers in the South were barred from the manufacturing of cigars and cigarettes, a white women's job; instead they did the preparatory work on the tobacco: "Tens of thousands of Negro women in the South are employed ten hours daily in old, unclean, malodorous buildings in which they are denied the most ordinary comforts of life. Either standing all day, in some occupations, or, in others, seated on makeshift stools or boxes with no back support, they toil incessantly throughout the long, tedious hours of the work day." For this seasonal labor, they earned only two dollars a week. The North was little better. In 1920, researcher Alma Herbst surveyed Chicago packing plants and slaughterhouses and found black women seasonally employed in the hogkilling and beef-casing section, "the most unattractive and disagreeable department," where they worked "under repulsive conditions." In both North and South, black women were segregated from white women, who generally refused to work with African Americans. Invariably, these white women had rest rooms, cleaner jobs, and better pay.

Some African American women were able to escape and achieve some spectacular successes. Madame C. J. Walker, who died in 1919, became a millionaire manufacturing and selling hair and cosmetic preparations to black women. Maggie Lena Walker (not related) was the founder and president of what became the Consolidated Bank and Trust Company, a blackowned and black-run bank. But most black women entrepreneurs were independent dressmakers or hairdressers. With the help of migration, black businesses in the North did expand in the 1920s, and thus opened a few clerical jobs to women. But opportunities were few—African Americans owned only 20 percent of Harlem businesses, and black women were almost completely shut out of clerical or sales work for white employers. The federal government largely excluded them after President Wilson had resegregated civil service. This exclusion from clerical work was especially egregious because many black women had attained educational equivalency to native white women in the 1920s.

Well-educated black women had some professional opportunities. Social work was expanding in the twenties, and organizations like the YWCA and the Urban League hired trained black women to serve their own community. Teaching was open to African Americans, but unlike white women, they had difficulty finding jobs, especially in the North. In 1920, for example, Chicago employed only 138 black female teachers. Nurses faced similar discrimination: they found it difficult to get public health jobs, and when they did, they were paid significantly less than white women. White nurses' organizations, then in the process of professionalizing the field, denied African American nurses membership. Repeatedly black nurses found, as their sisters in factories had discovered, that white women were unwilling to work with them.

Mexican immigrant women and their daughters shared with African Americans the experience of migration. In the early twentieth century, Mexican migration to the United States increased dramatically. Almost 10 percent of Mexico's population, over a million people, emigrated to the United States between 1910 and 1930. Some traveled to midwestern cities, but most congregated in the South and Southwest. Although many of these migrants worked in the expanding "factories in the field," the increasingly large agribusinesses of the West and Southwest, by 1930 half of the Mexicans in the United States lived in urban areas.

We know relatively little about Mexican women workers. Until 1930, the census did not enumerate people of Mexican descent as a group. In that year, the statistics for Mexicanas and Chicanas employed was among the lowest of all groups, around 15 percent, a figure that undoubtedly undercounted the most common form of female employment, agricultural labor. Most Mexican migrant women, continuing a tradition of a family economy, worked in agriculture as part of the family unit, and did not receive an individual wage. Throughout the West and Southwest, wages were so poor that families were dependent upon the labor of everyone—women and children—to maintain the minimum essentials of life. While these women worked in the fields, they struggled to raise their families in dismal conditions and dire poverty.

Although there was strong Mexican cultural resistance to married or single women working for wages, the necessity of supplementing the wages of men, who were often seasonally employed and whose wages were invariably low, led urban Mexicanas and Chicanas into the workforce. Historian Albert Camarillo found that in the small community of Santa Barbara, California, the large majority of women labored in unskilled or semiskilled jobs as servants, seamstresses, and so forth. The 1910s, however, saw a slight expansion of job possibilities. In 1920, 29 percent of working women of Mexican descent had clerical or sales jobs, mostly working for Mexicans or Anglos who owned businesses that required bilingual employees for their Spanish-speaking clientele. A 1928 study by economist Paul S. Taylor offered some details of women employed in industrial jobs in Los Angeles. Taylor reported that "in some cases the wife or mother sought the work; in others, the young daughters. In either case, poverty was the immediate incentive." Nine-tenths of the workers surveyed were unmarried young women, who despite cultural resistance to female employment "looked upon some sort of industrial work as they complete their basic education as in the natural course of events" before marriage. The greatest proportion "were employed in packing houses and canneries of various kinds, followed by the clothing, needle trades, and laundries," with relatively few working in manufacturing. Like black women, they were heavily concentrated in domestic labor: in 1930, 44 percent were servants.

Yet another group, Japanese women, found their opportunities severely circumscribed by racial discrimination and economic marginality, with domestic service their major form of employment. Next to black women, the Japanese were the most likely group of women to work outside the home: of the 25,000 Japanese women in America, 30 percent worked for wages. Most of these were Issei, or first generation, because the second generation, Nisei, were as a rule too young to work outside the home in the 1920s. And since most Issei women were married, most of these working women were also wives. A significant proportion of these employed women were engaged in agricultural labor, primarily on family farms. They and their children provided the unpaid labor that was crucial to the remarkable success of Japanese farmers on the West Coast who specialized in labor-intensive agriculture.

In the cities, the Issei women, limited by their lack of skills, difficulties with English, and racial prejudice, found few jobs open to them. As a rule, they sought positions that could be combined with their family responsibilities. Relatively few worked in manufacturing, the least flexible type of job. Some women worked as clerks or assistants in small family-owned enterprises. Others did piecework, especially garment sewing, in their homes. Sociologist Evelyn Nakano Glenn reported on a Japanese couple in San Francisco's Chinatown who sold hand-made kimonos in their gift shop. The wife cut out the fabric for each kimono, which was then distributed to women pieceworkers, who were paid three dollars for the completed garment.

The most significant employment for Issei women outside agriculture was domestic service. In 1920, 27 percent were servants; the figure dropped to 18 percent in 1930, probably reflecting an increase in employment in Japanese-owned retail establishments. Domestic labor, although difficult work that often required demeaning subordination to an employer, nonetheless had advantages. Women sought out day work, with relatively flexible schedules that would allow them to maintain their families and work at the same time. Those who worked did so primarily to supplement their husband's inadequate wages. Even wives of small entrepreneurs often found it necessary to help out. There were two main tracks for domestic employment. Some began as apprentices before they were married and continued to work most of their lives. Others began after marriage, when the financial pressures of children required additional income.

Domestic service was isolating and provided no avenue to better, more lucrative jobs. It was also difficult labor. According to the women Glenn interviewed, however, there were some advantages. Working in American homes gave them an opportunity to learn the English language and American ways. These women also expressed pride in their ability not only to work hard but also to figure out how to please each employer. In addition, they took satisfaction from their contribution to their family's welfare. Keeping their children in school was an important priority. Almost all Nisei did in fact graduate from high school, and their mothers' efforts surely were important to their achievement.

For all women of color, even the educated, the double burden of race and gender translated into few job options. In contrast, white women, especially native-born ones, had cleaner, better-paying, less demanding work. But despite the significant differences among women, all experienced the labor market as hierarchical, with women's labor largely devalued and poorly paid. As Emily Blair put it at the end of the decade, summarizing her and other feminists' disappointment over women's failure to make significant economic advances in the 1920s: "The best man continued to win, and women, even the best, worked for and under him. Women were welcome to come in as workers, but not as co-makers of the world. For all their numbers they seldom rose to positions of responsibility or power."

Women's work had changed and they had moved into the public sphere in greater numbers, but the belief that women's primary role was in the home had undergone less transformation. This persistence came out especially clearly in the heated debates over working wives. Throughout the decade, periodicals and books addressed the desirability of wives working outside the home. The attention was out of proportion, given the actual number of wives working, and clearly indicates that the issue struck a sensitive nerve in the American public. The climate was generally hostile. One of the most popular novels of the period was A.S.M. Hutchinson's *This Freedom,* a book extremely critical of the career woman as "a traitor to her sex." A 1924 survey of white-collar men found them resistant to the idea of wives working. Sixty-five percent said they should not work; 31 percent said it was acceptable for married women to work, but not mothers. These beliefs were echoed by marriage experts, such as Ernest Groves, who in 1925 declared: "When the woman herself earns and her maintenance is not entirely at the mercy of her husband's will, diminishing masculine authority necessarily follows."

Even observers supportive of working wives were ambivalent about the issue. Many commentators drew invidious distinctions between women who had to work out of need and those who did so out of choice. Social reformers who clustered around organizations such as the Women's Trade Union League, the National Consumers League, and the U.S. Women's Bureau were highly sympathetic to the working-class wife when they believed she worked out of necessity, yet regarded her as unfortunate. The Women's Bureau conducted over twenty-five studies during the decade, designed in part to demonstrate that these women did not work for "pin money," but were instead permanent workers, who deserved equal pay. It was concern for these women that prompted the intensity of these reformers' support of protective legislation and opposition to the ERA. Although these reformers recognized the legitimacy of working-class wives' work, their insistence that these wives worked because of an absent husband, or one unable to earn sufficient income, made it clear that they did not consider wives' work desirable or normal. These reformers might work for improved conditions for working women, but ideally an income provided by a male wage adequate for a family's support would solve the dilemma by taking wives out of the workplace altogether.

Attention was also focused on middle-class women who sought careers. These were few in number, probably less than 4 percent of all working women, but they had high publicity value. Many feminists insisted upon women's rights, whether married or not, to careers. Mabel Schwartz, of the Women's Trade Union League, argued that for professionals work provided "a development of their personalities, an enlargement of their lives." But many supporters of careers for wives revealed their reservations about combining a career and a home. In 1922, *The Literary Digest*, prompted by the tremendous success of *This Freedom*, wrote to married women listed in *Who's Who in America* to ask "Can a Woman Run a Home and a Job, Too?" Only a fifth of the answers were negative—not unexpectedly, given that most of the women they contacted had careers. The vast majority thought it was possible to do both, but many emphasized that the home must come first, and moreover, that it took an unusual woman to succeed in both arenas. As the *Digest* summed it up, most respondents believed "that, if a woman has brains, she can keep her place in the home and swing a bit of a career, too."

Many defenders of middle-class working wives invoked the "nervous housewife" syndrome. In a 1929 essay, social scientist Lorene Pruette noted particularly the sexual problems that arose between "the inattentive, hard-working husband and the idle, over-eating wife who fills many hours with erotic daydreams about that perfect lover who shows, alas, little resemblance to the husband." Pruette's solution for this bored, neurotic woman, however, was not a full-fledged career, but rather part-time work for wives: "Typing, sewing, preparation of gift cards, painted lamp shades and the like offer the advantages of a fixed return to be determined by the amount of time invested. Similarly, the wives of the faculty are often employed in college to read the class papers and examinations, payment being by the hours or a lump sum for the year."

Not surprisingly, the issue of careers and marriage was raised in women's colleges, where women for two decades had been trained for careers. In the nineteenth century, many college-educated women had not married, or done so late in life, choosing instead to pursue careers or social reform. By the 1920s, that trend had been reversed and educated women increasingly married. Many hoped to have both career and homes. As one Smith College student put it: "We cannot believe it is fixed in the nature of things that a woman must choose between a home and her work, when a man may have both. There must be a way out and it is the problem of our generation to find the way." At Smith, Ethel Puffer Howe directed the Institute to Coordinate Women's Interests, which hoped to do just that. The institute experimented with cooperative facilities—nurseries and kitchens—to devise means of simplifying housework and child care. But like Pruette, Howe emphasized part-time work and freelance activities as appropriate jobs for wives. And as limited as the view of the Smith plan was, it was far more progressive than what Vassar offered its students. In 1924 it set up a School of Euthenics to channel "education for women along the lines of their chief interests and responsibilities, motherhood and the home." Despite the existence of the Smith institute and the handful of champions of wives with careers, public sentiment in the 1920s was hostile to wives working out of a sense of personal fulfillment, rather than dire need. As historian Nancy Cott has pointed out, wives who pursued such an individualistic course were labeled "the enemies of society."

Clearly, ideas about women's primary duty to the home were intensifying in the face of underlying changes to the contrary. Husbands and wives often viewed the latter's work, whatever the reality, as temporary, and legitimate because it assisted the family. These powerful ideas affected the work experience of young single women as well. Although young women, especially those in the middle class, undoubtedly were taking a more individualistic approach to work than the nineteenth-century working daughter, most expected to quit work when they married or bore children, either out of preference or because of societal pressures.

This sense of women's work as a temporary removal from the home had been crucial in creating sex segregation in industrial labor in the nineteenth century, as women clustered in the lower-paid, unskilled jobs. Both employers and male employees had reinforced this view of women as marginal workers. For men, women co-workers could present a psychological threat; keeping women out of men's jobs helped maintain the linkage between male wage earning and masculine identity. Male workers also viewed women as economic threats and resisted their employment, especially in skilled trades. Many women, despite handicaps, were often eager to be organized, but they found most unions resistant or indifferent. Unions welcomed women primarily when they might otherwise threaten male unionists by working for lower wages. American Federation of Labor officials persistently insisted that men should be paid a family wage, which would keep women out of the workforce and allow men to be manly. Since women workers' marginal status made them a readily exploitable, plentiful source of cheap labor, employers encouraged sex-segregated labor; they had a vested interest in the notion of women as temporary workers whose major commitment was to the domestic sphere.

Relatively little had changed by the 1920s. Unions, with some notable exceptions such as those in the garment industry, continued their indifference to organizing women, and male workers were hostile to the idea of women in men's jobs. The sex segregation evident in factories in the nineteenth century was carried forward into the clerical fields and professions, with its accompanying wage differentials. The work that women did continued to be devalued. Although there were striking differences among women, based on class, race, and ethnicity, there

were also important similarities. The social attitudes that circumscribed women's opportunities affected domestics, factory
hands, clerks, and professionals. As historian Alice Kessler-Harris
summed up the decade of the 1920s: "Women were invited into
the work force and again invited not to expect too much of it."

But if women could not expect much from work, that did not
mean that the experience had no impact on them. Although
wage work had its limitations, as Julie Matthaei has argued,
working for wages could provide "a woman with an individual
public existence, a public identity of her own, and a sense of
her own worth." While working for wages may not have encouraged women to challenge the domestic ideal, this enhanced
sense of identity could affect patterns of authority in the family,
although probably not as dramatically as social observers of the
time who worried about the emasculated man feared. In many
instances, wage earning allowed women to challenge the patriarchal structure of the family. Observers of immigrant families
noted this phenomenon repeatedly. Evelyn Nakano Glenn
found that until World War II, the rigid patriarchal Japanese
family was still firmly in place in rural areas where Issei women
worked on family farms and did not earn separate wages. In
contrast, Issei women who worked as domestics for wages
gained a sense of independence that gave them more leverage
with their husbands. Rosalinda González found that Mexican
migrant men interviewed in the twenties were sometimes critical of Mexican women who had worked in America and were
too much " 'like American women,' independent, sassy, and no
longer content to remain submissively at home." This challenging of the traditional family may have been particularly true for
young women. Paul Taylor uncovered a significant number of
Mexican daughters in Los Angeles who wanted to work in order
to be independent of their parents, "with the clear implication
of dissatisfaction with parental authority, old customs, and
mode of living." Similarly, many young European immigrant
women workers interpreted wage work as an Americanizing experience which helped them to break away from old traditions
of female subordination and demand more social freedom for
themselves as they sought to participate in the heterosocial culture of dating and urban amusements.

Thus work could engender a break from parental authority. It also increasingly meant a means to participate, to the extent that their low wages would permit, in the consumer culture. Studies of working women repeatedly emphasize their interest in "putting on style." In Flint, Michigan, the Department of Labor found that women were eager to earn money for "independence and material gratification," and in particular they placed "an extremely high priority on buying new clothes to keep up with the latest fashions and they often went into debt to stay in style," and even in the remote, financially depressed Appalachian South, young women textile workers on strike appeared on the picket lines turned out in fashionable clothes. Thus, although women found limited economic reward or autonomy in the workplace, some sought compensation in the consumer culture, with its emphasis on leisure, pleasure, urban amusements, and acquisitions. This development was part of a broader change that transformed women's private lives. Far more so than in the public arena of politics and work, the new, modern woman emerged in the personal sphere of the home, courtship, and marriage.

THE NEW WOMAN IN THE PRIVATE SPHERE

It is clear that women (and the American public) persisted in traditional values: women's primary duty was to the home. As one might expect one of the most popular songs of the 1920s was "My Blue Heaven," an ode to domestic bliss: "Just Mollie and me / And baby makes three / We're happy in my blue heaven." But although old ideals remained, there were nonetheless significant changes in the home, family, courtship, and marriage that had important ramifications, especially for the white middle-class woman.

For most homemakers in the 1920s, caring for the home was much easier than it had been for their grandmothers or even their mothers. The middle class had fewer servants, but technology stepped in to make housework less arduous. Electrification of the home was crucial: in 1907, only 8 percent of

American homes had electricity; by 1920, more than half did. Electric lights in themselves tremendously simplified daily maintenance and kept homes cleaner. But in addition, there was a wide range of appliances available to the housewife: irons, toasters, sewing machines, refrigerators, washing machines, and percolators. The introduction of cheap mass-produced cast-iron enamelware in bathroom fixtures made bathrooms relatively easy to keep clean. Food preparation was simplified by new appliances and the widespread use of canned goods. Manufacturers touted these new products, from canned foods to refrigerators, as a means of providing the housewife with new leisure, and featured in their advertisements elegantly dressed women golfing, playing bridge, or enjoying their children with the spare time the products they bought saved them.

But although housework was made easier, it was not necessarily less time-consuming, because standards of cleanliness increased dramatically. In "Selling Mrs. Consumer," a *Ladies' Home Journal* author summarized the new demands: "Because we housewives of today have the tools to reach it, we dig every day after the dust that grandmother left to a spring cataclysm. . . . If our consciences don't prick us over vacant pie shelves or empty cookie jars, they do over meals in which a vitamin may be omitted or a calorie lacking." Nor did the new technology mean that housekeeping became less important in the wifely duties. Women's magazines, abetted by home economists, elevated homemaking to a career in this period. They glamorized the role of housewife, and depicted housework and cooking as an essential means to nurture her family while proving her self-worth. Emphasis on scientific management among home economists encouraged the wife to think of herself as a modern professional, relying on expert advice. The good wife and mother needed to have scientific knowledge of vitamins, food groups, and calories in order to feed her family properly. She needed to be a skilled hostess in order to promote her husband's career and her own social expectations. If she was not, advertisements offered assistance in proper etiquette and home style. Rogers Brothers Silverplate was not unusual in offering a free pamphlet, "Etiquette, Entertaining and Good Sense," which was full of "suggestions for successful entertaining."

Clearly an important component of the expert housewife's function was as consumer. Contemporaries estimated that women's purchases of consumer goods represented two-thirds of the $44 billion spent annually. Not surprisingly, advertisers wooed middle-class women shoppers assiduously. *Photoplay* ran an ad that summed up the sense of the new woman in the home: "Home Manager—Purchasing Agent—Art Director—Wife." Whether young or old, she had a tremendous responsibility. "She is the active partner in the business of running a home. She buys most of the things which go to make home life happy, healthful and beautiful. Through her slim, safe fingers goes most of the family money. . . . Advertisements are the wise counsellors in the spending of money that the clever housewife needs." Advertisements thus encouraged women to identify themselves with the products they bought. In addition, by exaggerating the importance of the choices women made when purchasing, advertisements gave a false sense of women's freedom, and trivialized the more significant arenas of women's choice, as this *Chicago Tribune* ad indicates: "Today's woman gets what she wants. The vote. Slim sheaths of silk to replace voluminous petticoats. Glassware in sapphire blue or glowing amber. The right to a career. Soap to match her bathroom's color scheme."

The new woman's importance as a consumer was linked to a broader pattern of changes in the family. In the twentieth century, family size continued the dramatic decline seen in the nineteenth century. In 1900, the average family consisted of 4.7 persons; in 1910, 4.5 persons; and in 1920, 4.3. Although family size shrank for the population as a whole, the change was especially noticeable among the urban middle class, who were likely to limit their families to one to three children. Beyond changes in size, at least for the middle class and perhaps some working-class people, the nature of families was shifting as well toward the "affectionate family." Smaller families, tending to emphasize the individual potential of each child, were less authoritarian and more democratic. Family functions also changed: by the twentieth century, not only did most families cease to exist as productive economic units but the social and educational activities associated with the family were absorbed by outside agencies. The family's main economic activity became consumption. In addition, the family became increasingly privatized, with the affectionate focus the psychological nurture of its members. By the 1920s, there was also a tremendous emphasis on expert child rearing. The U.S. Children's Bureau reported requests for hundreds of thousands of pamphlets on child care; *Parents' Magazine* got its start; and psychological experts wrote books and articles on proper child rearing, revealing an emphasis on child-centeredness and individuality that typified the new family.

Just as important as the changes in child-rearing advice were the new conceptions of marriage emerging in the early twentieth century. Although the age of marriage was dropping for both men and women and the percentage of married Americans was increasing, divorce rates also rose in the twenties, indicating a significant challenge to traditional views of the sanctity of marriage. The number of divorces began to accelerate in the late nineteenth century, when in 1880 one in every twenty-one marriages ended in divorce. By 1890, the figure was one in twelve, and by 1924, one in seven. Not surprisingly, disturbed observers placed the blame on the new woman and her new freedoms. While changes in women's experiences may have influenced divorce rates, there are other compelling explanations. One is the growing secularization of American society that was evident in the early twentieth century. Certainly religious faith persisted, but religion was less important in the public arena of American life. At the same time there was a decrease in the number of marriages sanctified by religious authority. In Middletown, the Lynds found that religiously sanctioned weddings accounted for 85 percent of the marriages in 1890, but only 63 percent in 1923. As marriage itself became less sacred, there was a rise in marriage dissolutions.

But perhaps the most crucial factor influencing divorce was the emergence of the affectionate family. As historian Elaine Tyler May has argued, popular ideals increasingly emphasized marriage as the source of personal satisfaction, in contrast to the Victorian ideal which had posited marriage as a matter of public duty. The changing nature of work, its increasing bureaucracy and regimentation, placed heavy emotional demands on marriage and the family as a source of personal fulfillment. Although many recognized this process and applauded it as an adaptation to modern times, great expectations, as May puts it, undoubtedly contributed to the rising divorce rate.

The growing assumption on the part of both experts and the general public that sex was a vital part of a good marriage signaled another source of changing expectations about marriage. Phyliss Blanchard and Carolyn Manasses, in a 1930 sociological study appropriately titled *New Girls for Old*, summarized the new way of thinking: "After hundreds of years of mild complaisance to wifely duties, modern women have awakened to the knowledge that they are sexual beings. And with this new insight the sex side of marriage has assumed sudden importance." At the root of the new weight given to sexuality in marriage was a changing notion of female sexuality. The Victorian moral code did not permit respectable middle-class women to admit to sexual appetites. Although it is possible to overstate the repressiveness of the Victorians, nonetheless it is true that they rigidly held that men were animalistic, aggressive creatures whose passions must be kept in bounds by chaste, genteel wives. For men, sexual intercourse was a necessary release; for women, it was a duty.

Many observers in the twenties, noting the emphasis on the new woman's sexuality, argued that the dislocations of war had turned traditional morals upside down. The causes, however, are far more complex and, moreover, predate the war. An emerging new morality was already evident in the 1910s. As one journal put it in 1913, the nation "has struck sex o'clock." The emphasis on women's sexuality coincided with the trend of women seeking more freedom in their social life. At the forefront of this change were the working-class young women who by the turn of the century were seeking, in historian Kathy Peiss's words, "cheap amusements." Looking for an escape in part from parental authority and in part from the harsh conditions of work, many young women took advantage of the new urban amusements—dance halls, amusement parks, theaters. This unchaperoned, relatively anonymous environment inevitably led to more sexual experimentation. Relaxing sexual standards may also have stemmed from the widespread practice of "treating." Poorly paid and often contributors to family incomes, these women had little left to pay for their entertainments. Men could and did "treat" them, but frequently with the implicit assumption of sexual favors as part of the exchange. These young women, then, lived in a society with more relaxed sexual standards than those of their parents.

By the 1910s those elite, radical women who clustered in bohemian centers like New York's Greenwich Village were also promoting a more sexualized personal life that included a rejection of bourgeois marriage. Many were self-styled feminists. Not all women's rights advocates embraced female sexuality, and indeed many shared a repressive Victorian sense that sexual freedom for women should mean freedom *from* sexuality. But for a small cadre of radical women, a commitment to women's equality included the right to both economic independence and sexual satisfaction. These women were heavily influenced by Sigmund Freud, Havelock Ellis, Ellen Key, and other intellectuals who provided evidence that women were sexual beings. In this early period, Freud was less important than writers like Ellis and Key, who tended to romanticize sexuality by investing it with mystical qualities, and who also insisted that sexual gratification was necessary for emotional health. These sexual radicals who embraced the sexologists' ideas about women's capacity for eroticism had great influence: they wrote novels, plays, and magazine articles that reached the middle-class parlor. These women, along with academic social scientists who were teaching the new sexual ideology in college courses, helped to spread a new ideal of womanhood.

By the twenties, these changes evident in both working-class women and elite sophisticates had filtered to large numbers of women. The legitimacy of female sexuality was furthered in part by the increased acceptability and availability of birth control devices, particularly the diaphragm. Birth control pioneer Margaret Sanger had begun her drive for contraception in 1913, primarily out of concern for poor women whose lives were overburdened by excessive childbearing. By the 1920s, she had become more conservative politically and, well aware of eugenics, now sought to reach poor women as a means of social control. Moreover, she increasingly targeted as her audience middle-class and elite women, who proved very receptive to means of controlling their fertility and exploring eroticism. Heavily influenced by Havelock Ellis's romantic notion of sexuality, Sanger promised that birth control made sex "a psychic and spiritual avenue of expression." Although many legal restrictions still limited the dissemination of birth control information or devices in the 1920s, Sanger persisted throughout the decade. Abandoning her early efforts to put birth control in the hands of poor women through public clinics, in part because it met with so much opposition, she strove to legitimate contraception by dispensing it through physicians. This was a successful technique, but one that limited easy access to birth control to patients with private doctors. It is not surprising, then, that the Lynds found in Middletown that all of the business wives whom they interviewed practiced birth control (27), but only 34 of the 77 working-class wives did so, and many of them used "primitive" practices. The Lynds listed a wide range of reasons working-class wives gave for not using contraception, including ignorance of methods, resistance by husbands, and personal repugnance. Whatever the reason, the class nature of contraceptive use suggests that the married women most likely to experience sexuality as liberating may have been middle-class and elite women whose matter-of-fact use of birth control allowed them to divorce sexual pleasure from reproduction.

The mass media proved to be as important as contraception in bringing about changed attitudes toward sexuality. If, in the 1910s, 23 percent of intellectual magazines had argued that sex was good for both men and women, now 40 percent of popular magazines did so as well. Moreover, sex adventure magazines like *True Confessions, Telling Tales,* and *True Story* proliferated, with suggestive story titles such as "The Primitive Lover" ("She wanted a caveman husband"), "Indolent Kisses," and "Innocents Astray." Although advertising broadcast a variety of images of women, an important motif was the glamorous woman, whose sexual appeal was undisguised. In a 1924 *Picture Play* ad Palmolive featured a barely clad woman in an exotic Egyptian setting and promised the "beauty secret of Cleopatra hidden in every cake."

Above all, movies projected a new version of womanhood. Historian Mary Ryan has commented that the rising female stars of the twenties, Madge Bellamy, Clara Bow, and Joan Crawford, with their physical freedom, energy, and independence, represented the modern woman. The new style of vibrant physicality included an emphasis on sexual attractiveness. Increasingly, young stars had to have what British novelist Elinor Glyn had termed "It." Personified by Clara Bow, the "It" girl possessed, as Glyn put it, the "animal magnetism" that is " 'the open sesame' to success in life and love." The movie industry promoted "It" by featuring displays of female flesh in lingerie and scenes set in opulent bathrooms. The plots invoked the new sexuality as well. Movie ads titillated fans with "brilliant men, beautiful jazz babies, champagne baths, midnight revels, petting parties in the purple dawn, all ending in one terrific smashing climax that makes you gasp."

Adultery and promiscuity were rarely condoned in the mass media, however. Movie adulteresses invariably paid for their sins, and heroines ultimately resisted temptation and were rescued by marriage or renewal of their marital commitment. Moral endings were also standard fare in the sex adventure magazines. There might be titillating stories of fallen women, such as "Her Morning After—Two Lives Transformed in One Night—Before the Volstead Act," or "My Own Story of Love," which asked, "Should a woman tell her husband all the secrets of her past? Should she uncover things gone—but not forgotten?" But at the end, the sexually active woman either paid a price for her lapse or achieved respectability through marriage. The purveyors of mass culture recognized changing sexual morality and, moreover, promoted it, but they nonetheless reveal a persistence of traditional values, especially the double standard.

That there were limits to the sexual revolution was also suggested by the lives of young unmarried women. The problem of wild, "abandoned" youth was a hotly debated topic in the 1920s. They had their defenders who welcomed their liberating influence, but traditionalists viewed modern youth as irresponsible, irreligious, and immoral. Invariably many placed the blame on the young woman, the flapper, who was such a vibrant symbol of the new generation. The flapper style entailed a minimum of undergarments, short skirts, filmy fabrics, and sheer hose. All this pointed to physical freedom and enhanced sexuality, even though the potential eroticism of their outfits was kept in bounds by the boyish look achieved by binding the breasts to make them appear flat. Bobbed hair, a release from the weight of tradition that required women to grow their hair long and then restrain it in chignons, buns, and the like, also represented female daring and eroticism. Smoking, drinking, and cosmetics, traditionally associated with prostitutes, further underscored young women's insistence on their right to sexuality and personal liberty.

A final indication of youthful insistence upon sexuality was the new dancing. For men and women alike, jazz was the craze. This was the period when whites went slumming to Harlem, an environment they viewed as erotic and dangerous, to go to cabarets for dancing, music, and other amusements. Whites sanitized the jazz they heard there and brought it into mainstream popular culture, where it set the tone for new, less inhibited dancing that shocked the older generation. As a writer in *The Ladies' Home Journal*, expressed it: "Anyone who says that 'youths of both sexes can mingle in close embrace'—with limbs intertwined and torso in contact—without suffering harm lies. Add to this position the wriggling movement and sensuous stimulation of the abominable jazz orchestra with its voodoo-born minors and its direct appeal to the sensory center, and if you can believe that youth is the same after this experience as before, then God help your child." Despite this lament, much of the new dancing, at least to present-day eyes, seems more boisterous than sexual. But to youth of the twenties, including young women, their dancing was symbolic, another badge of their rejection of traditional standards of behavior.

But it was not all symbolic. Rouged young women with bobbed hair, who smoked, drank, danced to jazz, and talked knowingly of sex, were also engaging in sexual activity. Charting something so private is difficult, but some concrete evidence exists. The Kinsey Report of the 1950s, which asked respondents for their sexual history, indicated an increase in premarital intercourse for the generation of the 1920s. Kinsey found that of the women born before 1900, 14 percent acknowledged premarital intercourse before the age of twenty-five, while those born after that date were two and a half times as likely (36 percent) to have had premarital intercourse. The latter group was also more likely to experience orgasm as well. Contemporary social scientists and sexologists, of whom there were many, also assumed a rise in premarital experience, further indicating that sexual norms and behavior were undergoing a significant transformation in this period.

This transformation had limits. The sexual double standard was still in place, with young women in the position of protecting their reputation by exercising discretion and restraint in their sexual activities. Moreover, it appears that according to prevailing norms, intercourse was still reserved as a prelude to marriage among engaged couples. Blanchard and Manasses found that the young women they interviewed approved of premarital sex, but only when a couple was deeply in love: "I disapprove of promiscuous relations on moral grounds; not, however, between a man and woman in love." As Blanchard and Manasses summed it up: "The code which the girls have worked out for themselves declares that sexual intercourse without marriage can safely be indulged in when it is a prelude to the more permanent arrangement of matrimony. Promiscuity is clearly differentiated, and largely condemned as 'cheap' and 'common.' "

As startling to contemporaries as changed attitudes toward premarital sex was the widely publicized form of sexual play known as petting, which included a variety of sexual activities short of intercourse. All contemporary sources indicate it was a widespread phenomenon. Advice columns frequently printed anguished letters in which young women bemoaned the fact that without petting they could not keep a boyfriend. In *Middletown*, the Lynds reported that in a survey of juniors and seniors in high school, 48 percent of the male students and 51 percent of the female students agreed with the statement that nine out of ten high school students had petting parties. That much petting apparently took place publicly during parties is significant. In her study of college sorority and fraternity youth in the twenties, historian Paula Fass has perceptively argued that the peer group was an important factor influencing new sexual standards among youth. It legitimated and even enforced new sexual norms. By sanctifying erotic play, while reserving intercourse for committed couples, the peer group set up guidelines for appropriate behavior that helped to keep erotic activity in check.

The new rules that took the place of old restraints nonetheless maintained some traditional standards. A letter to advice columnist Carolyn Van Wyck in *Photoplay* graphically illustrates both the changes in sexual patterns and the persistence of old ideas. As the young correspondent explained it: "Petting is my biggest problem. The boys all seem to do it and don't seem to come back if you don't do it also. We girls are at our wits' end to know what to do." So far she felt fortunate, because she had dated nearly fifty different boys, and "as yet I've never been out with anyone that got beyond my control." But her problem was not so much controlling young men as resolving her own confusion over what she wanted: "I don't seem to know what I want out of life. I want the thrills. I get a kick out of petting and I think all girls do no matter how much they deny it. What's to be done?" The key question for her came down to whether petting would damage her reputation and affect her ability to marry. "It makes me wonder how on earth you are to get a husband who respects you because you don't pet if you get turned down every time because you won't, before they have time to appreciate your sterling qualities. I'm sure that I don't want to marry anyone who is too slow to want to pet. But I want to discover what is right. Please help me." As the letter suggests, as significant a change as petting represented, it nonetheless included the persistence of the double standard and was a form of courtship linked ultimately for women to obtaining a husband.

Despite very real changes, the extent of the sexual revolution is easily overstated. Movies with moral endings, the persistence of the double standard, the limits on erotic experimentation set by group-sanctioned petting, all suggest limits to cultural change. Moreover, the new woman did not describe all women. The tremendous to-do in the 1920s about the new sexual woman was really centered on the "respectable" white middle-class women, because it was changes among them that were the most dramatic. For many in the working class, sexual norms had changed years earlier. Still others remained largely untouched by the new morality. A very low rate of illegitimacy for Italian immigrant daughters persisted into the 1930s, suggesting that among that group, young women remained outside the peer culture that sanctioned sexual activity for unmarried women. Many women may have been influenced by changing standards even if they did not embrace them. Elaine May has written about divorce cases in which wives, traditionally reared, could not comfortably accept the new sexual code, much to the dismay of their husbands, who had anticipated a highly sexualized marriage. The legacy of the Victorian moral code was not easily dismissed.

The concentration on women's sexuality in the twenties also disconcerted many women's rights activists, for whom equality in sexual matters had never been an issue. They worried that the pursuit of social pleasures and sexual activity led women away from more serious concerns such as social reform and women's rights. These women, often shaped by Victorian notions of female sexuality, were critical of women's "abuse of New Freedom." Charlotte Perkins Gilman in 1923 condemned the moral revolution, especially the misuse of birth control, which had become "a free ticket for selfish and fruitless indulgence, and an aid in the lamentable behavior of our times, affecting both men and women." Many older feminists, who came of age in a time when homosocial bonding was especially common among educated, professional women, were also disconcerted that the new psychology of sexuality made close relationships between women suspect as homosexual. It became increasingly common, moreover, for popular observers to analyze militant feminists as repressed lesbians. For homosexual

women, sophisticated urban environments gave them more opportunities to live the lives they wanted, but the relentless celebration of heterosexuality could only have been disconcerting.

For many African American women, the 1920s' emphasis on
sexuality was also problematic. Middle-class black women reformers traditionally had been eager to protect black women
from sexual exploitation and to counter stereotypes of them as
sexually permissive. Women authors of the Harlem Renaissance,
unlike men, tended to be uncomfortable with the emphasis on
the "primitive," especially when it touched on sexuality, because it seemed to reinforce unwanted stereotypes. Jessie Fauset's novels invariably featured light-skinned, upper-class,
genteel women, with the underlying message that African Americans could be people of culture and propriety. Nella Larsen's
characters were more complex and spoke to the dilemma many
black women faced. In *Quicksand*, Helga Crane, a well-educated
mulatto, struggles with her relationship to the white world and
the black world. Her sense of her sexuality is linked with this
struggle, and for the most part she represses her erotic feelings.
White society, as represented by Danish relatives of her white
mother, lionizes her as an exotic, sensuous creature. A Danish
painter, who executes her portrait, after first attempting to se-
duce her, offers marriage. Helga rejects him and the white society that has dehumanized her: "But you see, Herr Olsen, I'm
not for sale. Not to you. Not to any white man. I don't at all
care to be owned. Even by you." After returning to New York,
Helga's sexual reserve is broken in an orgiastic religious conversion scene. She surrenders herself to an uncouth southern minister, whom she marries and follows to the rural South. There
the novel leaves her, burdened by seemingly endless childbirth
and the responsibility of her children, presumably trapped by
her own body.

Helga's story by and large speaks to a rare dilemma, of a
woman caught between two societies, whose sexuality was
shaped in part by white society and its expectations of her.
Turning away from novelists to blues singers, as Hazel Carby
has done, can illuminate a strikingly different view of African
American women's perception of their sexuality. Blues singers

like Bessie Smith, Ma Rainey, Ida Cox, and Ethel Waters sang their music in vaudeville and carnivals throughout the North and South. By the late 1920s, "race records" and later the radio disseminated this music even farther. While many blues songs entailed descriptions of a masochistic woman clinging to the man who "done her wrong," a significant body of songs, often written by the performers themselves, painted a different picture. Some evoked an exuberant sense of women's enjoyment of their sexuality that spoke of resistance to sexual objectification and domination by men. There were songs that featured a woman demanding that her lover pay attention to her needs, such as "One Hour Mamma," in which Ida Cox reminded her man that

> I want a slow and easy man
> He needn't ever take the lead,
> Cause I work on that long time plan
> And I ain't a looking for no speed.
>
> I'm a one hour mamma, so no one minute papa
> Ain't the kind of man for me.
> Set your alarm clock papa, one hour that's proper
> Then love me like I like to be.

Others, like Ethel Waters' "No Man's Mamma Now," expressed independence from men: "I can say what I like, I can do what I like. / I'm a girl who is on a matrimonial strike; / Which means, I'm no man's mamma now." The blues, then, reveal a forum in which black women could not only celebrate their sexuality but claim to control it. Whether prescriptive or descriptive, these blues songs gave expression to black female desire that was distinct from that of their novelist sisters who focused on the burden of battling racial stereotypes.

As in work and politics, then, the new woman's sexuality did not resonate for all women. And as in politics and work, the question of how much liberation social change brought women is crucial. At the time most women identified the new sexuality as a form of freedom and equality, but a closer look paints a more complex picture. Film treatment of white women in this period is suggestive, for the new sexuality was often expressed through consumption. Indeed, most heroines attracted the opposite sex not through the body but through the clothes, jewelry, and cosmetics that adorned it. Films such as *Charge It* and *Gimme* underscored the point. In keeping with this theme of sexuality and consumption, many movies employed the "makeover plot" in which a dowdy, restrained matron traded her old-fashioned clothes for flapper attire to regain her husband. The makeover movies reveal the limits of women's film transformation. Films might feature sexuality, even infidelity, but women's goal in most movies was marriage or the maintenance of marriage. Despite the titillation these films offered, they, along with the other mass media, tended to tame sexuality and keep it from threatening the social fabric.

As the films suggest, physical attractiveness was a central component defining the new sexual woman. Beauty shops multiplied, expanding from 5,000 in 1920 to 40,000 in 1930. Similarly, the sales of cosmetics mushroomed, with sales in 1914 of $17 million, and in 1925, $141 million. And, inexorably, the purpose of these products was to produce a youthful appearance. The youth cult was pervasive. It appeared in films, books, magazines, and advertisements. Above all advertisements. The American Laundry Machinery Company used the appeal of youthfulness to promote commercial laundries, insisting that "the woman of America stays young because she keeps her mind young." The time she saves permits "the many things which bring happier days and longer youth." Metropolitan Life Insurance saluted the woman who concealed her age: "Through her determination to stay young—even to the point of denying the calendar—she has set up higher health standards." More predictably, clothing and cosmetics manufacturers promised a youthful look. Addressing a middle-aged woman, Charis corsets acknowledged that "within this woman's soul burns still the flame of her desire for charm and beauty." Charis corsets not only would provide a youthful silhouette but would also improve the strength of the wearer's internal organs so that she is "younger in fact as well as in appearance."

Women were encouraged to identify their youth, and thus their sexual attractiveness, with the goods that adorned their bodies. This sentiment came out in a remarkable letter to the editor of *Picture Play*. A Kansas wife wrote in protesting a man's letter in the previous issue in which he complained that a Bebe Daniels film had compelled his wife to spend eighteen dollars for a new hat. The Kansas woman explained that the impulse to buy a hat comes from a woman's sense that she is no longer young, and that "motion pictures have sharpened this instinct by putting beautiful women before us every day." But rather than criticize the influence of the media, she insisted that it was a healthy influence. "The extravagant hat is just one flash of a great power which is keeping the modern woman slim and healthy and keen, as young at forty as her mother was at thirty and her grandmother at twenty. More power to the Gloria Swansons, the Elsie Fergusons, the Irene Castles, and the Viola Danas!" This woman's enthusiastic letter offers telling evidence of how successful the media were in convincing women that their attractiveness and self-worth were linked to the products they bought.

The new sexuality that led women to the cult of beauty and consumption also entailed a sexual objectification of women, an emphasis on their sexuality to the exclusion of other qualities. Many of the psychological works which championed women's right to sexuality also contained the seeds of objectification. Havelock Ellis, who was very sympathetic to women, nonetheless said that "their brains are in their wombs." The early feminists who had promoted sexual freedom had also envisioned it as part of a broad process of liberation that included economic and political freedom. The enthusiasm for women's sexuality as it developed among intellectuals like Ellis, but especially in the mass media of movies, advertising, and periodicals, co-opted this emphasis on sexuality, with little of its egalitarian content. As Nancy Cott has argued: "Advertising and mass media took up women's heterosexuality as their own agent, blunting the Feminist point that heterosexual liberation for women intended to subvert gender hierarchy rather to confirm it." The new woman's sexuality thus lost much of its radical potential. Most contemporaries may have viewed the changes for women as liberating, for many women did achieve more freedom in the personal arena, and in particular, the legitimation of their sexuality. However, enhanced freedom was within narrow boundaries. It was accompanied by sexual objectification and linked to consumerism, which ushered in the modern trend of defining women in terms of their sexual allure and adornment, both of which served to contain women's eroticism. Women's sexuality was also tamed, and its threat to male dominance reduced, by the persistence of the double standard and the insistence that marriage was a woman's ultimate goal.

The new woman's liberation was in some measure a cultural construct embroidered by movies, advertisements, and the popular press. To the extent that the image was accurate at all, it depicted white, relatively affluent women, and had relatively little meaning to poor women of color. Moreover, whatever a woman's race or ethnicity, significant limits to her freedom and autonomy were evident in politics, work, and the personal arena. Although minority women were the most exploited, almost all women confronted a labor hierarchy in which they faced discrimination and wage differentials. In the political world, the women's movement, beset by external constraints and internal divisions, was not able to construct an agenda that could provide the basis for expanding feminist consciousness to a wide range of women. In the personal sphere of home, marriage, and courtship, women may have rejected older notions of duty and sacrifice to demand independence and individualism, especially in sexual matters. But even in the private arena, their autonomy and freedom were circumscribed by widespread expectations that women's primary role was still as wife and mother.

But to minimize the liberation of the new woman is not to dismiss the significance of changes in women's lives. The rigidly separated spheres for men and women were being eroded. In politics, the existence of a separate women's political culture, based on the idea of women's special moral nature that put them above politics, was disappearing. Women activists, no longer part of a distinct separate sphere, became subsumed by the political parties, where they found little influence or power. In the workplace, the acceptability of employment for single women was a given by the 1920s. And despite the general disapproval of employed wives, the modern trend of their entering the workforce was well in place, with its long-range implications for women and the family.

Finally, another significant change in this decade was that, save for those in dire poverty, women became central to the consumer culture. The major purchasers of products, they constituted a crucial underpinning of the economy. Moreover, changing ideas about leisure and personal satisfaction that were an integral part of the consumer culture were evident in women's private lives, especially in the new emphasis on female sexuality. The fusion of sexuality with consumption also led to women's sexual objectification, and encouraged women to measure their self-worth by the goods that adorned their bodies. The twenties, then, witnessed a coalescence of factors that did not make women free, but did give their lives a modern contour.

THE ACIDS OF MODERNITY:
SECULAR AND SACRED
INTERPRETATIONS

Although changes in women's roles were circumscribed by traditional values, nonetheless contemporaries viewed them as symbols of a modern culture, and women's visible presence in the workplace and participation in new sexual mores were all the more striking because they formed only part of a long litany of social transformation. Mass culture and technology's impact on social organization and day-to-day life, the rise of an urban, more cosmopolitan culture, the spread of bureaucratization and standardization, also challenged the Victorian worldview that dominated nineteenth-century white middle-class America. That culture had honored order, stability, and hierarchy as Victorians drew firm lines of class, gender, and race, and assigned subordinate positions to immigrants, Native Americans, African Americans, white women, and workers. Clinging to the sense of a rational universe unfolding from God-given natural laws, mainstream Americans enshrined a belief in progress, a faith that placed their civilization in the vanguard of social, political, and cultural improvement. Well before the 1920s the disruption accompanying America's industrialization and urbanization unleashed serious challenges to this Victorian sense of order. Influenced by European "modernist" ideas in art, literature, and the sciences that were overturning conventional ways of seeing and thinking, intellectuals in particular were questioning received traditions. These fissures in Victorianism had widened perceptibly by the 1920s. By then, not only could many Americans look to symbols of the new order like flappers and Ford motorcars, but they had also gained access to new ways of understanding the world that before the war had mostly been the preserve of intellectuals. Three examples tell the story.

In the early twentieth century, the ideas of Sigmund Freud had become so familiar among intellectuals that therapeutic techniques like free association turned into parlor games at Greenwich Village parties. For many, Freud's theories of the unconscious translated into liberating insights that informed their work and their personal relationships; their fascination with Freud became part of their battle against the restraints of a repressed culture. For middle-class Americans in the 1920s, Freud became a household name: inferiority complex, fixation, and neurosis entered their vocabulary, and psychoanalysis came into vogue. When F. Scott Fitzgerald's flapper announced that she was "hipped on Freud and all that," he could be sure his readers knew exactly what she meant. Popularizers of Freud, who for the most part distorted his ideas, boiling them down to "repression is bad," were so thick on the ground that in 1929 humorists James Thurber and E. B. White could write a classic parody, *Is Sex Necessary?* Filled with Thurber's wicked drawings representing the "unconscious," the book spoke to the public desire to master the new psychology in order to live more fulfilling lives. And, as we have seen, the popularization of Freud challenged older notions of sexuality and helped to unseat the Victorians' code of genteel behavior, especially for women.

Simultaneously, another school of psychology gained widespread popularity: behaviorism, which took its name from John B. Watson's *Behavior: An Introduction to Comparative Psychology* (1914). Watson and other behaviorists described humans as hollow shells, formed by their environment, who responded to external stimuli. Although significantly different from the Freudian approach, behaviorism was similar in that it minimized men's and women's ability to control consciously their behavior and ideas. The popularizers of both approaches offered the individual's understanding of psychology as a means to self-improvement, but at the same time spread the notion of the inherent irrationality of the human psyche.

Similarly, Americans were exposed in the 1920s to the knowledge that developments in physics were fundamentally altering the way that scientists understood the universe. After the war, American newspapers and magazines publicized Albert Einstein's theories of relativity and the wave of controversy they set off. Although Einstein could allegedly joke that only twelve people understood his work, nonetheless many writers tried to interpret relativity to the general public. In 1921, *Vanity Fair* featured a page on "Rhyme and Relativity," offering parodies of what poets like T. S. Eliot and Carl Sandburg might write "after a course of easy lessons in Einstein." Einstein himself appeared in a 1923 film, *Relativity*. A *New York Times* review reported that the "film makes a brave attempt to explain to the popular mind the fourth dimension of space and how Einstein measures the universe by a space-time yardstick," and concluded that the various illustrations, including moving boats, stationary lights, and backward-walking men, were "clear as a bell." However, the report concluded, "it is what they are all about that foils the humble student of relativity." It is unlikely that any of these efforts imparted a clear understanding of relativity, but they did convey the notion that commonsense knowledge and ordinary experience were no longer adequate to understand the physical world, with the unsettling implication of a world more unpredictable and uncontrollable. According to philosopher Morris Cohen, relativity even undermined democracy itself: "Free civilization means that everyone's reason is competent to explore the facts of nature for himself, but the recent development of science, involving ever greater mastery of complicated technique, means in effect a return to an artificial barrier between the uninitiated layman and the initiated expert."

Finally, more dramatic than the popularizations of either Freud or Einstein was the renewed attention given to scientific challenges to religious ideas. Although many nineteenth-century educated Americans had been able to adapt Darwinian science, with its emphasis on gradual evolution, to their own notions of progress and ordered change, Darwin nonetheless undercut religious interpretations of human origin and sowed the seed for challenges to religious faith. The rise of biblical criticism and the study of comparative religions, with its emphasis on a historical understanding of world religions, had also undermined for many the sense of the unique truths of evangelical Protestantism. These issues, especially the implications of evolutionary theory, seemed to explode in the 1920s with the advent of the highly publicized 1925 Scopes trial (discussed in detail below), in which a young biology teacher stood trial for teaching evolution in violation of a Tennessee law. Reams of information on the trial, including detailed scientific testimony on the validity of evolution, flooded newspapers and periodicals, and may have undermined many readers' faith in the absolute truths of the Bible.

These three developments represented significant challenges to an older understanding—about the operation of the universe, the origins of humanity, and indeed the very nature of humankind. They formed an important part of what Walter Lippmann in his 1929 *Preface to Morals* called the "acids of modernity," a shorthand term he used to invoke the wide-ranging forces that were disrupting the certainty and stability of modern men and women. What were the implications of these corrosive acids? For many Americans, the 1920s brought an acute consciousness of social and cultural change that challenged tradition, religion, rational order, and progress. Some—especially the young—reveled in modernity. They viewed their own time as a demarcation, a release from the restraints, especially the Victorian moral code, of the past. Fluidity translated into freedom. Many in the middle and upper classes may well have worried about some aspects of modernity, but with their enthusiasm fueled by prosperity and such dramatic technological developments as movies, automobiles, airplanes, and radios, they maintained a belief that practical guidelines for living could be found, that modern people could adapt to the transformations in their society. Popular journals like *The Saturday Evening Post* encouraged them in this complacency. And *Vanity Fair*, a more sophisticated sleek periodical that straddled the line between popular culture and the avant-garde, also celebrated the modern spirit enshrined in mass-culture artifacts such as jazz, spectator sports, and comic strips. But many other Americans resisted change. Defensive social movements, like the Ku Klux Klan (discussed in the following chapter), bear strong witness to the desire to maintain traditional order and values. The response to modernity was thus complex and ambivalent. Two key arenas, intellectual and religious life, illuminate with particular clarity how Americans interpreted social and cultural change. The two were not necessarily mutually exclusive, but most intellectuals of the 1920s were self-consciously secular, in itself suggestive of the decline of the Victorian order.

INTELLECTUALS

Intellectual life in the twenties—like so many other aspects of the decade—was extremely diverse. Social scientists, pursuing new developments in their disciplines, struggled to understand the nature of modern society and culture. Artists of the Lost Generation, shaped both by war and by the prewar intellectuals' critique of the Victorian order, created a powerful literary legacy that helped to set the tone for the decade. The writers of the Southern Renaissance condemned the modern world and enshrined the traditionalism of the agrarian South. Other intellectuals explored the pluralism of American culture, most notably participants in the Harlem Renaissance who sought to define the distinctive contribution of blacks to American culture. Despite their particularistic concerns, these intellectuals may be loosely tied together by their shared consciousness of modern times and their role as interpreters of their culture.

THE LOST GENERATION AND
THE MODERNISTS

The group of intellectuals most associated with the twenties was the one Gertrude Stein labeled the Lost Generation—the white writers and artists who came to maturity with World War I and whose disaffection with American culture led many to artistic exile in Paris and elsewhere in Europe. The Lost Generation was deeply influenced by the prewar intellectuals' revolt against the Victorian "genteel tradition" and the stultifying culture that had produced it. Challenging the idea that art must serve a didactic purpose of moral improvement, writers like T. S. Eliot, Gertrude Stein, Ezra Pound, and Amy Lowell had joined the wave of European modernists who experimented with form and language and celebrated experience and individual liberation. The Lost Generation authors took up the mantle of these predecessors. Determined to create a new and vital American artistic culture, free of the complacency and repression of the Victorian tradition, they explored the crisis of the individual in a modern world of machines and mass culture, of uncertainty and spiritual malaise.

This sense of crisis was expressed in the rootlessness and world-weary cynicism that pervaded the works of the most famous of the Lost Generation. F. Scott Fitzgerald penned a colorful and popular version of the youthful pursuit of experience and excitement. Beneath the glamour of his flappers and jazzhounds lay a fragility rooted in their failure to find meaning or purpose amid the uncertainty of modern life. In *This Side of Paradise* (1920), a novel of complex romantic entanglements, booze, artistic desires, and money, Gloria Patch reflects, "There's only one lesson to be learned from life anyway. . . . That there's no lesson to be learned from life." Fitzgerald's most famous novel, *The Great Gatsby* (1925), is peopled by empty, superficial characters, especially the rich, and especially women. Gatsby's fatal tragedy hinges on his futile effort to win the woman he lost as a young man and the social status she embodies. Critic Frederick J. Hoffman traces the failure of Gatsby and other Fitzgerald characters to "a fundamental lack of a clear moral sense, a lack really of cultural tact, which had caused men in the very beginning to have the wrong dreams, and which gave them no proper way of judging them." Fitzgerald not only interpreted youth and the extravagance of a class of wealthy people to Americans—the rootlessness and the pursuit of "the most expensive orgy in history"—he lived that life as well. With his wife, Zelda, he enjoyed the high-flying, fast-paced world of the expatriates, who wandered from watering hole to watering hole, from experience to experience.

The expatriate appears most memorably in the pages of Ernest Hemingway's novels, especially *The Sun Also Rises* (1926). There, characters like Jake Barnes and Lady Brett Ashley range from Paris to Pamplona in an alcoholic haze. A central metaphor in the book is Barnes's war injury, a wound that has left him impotent both physically and emotionally, a symbol of the psychic wounds of a generation that experienced war. This theme appears repeatedly in Hemingway's work. In the short story "Soldier's Home" (1925), Harold Krebs returns well after the armistice to small-town America to find himself totally out of sync with his family and community. Disaffected and emotionally impaired, Krebs "did not want any consequences. He did not want any consequences ever again. He wanted to live along without consequences."

The search for meaning of some of Hemingway's characters takes them far afield from modern industrial society. Jake Barnes hopes to find it in the bullfights of Spain, which he experiences in an almost religious fashion, reveling in the rituals and authenticity of the tradition. Similarly, the only point in the novel at which he seems to enjoy any peace of mind comes when he and a male friend go fishing in a remote spot in the Spanish countryside. The possibilities for connection found in nature, the woods and rivers, also pervade an important collection of short stories, *In Our Time* (1925), about Nick Adams, another war veteran whose memories of Michigan and the masculine outdoor life powerfully mingle with his experiences in battle.

The exploration of the dilemma of the individual in the modern world was often expressed in the context of the shattering experience of World War I, which had left an indelible stamp on most Lost Generation authors. Several, including Hemingway, e. e. cummings, and John Dos Passos, had volunteered early on to be ambulance drivers. They approached the war, not convinced by the rhetoric that described it as a battle for democracy, but rather with the belief that for fledgling writers war represented something essential that they must experience first-hand. They emerged with grist for their artistic mills, but also with their senses profoundly shocked by the brutality of combat and of the war machinery itself. Their critique, however, had deeper roots than the war itself. Like the older generation of modernists, they condemned not just war, but the societies that had produced it. The war became a metaphor for far-reaching condemnation of modern culture. In the words of expatriate poet Ezra Pound in *Hugh Selwyn Mauberley* (1920), men had died "For an old bitch gone in the teeth, / For a botched civilization."

A more narrowly construed critique of the contemporary world focused on the sterility of American culture in particular. A theme that historians have called the revolt against the village pervaded the literature of the twenties. Both the young members of the Lost Generation and an older cadre of writers inveighed against the crudeness, materialism, and repression of their own society. The Red Scare, the Ku Klux Klan, prohibition, and the anti-evolution campaign were widely interpreted as examples of the power of rural provincials in particular to stultify American culture. This provincialism, combined with the overwhelming philistinism and commercialism of the "respectable" middle class, led many intellectuals to despair of American culture and the place of the artist in it.

This interpretation emerged most stridently in Harold Stearns's anthology *Civilization in the United States* (1922). Arguing that American culture had precious little "civilization," the contributors described a sterile society, marred by traditions of the New England Puritan and the hardy pioneer whose practicality and repression had merged to create a stony soil which discouraged artistic endeavor. The problems were compounded because the centrality of commercial pursuits meant that culture had been relegated to female guardians who were more concerned with morality than art. Hence women were behind the "genteel culture" that proved so crippling to artistic achievement. Other observers, notably H. L. Mencken, whose magazine *The American Mercury* was a must among the cosmopolitan set, echoed the condemnation of the village.

In fiction, Sherwood Anderson continued themes he had developed before the war which centered on the repression, especially sexual repression, of the village and of contemporary society more generally. Like many other writers of the period, Anderson, with his emphasis on individual freedom, was heavily influenced by Freud. As one of his characters put it: "If there is anything you do not understand in human life, consult the works of Dr. Freud." In *Winesburg, Ohio* (1919), *Dark Laughter* (1922), and *Many Marriages* (1923), Anderson fashioned dark, brooding stories dealing with marriage, morality, and individuals destroyed by success. In *Many Marriages*, the protagonist, in the midst of a passionate affair and on the verge of leaving a joyless marriage and a dull business, feels that "he himself wanted, more than anything else, to give way to the impulses within himself," and ruminates that others shared his boxed-in feelings: "Men and women either spend their lives going in and out of doors of houses and factories, or they own houses and factories and they live their lives and find themselves at last facing death and the end of life without having lived at all."

The novels of Sinclair Lewis were less dark than Anderson's, suggesting a greater ambivalence on Lewis' part about the unalloyed damage of the small-town mentality. Nonetheless, his parodies of both the village (Gopher Prairie in *Main Street* [1920]) and the small city (Zenith in *Babbitt* [1922]) dissected the way in which conformity, stunted lives, and dull practicality, coupled with the pursuit of the dollar, dampened the individual spirit. Yet *Main Street* was also notable for its generally sympathetic treatment of a woman, Carol Kennicott, the town doctor's rebellious new wife, who tries to shake Gopher Prairie out of its complacency. She hopes to bring beauty, art, and cosmopolitan values to the dreary, stuck-in-a-rut town, but ultimately an ambivalence about her mission prevails and she succumbs to the town's conventions. The novel ends with her pinning her hopes for change on her infant daughter.

Given the flourishing of feminism before the war and the widespread perception of a new woman in the 1920s, it is at first surprising how little attention was paid in the most critically acclaimed work to the new woman or to women artists. But, as

Elaine Showalter has argued, the Lost Generation was "a community of men," who tended to be dismissive of women, in part out of the broader revolt against the village and the "feminine" genteel culture of the nineteenth century. Moreover, critics and writers alike tended to view women primarily as midwives to art. And indeed, many women filled that role. Margaret Anderson served as editor of *The Little Review* and Marianne Moore of *Dial*; Elinor Wylie and Jessie Fauset were literary editors of *Vanity Fair* and *The Crisis*, respectively. Other women, such as Gertrude Stein and Natalie Barney, acted as critics, go-betweens, and promoters of a variety of artists.

Although the male-dominated literary world generally devalued women, most of these women were artists in their own right. Many of them, especially those attracted to the left, like Genevieve Taggard and Lola Ridge, reflected a feminist consciousness, as this passage from "Sun-Up" (1920), a poem by Ridge, suggests:

> When you tell mama
> you are going to do something great
> she looks at you
> as though you were a window
> she was trying to see through,
> and says she hopes you will be good
> instead of great.

Lesbian women, part of an expatriate community in Paris like Djuna Barnes and Janet Flanner, also explicitly criticized the patriarchal restrictions on women. But for the most part, their overt criticism was muted. As we have seen, feminism floundered in the 1920s, and its decline hampered many women artists' efforts to arrive at a distinctive woman-centered voice. In a male-dominated canon, women poets also struggled to be taken seriously. In part because of the association of women artists with sentimentality, many of them, including Elinor Wylie, Marianne Moore, and Hilda Doolittle ("H.D."), often avoided themes that directly acknowledged gender, a tendency that gave their work a guarded, evasive quality, a "film of distance," as critic Alicia Suskin Ostriker has noted. Although few poets explicitly explored women's subordination, recent feminist critics have uncovered distinctive female language and concerns—a resistance to what Gertrude Stein called "patriarchal poetry"— embedded in much of their work. Their poetry, like that of male artists, was also informed by tangled personal lives. Conflicts surrounding childbearing, marriage, and sexual orientation shaped their poems and reflected very modern sensibilities.

The most famous example of the literary new woman was poet Edna St. Vincent Millay, who flouted convention in her personal life and in her poetry expounded on women's sexual freedom and equality. "First Fig" ("My candle burns at both ends; / It will not last the night; / But ah, my foes, and oh, my friends— / It gives a lovely light!") seemed to speak to the era's youth, who eagerly memorized it. One contemporary reported that Millay "became, in effect, the unrivaled embodiment of sex appeal, the It-girl of the hour, the Miss America of 1920." Despite this insistence on female sexuality, Millay's message was ambiguous, for her work often reflected a commodification and objectification of women's bodies that undermined its liberating possibilities.

At the time, older women writers were also uncomfortable with the new woman that Millay symbolized. Talented novelists like Willa Cather and Edith Wharton produced important works in the period, such as *Death Comes for the Archbishop* (1927) and *The Age of Innocence* (1920), respectively, but found their critical reputation diminished. Neither revealed a feminist consciousness or celebrated women's freedom, but, unlike most male writers, they did portray strong women who sought control over their lives, or criticized the social milieu that turned many middle-class women into shallow fashion plates and followers of convention.

The sense that Cather and Wharton were outdated in the 1920s derived in part from the fact that they were middle-aged, in part from their increasing preoccupation with the traditions and stability of the past. But Cather and Wharton were also out of sync with the prevailing emphasis on modernist forms in art and literature. Following trends begun by the Greenwich Village artists in the prewar years, younger artists avidly sought new modes of expression that could capture what it meant to be modern. One central motif in this quest was the depiction of the machine and industrial culture. Many artists condemned the machine for crushing the human spirit and used it as a metaphor for standardization and sterility. Carl Sandburg's poem "Smoke and Steel" (1920) invoked the human costs of the industrial age as he described a steel bar as having "smoke at the heart of it, smoke and the blood of a man." Hart Crane exemplified those artists who believed that the machine had liberating, exciting possibilities for civilization, and that the function of the poet was to absorb the machine "as naturally and as casually as trees, cattle, galleons, castles and all other human associations of the past." In his epic poem "The Bridge" (1930), Crane used the Brooklyn Bridge as a metaphor for America, as a means of exploring the pioneer past and the industrial urban present. In a motif that would appear in the works of many other writers, he underlined the centrality of technological artifacts by using religious imagery to describe the bridge: "O Sleepless as the river under thee, / Vaulting the sea, the prairies' dreaming sod, / Unto us lowliest sometime sweep, descend / And of the curveship lend a myth to God."

Painter Charles Demuth explored the machine age on canvas. In the postwar period his art was "precisionist," as was appropriate for a society of mass production and standardization, and featured industrial urban scenes. In some of his most important paintings, he portrayed industrial buildings as religious symbols. Thus in "Incense of a New Church," the smokestacks of a steel factory resemble church towers and are engulfed by billowing clouds of smoke. Demuth underlined the symbolism by placing a chalice in the foreground. Like many other artists and writers, Demuth was ambivalent about the machine and its potential for dehumanizing culture, but he also recognized that it embodied the essence of a distinctly modern American culture.

Modernists also attempted to capture the essence of modern times by experimenting with modes of expression. In the poetry of Crane, e. e. cummings, William Carlos Williams, and Marianne Moore, one finds new rhythms as they challenged traditional lyric forms. In works like "Marriage" (1923) and "New York" (1921), Moore's "disruptive verse, with lines consistently organized into unusual stanza forms and language frequently freed from traditional associations," led William Carlos Williams to hail her as "one of the main supports of the new order." Cummings, influenced by the European Dadaist, antirationalist, anti-art movement, experimented exuberantly with form and language. He ran words together, dismissed rules of capitalization, and used unconventional punctuation. Strings of nonsense—"@1/4%&:1/4/?@3/4)"—underlined his sense of irrationality and playfulness, and like many other artists, he incorporated advertising jingles, popular songs, and comic books into his poems, as the following from the 1922 "Poem, Or Beauty Hurts Mr. Vinal" suggests:

> *take it from me kiddo*
> *believe me*
>
> *my country, 'tis of*
> *you, land of the Cluett*
> *Shirt Boston Garter and Spearmint*
> *Girl With The Wrigley Eyes (of you*
> *land of the Arrow Ide*
> *and Earl &*
> *Wilson*
> *Collars) of you i*
> *sing: land of Abraham Lincoln and Lydia E. Pinkham,*
> *land above all of Just Add Hot Water And Serve—*
> *from every B.V.D.*
>
> *let freedom ring . . .*

The search to express modern sensibilities in artistic form that drove the poets and painters also influenced novelists. Hemingway was just one of many artists who went to Paris to learn how to write, to find out, in Frederick Hoffman's words, "what the twentieth century was all about and how it might be articulated and formalized." Hemingway gleaned from Gertrude Stein an understanding of immediacy, of viewing time, not as "quick breaks of narrative or of 'fill ins' of external events, but a flow of time, of which the style is an index." With his stripped-down sentences and his crisp prose, Hemingway also perfected an economy and precision of language that was typical of many of the self-consciously modern writers.

Others experimented with the form of the novel itself. Among the most innovative was John Dos Passos, who viewed himself as much historian as novelist. In his powerful trilogy, *U.S.A.* (*The 42nd Parallel, 1919,* and *The Big Money*), published in the early 1930s, but a product of the 1920s, Dos Passos was far more concerned than most of his contemporaries with politics and class conflict. But he also explored familiar themes such as the impact on the individual of money, commercialism, mass culture, war, and the machine. His books are peopled with rootless characters who embark on a failed search for meaning in an inhospitable, dehumanizing, and corrupt culture. Merging modern themes with new novelistic forms, Dos Passos interwove several different story lines about individuals whose lives only tangentially intersected, and interrupted these narratives with pithy and sardonic biographies of central figures of modern times: "Tin Lizzy" (Henry Ford), "Adagio Dancer" (Rudolph Valentino), and "The Electrical Wizard" (Thomas Edison). Segments entitled "Newsreel" pulsed with snippets of popular songs, advertisements, and tabloid journalism, and "Camera Eye" sections offered stream-of-consciousness fragments that often included pieces of Dos Passos' own autobiography. The fragmentation and the pace of the books further evoked modern life.

The search for experimentation, authenticity, and the essence of what it meant to be modern multiplied in every art form. The music of Aaron Copland, who used jazz and other popular forms in symphonic music; the photographs of Alfred Stieglitz and the expressionist painting of Georgia O'Keeffe; the innovative plays of Eugene O'Neill; and the dances of Martha Graham—all throbbed with modern themes and modern forms. The optimism of many prewar intellectuals was replaced by the deep pessimism of a new generation of artists who explored the impact on the individual of war, of mass industrial culture, of American provincialism, or of the patriarchal order. Nonetheless, the artistic world of the twenties was also characterized by excitement about its role in shaping a new art appropriate for the twentieth century.

Just as these artists embraced the modern world for its possibilities for individual freedom and artistic innovation, there were major pockets of traditionalism as well. As Roderick Nash has reminded us, for all the critical attention given to the Lost Generation, with its themes of alienation, experimentation, and spontaneity, most of the popular literature of the period remained totally conventional. Among the most frequently read were Harold Bell Wright, who often addressed religious themes; Gene Stratton Porter, whose novels were nostalgic, cheerful productions; Zane Grey, whose tales of the West emphasized traditional values; and Edgar Rice Burroughs, whose 1914 *Tarzan of the Apes* inspired a nationwide Tarzan mania that flourished in the twenties.

THE SOUTHERN RENAISSANCE

In a different vein, a voice of traditionalism emerged from an interesting group of writers who had begun to coalesce into a self-conscious Southern Renaissance that prided itself on its resistance to trends in modern society and art. Poets like Allen Tate, John Crowe Ransom, Robert Penn Warren, and Donald Davidson published in the journal *The Fugitive* between 1922 and 1925, but the major statement of their ideas and those of eight other men appeared in the 1930 anthology *I'll Take My Stand: The South and the Agrarian Tradition* by "Twelve Southerners." The authors articulated a defense of the South and its traditions that had been prompted in part by the national attention focused on the South during Tennessee's famous Scopes trial. Much of the northern media pictured this evolution controversy as a product of ignorant southern yokels. Stung by this immediate insult, the authors of *I'll Take My Stand* also harbored long-standing resentment against the North, most obviously based on the Civil War and Reconstruction, which had permanently disrupted the South's economic and racial order. Contemporary efforts by both northern and southern business- men to develop an industrial and modern "New South" seemed the fruition of a long process of northern corruption of the South, a threat made palpable by the labor unrest emerging in places like the textile miles of Gastonia, North Carolina.

As they defended the South, the twelve men indicted the modern urban industrial society that had left individuals alien- ated and dispossessed. They explored the implications of factory work and consumer culture. As the introduction to the volume put it: "We have more time in which to consume, and many more products to be consumed," but labor had become less sat- isfying, "brutal and hurried." The worker "has to pay the pen- alty in satiety and aimlessness. The modern man has lost his sense of vocation."

Superficially, this critique was not very far removed from those of the Lost Generation and the modernists. But the Southerners' argument diverged significantly; even as they con- demned the new order, they glorified southern culture and so- ciety, specifically the "theory of agrarianism" that holds that "the culture of the soil is the best and most sensitive of voca- tions, and that therefore it should have the economic preference and enlist the maximum number of workers." As technology and northern urban mass culture continued to spread, bringing industry and a cult of science and efficiency, the Agrarians be- moaned the loss of tradition, community, stability, and religion rooted in the land and the past.

THE HARLEM RENAISSANCE

The changes in the South that encouraged the rise of the Agrar- ians included incipient challenges to the racial order that came with the wartime military service and migration of African Americans. A more militant "New Negro" was emerging in both North and South. One of its most important manifestations was literary and artistic. Poets Langston Hughes and Countee Cul- len, novelists Claude McKay, Jean Toomer, Jessie Fauset, and Zora Neale Hurston, and artists Aaron Douglas and Augusta

Savage were only the best-known of the hundreds of young men and women who flocked to Harlem to be part of the colony of black intellectuals who were consciously forging a Harlem Renaissance. For the most part, these artists did not center their energies on the themes that their white counterparts classified as modernism. However, in the long view, as they focused on the issues of racial identity and community, their concerns were quintessentially "modern." As W.E.B. Du Bois said in 1903: "The problem of the twentieth century is the problem of the color-line," and it was this problem that preoccupied the majority of African American intellectuals in the 1920s.

The coalescence of the artistic and literary expression of the New Negro was not altogether spontaneous, for the Harlem Renaissance had many midwives. Black magazines like *The Crisis, Opportunity,* and *The Messenger* provided showcases for writers and celebrated their talents. Philosopher Alain Locke, perhaps the most important mentor of the movement, edited *The New Negro* (1925), a volume of essays, stories, and poetry that attempted to express and explain the sources and nature of the current wave of black art, and in her role as literature editor of *The Crisis,* Nella Larsen played an indispensable role in nurturing black talent.

Whites also served the Renaissance by providing introductions, arranging publication, and buying books. Their patronage extended to financial gifts to writers and artists that enabled many to devote their time to their work. For many whites, the attraction of the Renaissance stemmed from the trendy fascination with blacks and black culture. This was a period of "slumming" in Harlem, when whites sought out its nightspots for jazz, uninhibited dancing, alcohol, drugs, and sex. To the white intellectuals and sophisticates in full rebellion against the constraints of "civilization," Harlem and African Americans represented the exotic, the sensual, and the free, themes evident in the works of a number of white authors, among them *The Emperor Jones* and *All God's Chillun Got Wings* by playwright Eugene O'Neill and *Nigger Heaven* by Carl Van Vechten.

The white world's significance to the Renaissance went beyond its patronage. Like other black leaders in the 1920s, black artists were struggling to legitimate blacks' place in American society. They had the excitement and the burden of believing that their efforts to spawn a vibrant black intellectual culture would be the ultimate proof of their equality, indeed of their humanity. This expectation often produced an identity crisis. They had no doubt that blacks were part of America. As Alain Locke put it: "The Negro mind reaches out as yet to nothing but American wants, American ideas." Some authors chose to emphasize the essential sameness of blacks and whites. But more typically, Harlem Renaissance artists sought to find something distinctive about black culture, to locate an essential black spirit that would be a source of pride and an indication of the contributions blacks had made to American culture.

The theme of Africa emerged in many works. Artists were not alone in attempting to forge links between American blacks and Africa. This was a period of increased recognition of the possibilities of Pan-Africanism. W.E.B. Du Bois, for example, sponsored several Pan-African Conferences in this period and was one of many black leaders who had hoped to influence the postwar Versailles Peace Conference to provide self-determination for former German colonies in Africa. Artists sidestepped the realities of contemporary African politics and attempted to invoke a more abstract connection between American blacks and Africa. The stark black-and-white drawings with African motifs that decorated Locke's *The New Negro* were the work of Aaron Douglas, the best-known artist to use African motifs and styles. In "The Negro Sings of Rivers," Langston Hughes also expressed the black link between America and Africa, as he invoked the "ancient, dusky rivers" of the Euphrates, the Nile, and the Mississippi.

But as Nathan Huggins has pointed out, the African theme ran false in much of the Harlem Renaissance. Africa was merely an abstraction—few American blacks knew much about it, and demonstrating the spiritual link between American blacks and Africa was fraught with difficulty. In other attempts to express the distinctive quality of African Americans' contribution, writers focused on the spiritual, creative character which was commonly believed to be the essence of black culture. In search of this spirit, many black writers, notably Zora Neale Hurston and Jean Toomer, turned to folk culture and the rural South. Spirituals were also viewed as a source of inspiration and understanding of black culture. In a somewhat related vein, the idea of blacks as innately sensual, creative, alive people emerged as a prevalent theme in the decade's writing. Although some writers merely tended to celebrate this perceived aspect of African American culture, others like Nella Larsen and Claude McKay offered more thoughtful insights that spoke to the dilemma of the educated black person cut off from his or her ancestral roots.

The quest for the primitive presented problems for many black authors, because it came so close to pejorative stereotypes that blacks had been trying to lay to rest. Many resented the fad of emphasizing black exoticism and sensuality, especially the white audience's enthusiasm for it. This type of imagery was especially problematic for women artists. Sensitive to the sexual exploitation and stereotyping of black women, they were uncomfortable with "tom-tom" themes and evoked them far less frequently than men. Sharing some of the problems of their white women contemporaries—the Harlem Renaissance was as male-dominated as the Lost Generation—African American female artists also tended to be subtle in their criticism. In Maureen Honey's words, their work was "indirect, coded, wrung free of overt anger," yet contemporary critics have found much subversive content, a challenge to racial and gender hierarchies in prose and poems that superficially seem conventional and conservative. And while they rejected primitive imagery, some women—like poets Angelina Weld Grimké, Mae V. Cowdery, and Virginia Houston—often employed overtly erotic imagery, in which they portrayed their sexuality in their own terms, not those of white patrons or male colleagues.

Helene Johnson, one of the more innovative, though not very prolific, women artists, satirized the primitive theme. In "Poem," a dialogue with her "jazz prince," she wrote: "Gee, boy, when you sing, I can close my ears / and hear tom toms just as plain. / Listen to me, will you, what do I know / About tom toms? But I like the word, sort of, / Don't you? It belongs to us." Johnson also incorporated urban street slang, sharing with better-known artists like Langston Hughes and Claude Mc-Kay an appreciation of vernacular black culture.

In the search for distinctive black contributions, Hughes was one of a handful of intellectuals to explore jazz and the blues as examples of indigenous black culture. In *The Weary Blues* (1926), he not only conveyed a bluesy tone but underlined the importance of performance in black popular culture as he described a Lenox Avenue piano player in Harlem:

> *He made that poor piano moan with melody.*
> *O Blues!*
> *Swaying to and fro on his rickety stool*
> *He played that sad raggy tune like a musical fool.*
> *Sweet Blues!*
> *Coming from a black man's soul.*
> *O Blues!*

Hughes joined other artists, including Helene Johnson, Zora Neale Hurston, and Wallace Thurman, in establishing the short-lived journal *Fire*, which called for a more innovative approach to framing African American art. This celebration of the themes and forms of the urban masses met with much criticism by the older black intelligentsia, for while many were willing to romanticize the southern past with its folklore and spirituals, they were uncomfortable with the new urban culture of the black masses. This blindness to jazz and the blues in part reflects the class divisions that separated intellectuals from the vast majority of blacks, but it also suggests, as Nathan Huggins has argued, that many members of the Harlem Renaissance were too wedded to the Western European cultural canon to find jazz "useful." Mastery of high culture was the proof of black attainment. In their avoidance of jazz, Huggins convincingly argues, they missed possibilities for more innovative work and particularly for finding black contributions to American culture. The few who challenged the canon staked out new territory. Hughes recognized that the expression of urban culture was central to interpreting the modern black experience: in the blues, as Arnold Rampersad put it, "he found the tone, the texture, the basic language of true black modernism."

OTHER VOICES: PLURALISM AND MODERNITY

African Americans were not alone in the struggle over questions of identity vis-à-vis the mainstream. A variety of ethnic writers such as Ludwig Lewisohn, Ole E. Rölvaag, and Abraham Cahan also addressed this theme. Most notably, this period marked the first novel by a Native American woman (Mourning Dove's *Cogewea*) and the first English-language book by a woman of Japanese descent (*A Daughter of the Samurai* by Etsu Sugimoto). One novel in particular has emerged as an American classic. In *Bread Givers* (1925), Anzia Yezierska tells the story of a Jewish immigrant family in New York through the eyes of a daughter, Sara. Sara's desire to "be a person" speaks to her marginal status as an immigrant, but also as a woman. To achieve an individual identity, she must challenge the autocratic power of her father, an Old World patriarch. Through extraordinary hard work and determination, she realizes her dream: education and a job as a schoolteacher. At the end of the novel, having achieved her Americanization and acquired a fiancé, Sara becomes reconciled with her father, an act that suggests an acceptance of her Jewish ethnicity as part of her American identity.

Other ethnic offerings appeared in specialized periodicals. Self-consciously Catholic writers (a number of the Lost Generation writers, Fitzgerald among them, were Catholic, but did not write from the perspective of the church or from an ethnic tradition) congregated around *The Commonweal*, a journal that focused on delineating the contributions of Catholicism to American culture. Authors such as Michael Williams and George N. Schuster sought to counter contemporary disillusionment, despair, materialism, and what Williams called "the new paganism" by promoting a Catholic organicism rooted in the romance and order of medievalism. They were optimistic and self-confident about a Catholic coming-of-age in America, which represented, as Michael Halsey has put it, "the survival of American innocence."

The twenties found Jewish intellectuals in transition. Yiddish and Hebrew writers were being replaced by a new generation of English speakers, many of whom found a home in the *Menorah Journal*. The magazine came out of a network of college students' Menorah Associations, and helped to launch writers who by the 1930s would become a recognizable coterie of left-leaning New York intellectuals, profoundly influential in American arts, letters, and politics. In the 1920s, these mostly secular writers, including Horace Kallen and Lionel Trilling, examined the place of Jews in American culture, and "aspired to cultivate respect for the Jewish past while also responding to the American present."

Kallen has come to hold a particularly important place in the history of ideas about ethnicity. Along with Randolph Bourne, he was one of the leading proponents of cultural pluralism in the early twentieth century. Although it was Kallen who actually coined the term in 1924 in *Culture and Democracy in the United States*, both men, contending that nativists' insistence on uniform assimilation was detrimental to society, stressed the maintenance of European immigrants' ethnic identity. Instead of being a melting pot, America was a federation of nationalities that should be celebrated, not denigrated. The cultural pluralism of Bourne and Kallen was not just a plea for tolerance, but a program for reform that would enhance equality and democracy. In Kallen's words: "Democracy involves not the elimination of differences but the perfection and conservation of differences." Tolerance had its limits, however: this view of pluralism did not embrace African Americans or immigrants of color.

Cultural pluralism did not attract much attention in mainstream artistic circles until after World War II, but it did surface in the works of many social scientists in the twenties. Robert Park, a leader of the Chicago school of sociology, helped to channel academic investigations away from the idea of innate racial or ethnic traits and toward the examination of relationships between groups. He described an urban race relations cycle consisting of contact, competition, accommodation, and assimilation. At a time when many suspected that ethnic institutions were "un-American," Park insisted that they were in fact beneficial. Newspapers, fraternal organizations, and ethnic literature, he argued, helped the individual to find identity, self-esteem, and order in the complex urban world. Moreover, the separatist institutions of European and Asian immigrants and African Americans could be way stations for incorporation into the mainstream: "The fact that the individual will not be respected unless his group is respected becomes, thus, perhaps, the most sincere source of nationalistic movements in America. To this extent the nationalistic movements represent an effort to increase participation in American life." Optimistic in his cultural pluralism, Park was nonetheless acutely aware of the impact of racism, and recognized that for African Americans and Asians, a "racial uniform" hampered the process of incorporation.

Anthropologists were also instrumental in challenging older views of human difference. After decades of American academics who contributed to racism by offering "scientific" justification for it, Franz Boas and his students led the way in challenging hierarchical assumptions about race. Drawing upon a notion of the plasticity of cultures derived from extensive fieldwork, they denied that biological factors determined human society or individual personality. Although these ideas about the centrality of culture were formulated well before World War I, they were not widely disseminated until later. The climate of nativism and racism of the 1920s led Boas to be outspoken in his insistence that there was no scientific basis for hierarchical racial assumptions. He provided data to congressional supporters of immigration and in particular refuted the validity of IQ tests that purportedly proved the racial inferiority of new immigrants and African Americans. Anthropologists and other social scientists were far from successful in dispelling racism or nativism, but they did ensure that by the end of the decade "scientific" racism was no longer respectable in academic or intellectual circles.

Beyond the issue of race, the new anthropology presaged new ways of thinking about society and knowledge itself. In their explorations of the sources of behavior, beliefs, and rituals in non-Western, premodern societies, Boas and his students Ruth Benedict, Edward Sapir, and Margaret Mead unseated older hierarchical distinctions between "primitive" and "civilized" societies. Drawing implicit or explicit comparisons, they suggested that the former were no more or less rational than the latter. Margaret Mead did much to popularize the notion that Americans should view their own culture in relative terms. In her best-selling *Coming of Age in Samoa* (1928), Mead detailed Samoan child-rearing practices and inferred that the "primitive" culture produced better-adjusted people than her own. Cultural relativism did more than challenge Victorian hierarchies about race or civilization. Like relativity in the sciences, it also undercut belief in the certainty of what could be known.

Another best-seller of the decade used the ethnographic approach to study a small city and offer a critique of modern American culture. Helen and Robert Lynd approached Muncie, Indiana, which they called Middletown, as a typical American community caught in the throes of significant modern development—changes in work, family, and culture. Central to the Lynds' interpretation was the idea of cultural lag—an idea first formulated by sociologist William Ogburn. In *Middletown* (1929), the Lynds argued that the tension caused by changes in structure—work, mass media, industrial developments—had proceeded faster than culture—ideas about family, religion, sexuality—could keep up with. In many ways, they sketched a bleak picture of confused individuals trying to re-create community and find meaning in the "all-too-bigness of things." But in the final analysis, the Lynds optimistically hoped that, in Richard Fox's words, the people of Middletown could resist the effects of modern commercial culture with a "voluntary adaptation of a new ethic of self-sacrifice, of putting the community welfare ahead of individual gain."

As an exemplar of modern culture, Muncie was in many ways a flawed choice. The Lynds deliberately sought a relatively homogeneous community with little ethnic or racial variety as a means of limiting the variables they needed to assess in evaluating social change. By this omission, of course, they excluded a central factor that was helping to make America modern—the ethnic and racial pluralism of its cities. But in other ways, the Lynds successfully captured the major components of twentieth-century society: changes affecting the economy, work, leisure, consumption, religion, sexuality, and the family, and the value shifts that accompanied these transformations. They, like other intellectuals, critics and creative artists alike, struggled to comprehend and express the modern temper and its implications for the individual, the community, and the culture.

RELIGION

Although the world of preacher and pulpit was far removed from that of intellectuals and bohemia, nonetheless a common thread unites them. The erosion of Victorian absolutes that so powerfully transformed intellectual assumptions also profoundly affected religion and the moral code associated with it. And, similar to what was happening in the intellectual arena, many of the changes shaping religion had predated the war, yet seemed to crystallize during the 1920s. On the one hand, American culture seemed increasingly secularized. Even religion lost some of its sacred aura as many urban ministers adopted modern business techniques and businessmen drew upon a religious vocabulary to promote their respective enterprises. On the other hand, there is much evidence of the continued strength of religious faith. Within Catholic, Jewish, and African American communities, pockets of traditionalism persisted, and among evangelical Christians in particular, a militant defense of old-time religion flourished as they resisted the efforts of other Protestants to update the Christian message to make it more relevant to the modern world. This conflict between traditionalists and modernists was just one sign of the considerable religious ferment of the 1920s. The religious history of the period underscores the weighty impact of social change and the varying responses to it, as Americans struggled to reaffirm their traditional worldview or to adapt ideals to meet the challenges posed by the acids of modernity.

THE RISE OF A SECULAR SOCIETY

In 1933, the President's Research Committee on Recent Social Trends described the previous decade's religious climate as "one of extreme unrest." The country's Protestant churches in particular were rocked by a variety of assaults on traditional faith. At the center of the ferment was the shock of World War I's carnage, as well as long-standing scientific challenges to religious conceptions of the world and humanity and the continued expansion of an urban, materialistic culture. Ministers across the country bemoaned the spread of apathy, skepticism, and secularism, and historians have concurred that the decade experienced, in historian Robert Handy's words, a "religious depression."

On the surface, the fortunes of organized religion do not appear that bleak in the 1920s. The number of church members —representing roughly 55 percent of the adult population— continued to increase, and churches prospered financially as well. Their coffers fattened by aggressive membership drives, many urban churches embarked on ambitious building programs, erecting not just places of worship but elaborate complexes to accommodate social, recreational, and educational programs. But even as the material fortunes of churches improved, many ministers decried the poor attendance that left the new sanctuaries half empty on Sunday mornings and forced the cancellation of Sunday-evening services altogether. Protestant and Jewish leaders alike worried about diminishing attendance. Another visible sign of the religious depression was the eroding support for missionary activities. Contributions were down, and so too were the number of individuals signing on to serve abroad. In 1928, only 225 students, as opposed to 2,700 in 1920, volunteered for foreign missionary service.

These measurable signs formed only part of the religious malaise that seemed to pervade the decade. The highly materialistic tenor of the period—the pursuit of the dollar, the huckstering mentality that was so much a part of the popular culture—also suggested that religious values were in decline. Charles Fiske, in his *Confessions of a Puzzled Parson* (1929), lamented that the enthusiasm for business had become so strong that it had invaded religion itself: "America has become almost hopelessly enamored of a religion that is little more than a sanctified commercialism; it is hard in this day and this land to differentiate between religious aspirations and business prosperity." In a related vein, the ebbing interest in social reform that many churches had backed under the rubric of the social gospel, indicated a turning away from the moral imperatives of church teachings.

That religion was losing its hold on many Americans also seemed evident in changing sexual standards—especially in the conduct of young women—which suggested that people were breaking away from the religious proscriptions that had been bound up with Victorian morality concerning home and family. The rise in civil marriages and divorce further reveals the eroding ability of traditional religion to determine people's daily conduct. And although Sabbath observance laws, which regulated what business and entertainment activities could be carried out on Sunday, still existed in many communities and states, churches increasingly competed with commercial amusements —movies, sporting events, and the like. Similarly, prohibition— largely the result of Protestantism's campaign for moral and social reform—was the law of the land in the 1920s, but it was widely flouted, not just by the immigrants and the working class but also by the nation's trendsetters—the respectable urban middle class. By the 1920s, as America had became more secular, religion—and Protestantism specifically—no longer dominated public life and cultural norms.

For many ministers, the crisis was in fact a crisis of Protestantism. Not only was the Protestant moral code deteriorating but decades of immigration had transformed the nation's religious makeup. While only 5 percent of the nation's church members were Jewish, almost a third were Catholics. Diversity in itself contributed to secularization. The tolerance that peaceful coexistence required made it more difficult to enshrine one specific set of beliefs. The growing interest in the history and sociology of world religions not only further weakened Protestantism's special position in the culture but also promoted the view that religions were not divinely ordained but were socially constructed.

A number of sociological studies addressed the state of American religion in the 1920s. In Middletown, the Lynds found mixed religious messages. Especially among their working-class interviewees, they uncovered a persistence of traditional religious beliefs; among the business class, more ambiguity and uncertainty. For the most part, the religiosity of the working class aside, the Lynds confirmed contemporary observers' perception of a rising tide of secularism. The Lynds' sampling revealed that Middletown's church attendance was low: an average of 11 percent of males and 18 percent of females in the community attended Sunday-morning services. They suggested that at least part of the explanation was the competing attraction of modern leisure—golfing and motoring took many a family away from the church.

The Lynds also recognized that among the middle class, ministers enjoyed a lower social status than the business and professional class, a factor perhaps of special interest to Robert Lynd, himself an ordained Presbyterian minister. Declining prestige, combined with poor salaries and ever-increasing duties, was a source of considerable lament throughout the country, and suggested, as one contemporary analysis put it, that ministers were "commonly supposed to be losing their influence in American life." Historian Paul Carter reports that the denominational press repeatedly claimed that talented young men were avoiding the ministry "because 'the man of affairs,' who was the culture-hero of the age, seldom 'says or does anything to indicate that he regards the Christian ministry as a real challenge to a man who wants to do big worth-while things with his life.' " The low salaries of ministers, according to Carter, placed the clergyman and his family in an awkward position among his middle-class parishioners, who customarily judged a man's value by his income and possessions.

Class was one factor that shaped attitudes toward organized religion; gender was another. Many scholars have noted the feminization of American Protestantism. In the nineteenth century women parishioners and male ministers allied to construct a sentimental, emotional religion that may have disaffected many men. Some found alternative religious experience in all-male fraternal organizations like the Freemasons and the Knights of

Pythias. Many churches, concerned about this disaffection, framed revival campaigns explicitly to recapture the interests of men. Thus there was nothing new about male discontent with the churches, but in the 1920s complaints became more overt and specific. A much-quoted survey of servicemen during the war, *Religion Among American Men* (1920), lamented their religious ignorance as well as their vague beliefs and concluded that many saw the church as a place for marrying and burying, but not connected to the "real business of life." Ministers, not part of the practical side of life, were not altogether male, and religion was not manly. Statistics confirm that women were more likely than men to be church members: 62 percent of white women and 73 percent of African American women were on church rolls, compared with 49 percent of white men and 46 percent of African American men.

In addition to the competition of secular attractions and the disaffection with the institutional churches and the ministry, spiritual considerations are equally significant in understanding religion's slipping hold on many Americans. Some observers, like the editor of *The Christian Century Pulpit*, suggested that a widespread crisis of faith had followed World War I: "A cynical generation like that which emerged from the great war weakened the supports of faith in the soul of every man." Others recognized that secular trends came from deeper sources that predated the war. Walter Lippmann, in the best-selling and Book-of-the-Month Club selection *Preface to Morals* (1929), suggested that church attendance had declined because people were no longer certain "that they are going to meet God when they go to church." The statement neatly summed up the spiritual uncertainty of the time that Lippmann attributed primarily to the expanding scientific understanding of the universe, scholarly analysis of the history of mankind and its religions, and the fluid conditions of urban industrial life. These changes had knocked the props out from under many Americans' faith: "This is the first age, I think, in the history of mankind when the circumstances of life have conspired with the intellectual habits of the time to render any fixed and authoritative belief incredible to large masses of men." Lippmann ended on an optimistic note, however. Hypothesizing an audience of "unbelievers . . . perplexed by the consequences of their own irreligion," he proffered his version of secular humanism to give structure and meaning to modern life.

Joseph Wood Krutch's *The Modern Temper* (1929) addressed similar issues, but in a far darker tone. Krutch traced the theme of man's struggle to construct a sense of meaning in the face of scientific evidence that undermined faith in God and humanity's central place in the universe. According to Krutch, the social sciences contributed to the sense of disorder, and in particular the spreading acceptance of Freudian psychology's understanding of the irrationality of human actions furthered the perception of how little control men and women had over themselves or their environment.

Unlike Lippmann, Krutch offered no way out:

> Weak and uninstructed intelligences take refuge in the monotonous repetition of once living creeds, or are even reduced to the desperate expedient of going to sleep amid the formulae of the flabby pseudo-religions in which the modern world is so prolific. But neither of these classes affords any aid to the robust but serious mind which is searching for some terms upon which it may live.

Dismissing both humanism and metaphysical approaches to a new sense of order, he wryly concluded that "if we no longer believe in either our infinite capacities or our importance to the universe, we know at least that we have discovered the trick which has been played upon us and that whatever else we may be we are no longer dupes."

Few observers painted as bleak a scene as Krutch, but many commented on contemporary men and women's struggle with uncertainty, with the ensuing fuzziness of religious belief. "People are questioning and wondering now about religious matters," one middle-class woman told the Lynds. "There are just a lot of things you have to try not to let yourself think about." The Lynds concluded that "doubt and uneasiness among individuals may be greater than a generation ago."

TRADITIONAL FAITHS

Lippmann's audience—as the Book-of-the-Month Club choice suggests—was primarily the educated middle class. For the most part, it was this group, especially Protestants, that secularizing trends most profoundly affected. Among Jews, the story is complex. Secularization had to compete with many other issues that concerned leaders. As Chapter VI argues, the Jewish community was divided along several lines. German Jews, "old settlers," who had arrived in the mid-nineteenth century, were more assimilated and had adopted a highly Americanized form of religion, Reform Judaism. They were often in conflict with newer immigrants from Southern and Eastern Europe, who had immigrated after 1880. The latter continued to be connected to Old World Yiddish culture and attempted to re-create the religious and cultural world of the shtetl. For the most part they practiced Orthodox Judaism. Tensions erupted between the groups over claims to leadership of the community, over definitions of American and Jewish identity, and over commitment to Zionism. In addition to internecine struggles, Jewish leaders in the 1920s also focused on combating the pervasive anti-Semitism of the decade.

In common with Protestants, rabbis and other religious leaders worried about declension, especially among the young. Mordecai Kaplan was a particularly important influence in the effort to adapt Judaism to American conditions as a way of preventing the disappearance of young Jews into the American melting pot. In the 1920s he proposed "Reconstructionism," a modification of religious laws and theology to fit with the realities of contemporary culture. De-emphasizing the belief in the supernatural, the idea of Jews as a chosen people, and adherence to archaic Jewish law, he substituted the promotion of Jewish ethnic identity based on a shared past and tradition. Part of his program included the construction of Jewish Community Centers which would supplement religious functions with social and educational ones. Kaplan's ideas met with criticism from the more orthodox who lamented that the centers transformed the temple into a "shul [synagogue] with a school and a pool." In time, Kaplan's ideas would prove quite influential, but in the twenties they made inroads only among a small group of well-educated, secularized Jews.

Despite worries about the younger generation, as second and third generations began to achieve occupational mobility and move out of the ghettos of original settlement, many did join synagogues and pay for the expensive building programs of the postwar decade. Their transition helped spur the growth of a third major religious component of Judaism, the Conservative movement. Although they were not as radical in their innovations as Reform Jews, Conservative congregations modified the traditional orthodoxy of their Southern and Eastern European parents to make it more palatable to modern Americans. However, although middle-class and Americanized Jews might join these synagogues, according to most observers at the time they infrequently attended them. For many, religious observance increasingly meant occasional attendance, usually during the Jewish New Year or Passover. Jewish identity became for them a semisecularized form of ethnicity. But not all Jews became so secularized or assimilated. For the first generation in particular, religion continued to play a vital part in everyday life. A commitment to orthodoxy formed part of the worldview that allowed many immigrants to maintain their traditional culture in an alienating environment.

Roman Catholics experienced comparatively little theological controversy or ferment during the 1920s. In his role as infallible spiritual leader, the Pope had already condemned modernism and efforts to reconcile faith with science, and thus the Catholic Church escaped much of the doctrinal discord that disrupted Protestantism, although certainly many Catholics may have waged their own private battles of faith. For the most part, the mood was optimistic, and the hierarchy concentrated on consolidating the rapid membership gains of the early twentieth century. Bishops embarked on extensive building campaigns and dramatically expanded the parochial school system, which doubled in size during the decade. In this period, the hierarchy also extended its control over the country's parishes and priests through increased centralization and bureaucratization of the church and its institutions.

In the 1920s, the church was still primarily an immigrant, working-class institution, and Catholic leaders occupied themselves with issues linked to their minority status vis-à-vis American society. Within the church, they pursued Americanization measures; outside, they vehemently resisted anti-Catholicism. Given the trend toward irreligion in modern society, Catholic leaders did express some concern about keeping the faithful within the fold. The Irish-dominated hierarchy particularly worried about apostasy among newer immigrants, especially Italians and Mexicans. But although the hierarchy was correct in their view that many Italian and Mexican immigrants were indifferent to the Irish American version of Catholicism, the elaborate rituals of their feast days and processions, adapted from patterns in their native country, testified to an ongoing identification with their traditional religion that in the new country became closely intertwined with ethnic identity. Indeed, immigrant communities all over the country—both Catholic and Jewish—represented strongholds of traditional faith.

The Protestant followers of old-time religion—an evangelical faith centered on a literal interpretation of the Bible which lent an absolute certainty to their beliefs about the life, birth, and death of Christ and his message of sin and salvation—constitute another significant example of the persistence of faith. For these believers, religion was something lived, not compartmentalized into Sunday observance. This was particularly true of the Holiness-Pentecostal movement, consisting of mostly poor and working-class men and women who left more established Protestant churches for the purity and intensity of newer sects that flourished in the 1920s.

The Holiness movement developed in the late nineteenth century as a protest against the increased worldliness of mainline denominations such as the Methodists. Although it began as an interdenominational movement within established churches, it broke into separate holiness sects. Followers embraced the literal interpretation of the Bible, especially the prophecy of a second coming of Jesus Christ, and were exceptionally concerned with a second blessing or "sanctification"—a process that followed conversion and confirmed it. In addition, disturbed by what they considered to be the immoral trends of the secular world, Holiness churches inveighed against drinking, gambling, dancing, and similar amusements. Pentecostalism emerged from the Holiness sects in the early twentieth century and was distinguished by its insistence upon glossolalia—speaking in tongues—as a sign of sanctification and baptism with the Holy Spirit, and the only incontrovertible evidence that one would be saved. Most Pentecostals also emphasized divine healing, another example of the search for visible, experiential evidence of salvation. Pentecostalism, like Holiness, was a highly expressive emotional form of worship, characterized by music, singing, shouting, and frenzied body movement.

Both Holiness and Pentecostals had strong egalitarian components. In keeping with their stress on the experience of faith, of baptism in the Holy Spirit, they placed little emphasis on formal religious training; few of their early religious leaders were educated to the ministry. Since this characteristic, along with their egalitarianism, gave women an outlet for leadership denied them in traditional denominations, women often occupied major positions, as either ministers, evangelists, or teachers. Pentecostalism initially carried egalitarianism even further: originating in the South and West in the early twentieth century, it began as an interracial movement. By the 1920s, however, racial segregation had become fairly well established. Although many different branches flourished under the broad rubric of Pentecostal, the major black group was the Church of God in Christ. Among whites, the Assemblies of God was one of the most important denominations. Just as racial lines hardened, by the 1920s, as sects became more organized and bureaucratized into churches, female leadership also began to decline. A major exception to this pattern, however, was the ministry of Aimee Semple McPherson.

McPherson began her calling firmly in the Pentecostal tradition. She accepted the belief in glossolalia and won her initial fame as a faith healer of exceptional power. After conducting revivals in various parts of the country, she settled in Los Angeles and in 1923 founded the imposing and expensive Angelus Temple dedicated to the "Four Square Gospel"—divine healing, regeneration, baptism in the Holy Spirit, and the second coming. Although McPherson had begun under the auspices of the Assemblies of God, eventually her church became a distinct and major international branch of Pentecostalism.

Her flamboyant style and publicity seeking made "Sister Aimee" a major celebrity. She brought Hollywood into the temple. She was most famous for her illustrated sermons, elaborate productions in which she would interpret biblical messages with professional stage sets, musicians, and actors, with herself as a major player. McPherson also proved a genius at using the new medium of radio. In 1924 she established her own powerful radio station, describing the enormous antenna towers as "alive, tingling, pulsing spires of steel, mute witnesses that at Angelus Temple every moment of the day and night, a silent and invisible messenger awaits the command to carry, on the winged feet of the winds, the story of hope, the words of joy, of comfort, of salvation." As the antennas projected her message, Sister Aimee skillfully brought her radio audience into the temple with her and established a sense of intimacy. She urged her listeners to put their hands on their radio and kneel in prayer with her. According to J. Harold Ellens: "Hundreds of thousands of people were electrified with the certainty that the broadcasts represented God's invasion into their personal lives. Thousands believed they were miraculously healed."

With all the hoopla, it would be easy to dismiss McPherson's calling as more show business than religion. But despite her emphasis on staged theatricality, Sister Aimee operated within the traditions of what she and her followers called "the old-time religion." She criticized modernist trends and insisted upon a literal interpretation of the Bible, and the faith and commitment to a moral code that went along with it. Like many Pentecostals and fundamentalists, she invested the old-time religion with more optimism and comfort than its Calvinist roots possessed. In William McLoughlin's words, she "emphasized the love of Christ, the joys of heaven, and the triumph of the millennium for the true Christian. Hers was a gospel of hope, of faith, of good times ahead, of rejoicing with loved ones in heaven, of a great day coming."

In keeping with this comforting hopefulness, healing continued to be a mainstay of her ministry. The lame and infirm flocked to Angelus Temple to experience her touch. Healing suggests an important clue to her (and other Pentecostal's) appeal: she offered a faith that worked, one that could be experienced. As physical evidence, she maintained a Miracle Room at the temple where she displayed the abandoned crutches and other accoutrements of infirmity that her followers no longer needed. She also constructed a prayer tower in which volunteers worked twenty-four hours a day: "We get requests from all over the country for special prayers—mountains of daily letters; prayers for the sick, prayers for the unhappy, prayers for wandering sons and daughters and husbands, prayers for agonized souls." As evidence for the efficacy of this prayer, she maintained a record of the many thousands of answered prayers.

Sister Aimee clearly touched a nerve. While some of the thousands of people who flocked to Angelus Temple went in the manner of tourists to witness the show, by all accounts McPherson also attracted a large, devout following. She especially appealed to midwestern migrants who were pouring into Los Angeles in this period. For these people, she offered a version of the old-time religion and morality that was familiar. Angelus Temple also formed the center of well-organized social and charitable activities that gave followers an opportunity to participate in a shared community of believers. At the same time, her Hollywood style satisfied a desire for novelty that must have accompanied the decision to uproot and transplant oneself in a new environment. Sister Aimee's followers could partake of some of the excitement of the new amusements without feeling they were compromising their traditional faith.

Aimee Semple McPherson was so beloved that even her celebrated 1927 kidnapping story, which the media exposed as probably a cover-up for a love-nest getaway with an employee of her radio station, did not seriously undermine her credibility among her followers, although it did mark an end to the heyday of her popularity among the general public. While she was certainly one of a kind, her success testifies to the vitality of religious faith during the period. Despite scientific and other challenges to old-time religion, Sister Aimee, with her stacks of discarded crutches and scrapbooks of answered prayers, demonstrates the attractiveness of an optimistic faith that could be experienced and even "proved."

McPherson's success serves as an important reminder that although traditional religion had deep roots in rural areas, it could and did flourish in the cities, especially among migrants seeking accustomed values in a new environment. Outside the South, Pentecostalism, for example, was overwhelmingly urban. The multiplication of small (usually under fifty members) "storefront" churches in the cities touched off by the mass migration of African Americans from the rural South in the teens and twenties represents another example of the vitality of urban religion. Chapter VI analyzes the implications of the movement to the cities of over a million African Americans. What is important here is that in the process of transplanting themselves, the migrants experienced tremendous disruption. Among the resources they drew upon to ground themselves in a new urban culture was a familiar religion.

Many African Americans sought out the already established black churches, especially the Methodists and Baptists, which were the most numerous denominations in the South. In Chicago, Olivet Baptist expanded dramatically during the northward migration, adding 5,000 members between 1916 and 1919. Adam Clayton Powell's Harlem Abyssinian Baptist Church constructed an imposing 2,000-seat sanctuary to accommodate its growing numbers and wealth. Featuring elaborate facilities and well-organized social activities, it provided many social services designed to assist youth, the elderly, and the poor.

But many Southerners found these large northern churches uncomfortable. The dissatisfaction stemmed in part from class differences. An emerging black middle class increasingly dominated the larger northern churches. Although sympathetic to the migrants, they were also embarrassed by them and their "peasant ways." In addition, the class differences played out in the matter of religious style. Southern rural churches, whether Baptist, Methodist, Holiness, or Pentecostal, tended to have a much more expressive and emotional style of worship, and featured spontaneous singing, shouting, and movement. Even if northern churches permitted more enthusiastic worship—as Harlem's Abyssinian Baptist did, for example—the large churches presented other problems. Small storefront churches gave vent to individuals' desire to be somebody, to resist the anonymity of the large city and church. One Chicago woman explained why she left the first church she had joined. It was "too large—it don't see the small people. . . . The preacher wouldn't know me, might could call my name in the book, but he wouldn't know me otherwise. Why, at home whenever I didn't come to Sunday school they would always come and see what was the matter."

In establishing these new churches, worshippers might bring ministers up from home or start their own around a core of like-minded devout people. Although many storefront churches were organized as Baptist or Methodist entities, Holiness-Pentecostal was very well represented. Among the latter, women often served as founders and ministers. In Philadelphia in 1924, Ida Robinson founded the Pentecostal Mt. Sinai Holy Church, which eventually had many branches. Lucy Smith, especially noted for her divine healing, staged prayer meetings in a single room in Chicago before she started the All Nations Pentecostal Church. As St. Clair Drake and Horace R. Cayton reported in *Black Metropolis* (1945), Smith explained what attracted her followers: "The members of my church are troubled and need something to make them happy. My preaching is not about sad things, but always about being saved. The singing in my church has 'swing' to it, because I want my people to swing out of themselves all the mis'ry and troubles that is heavy on their hearts."

Smith's description captures the appeal of such intense religion to the impoverished and oppressed. The reference to "swing" is also revealing. The storefront Holiness and Pentecostal churches emphasized music. There was an irony here, because most of these sects strongly disapproved of the worldly sounds of jazz, blues, and ragtime and the dancing that went with them. But the songs they sang, the instruments they used, and the ecstatic "dancing" of the sanctified were shaped by and in turn influenced black secular music. As one observer of the New York music scene put it in 1919: "They sang the blues in church; the words were religious, but it was the blues. They often had a drummer and a trumpet player." The music forged in these small churches was also the source of gospel, which dominated black religious music beginning in the 1930s. Storefront worship thus drew upon both sacred and secular African American cultural traditions and in the process helped to create new religious and musical styles.

The Holiness and Pentecostal storefronts were firmly within a familiar Protestant tradition, but urban settings also encouraged the proliferation of hundreds of cults that were clearly alternatives to Protestantism. Spiritualist churches merged a mélange of Catholic, Protestant, and vaguely Caribbean obeah ("voodoo") to promise practical, secular results from religious ritual. They flourished in cities North and South, and were heavily dominated by female leaders. Mother Leafy Anderson had her own church in New Orleans, a major Spiritualist center, where she trained numerous other women. In addition, she headed an association of churches in numerous other cities, including Chicago and Memphis. According to scholar Joseph R. Washington, Jr., the Spiritualist churches provided a form of counseling that was the poor black person's "positive thinking." Spiritualists used charms and amulets, and sometimes séances, "to fit the desires of blacks for success in love, marriage, gambling, employment and healing."

Other cults centered on charismatic individuals whom their followers worshipped as God. George Baker, Jr., more widely known as Father Divine, did not achieve national fame until the Great Depression, but he began his ministry in the teens. Divine blended New Thought ideas popular in the white mainstream—an emphasis on God's immanence in each individual, the power of positive thinking, and the healing power of individuals—with Holiness-Pentecostal religious enthusiasm to fashion his own theology. He attracted both whites and blacks, especially women, to his communal living colonies that featured a strict moral code (including celibacy), employment assistance, and a holy supper every evening. Divine offered an expressive religious experience combined with practical assistance in day-to-day life.

Followers of Spiritualists and leaders like Father Divine suggest the search for alternative religions. They indicate dissatisfaction not just with the "coldness" of big urban churches but with Protestantism and its focus on sin, sanctification, and otherworldly salvation. Most of the cults overtly included a concern with what might be called secular salvation. This emerged quite clearly in the proliferation of religions based on the notion that African Americans must find a faith divorced from the Protestantism white Americans had forced upon them, and in the process achieve a new identity. Thus dozens of groups centered on the idea that blacks were in fact the "real" Jews of the Bible, the chosen people. Others, like Detroit's Noble Drew Ali, constructed a version of Muslim faith. These groups emphasized rigid moral codes, a strong sense of community, and the racial pride and identity usually associated with black nationalism.

The premier black nationalist organization of the period was Marcus Garvey's Universal Negro Improvement Association (UNIA). Garvey did not expressly constitute the UNIA, a social and economic organization that fostered black pride and self-help, as a religious movement. Nonetheless, it had strong religious overtones. UNIA meetings were patterned after church services, complete with hymns, chaplains, prayers, offerings, and sermons. Religious themes figured in the content as well. Garvey drew primarily on Christianity, but insisted upon a religious conception broad enough to include blacks outside the Christian fold.

Intense racial pride permeated the religious message of the UNIA. Garvey and UNIA religious leaders insisted that their followers reject white images of Jesus and God. Moreover, central to the movement's message was a vision of Africa based on the biblical prophecy in Psalms 68:31: "Princes shall come forth from Egypt; Ethiopia shall soon stretch forth her hand to God." Garvey promised a black resurrection of Africa that would lead to the redemption of blacks everywhere. He offered hope, not of individual salvation, but of corporate salvation. An intensely spiritual movement, the UNIA achieved its success as the first genuine mass movement of African Americans in part by channeling the commitment and dedication associated with the black church. Fusing racial pride to a sense of spiritual and secular mission, Garveyism constituted a powerful civil religion for many African Americans.

African American religion eludes easy generalizations. Class, region, personal predilection—all shaped individuals' spiritual choices. Like their white counterparts, black ministers in this period worried about religious decline. An encroaching secular worldview, the appeal of jazz, blues, and leisure time, may well have undercut the faith of many African Americans. But for others, especially the migrants, the 1920s were a period of ferment, as they sought variously to maintain traditional religion or adapt it in the face of the new culture they were experiencing.

THE FUNDAMENTALIST CONTROVERSY

Many Americans adamantly resisted the prospect of adapting faith to a new culture. The most explosive confrontation between religion and "modern times" was the fundamentalist controversy. Fundamentalists, evangelical Christians within the mainstream denominations, worried about declension both in American society and in the churches, and feared that the country was slipping into a moral and spiritual decline that signaled Protestantism's diminishing role in defining the culture. Tracing immorality and irreligion to the changing worldview brought about by Darwinian science, they directed their greatest animosity toward leaders within the churches—"modernists" and liberals who had modified their religious views to conform to new knowledge and ways of thinking. The movement began to coalesce in the early twentieth century as church leaders in various denominations became concerned that the churches themselves—and their seminaries and missions—were being captured by the modernists. The movement got its name from the publication of a series of articles (1909–15) under the general title "The Fundamentals" that brought together essays by distinguished conservative scholars on theological doctrines they felt were being threatened by unorthodoxy. Unlike the Holiness-Pentecostals, with whom they shared many religious ideas, fundamentalists sought to recapture their churches, rather than secede from them to found purer congregations.

Despite the perception that World War I promoted secularism, it may have served as a catalyst for a new militancy among fundamentalists who interpreted the war as a fulfillment of Bible prophecy and specifically a judgment on Germany, which they viewed as deeply entrenched in modernist views of the higher criticism and Darwinian science. The battle against Germany became a holy war against modernism and confirmed them in their conviction that it must be routed in America as well. William Bell Riley, a Minneapolis Baptist minister, assumed a leadership role when he formed in 1919 the World's Christian Fundamentals Association, a group that organized conferences all over the country to call true Christians to battle. By the 1920s, working through interdenominational groups like Riley's, as well as through their denominations, fundamentalists had assembled a formidable institutional network of Bible institutes, local associations, newspapers, and periodicals to challenge the modernists. The confrontation between the two groups disrupted denominations with strong modernist leanings, especially the northern branches of the Baptists and the Presbyterians, and to a lesser extent the Disciples of Christ. Although the movement had its greatest strength in the Midwest and rural South, fundamentalism also surfaced in the North and in the cities, and appears to have been a movement consisting primarily of lower-middle-class and working-class people.

Fundamentalists were far from monolithic; they included conservative theologians like Gresham Machen of Princeton Seminary and flamboyant revivalist preachers like Billy Sunday. Although there were doctrinal differences among them, fundamentalists agreed on several principles, including the virgin birth and bodily resurrection of Christ, atonement, miracles, and a literal interpretation of the Bible. Further, most believed in premillenarianism, an expectation that fueled the intensity of their militancy as they prepared for the imminent second coming of Christ. Much of their energy concentrated on the inerrancy of the scriptures. For the Bible was at the center of the certainty that orthodox Protestantism promised its adherents: accept the word of God as revealed in the Bible and have a guide to true faith and salvation. Fundamentalists emphatically denied the validity of scientific theories that disputed their understanding of biblical truths, including a literal reading of the Genesis account of creation.

In the 1920s, the challenge of evolutionary science to the biblical story of creation, only a minor theme before World War I, became a central focus of many fundamentalists as they struggled to maintain the old-time religion, both in the churches and in American society at large. The evolution controversy was dramatized in the small Tennessee town of Dayton, where high school biology teacher John Scopes was prosecuted in 1925 for violating the Butler Act, recently enacted by the state legislature, which forbade teaching "any theory that denies the story of the divine creation of man as taught in the Bible, and teaches instead that man has descended from a lower order of animals." Although the state had not actively enforced the legislation, the American Civil Liberties Union encouraged Scopes to serve as a defendant in a test case.

Hundreds of reporters, who wired over two million words from Dayton during the eight-day trial, helped to turn it into a modern major media event. The fame of the lawyers on both sides of the courtroom guaranteed national attention. William Jennings Bryan volunteered for the prosecution. A major political figure since 1896, when he ran for President as a candidate of both the Democratic and the Populist parties, Bryan's most recent public office was Secretary of State under Woodrow Wilson, a position he resigned when he felt Wilson was not adhering sufficiently to neutrality before America's entrance into the war. After his resignation, Bryan continued to promote a variety of social and political reforms, but had become increasingly interested in religious questions, which were linked in his mind to a need for economic and social reform. Bryan shared with many evangelical Protestants a sense of the profound religious and moral decay of American society and the belief that the spread of evolutionist teaching in the colleges and public schools epitomized the threat to religion and civilization itself.

Although a latecomer to the anti-evolutionist movement that

had begun before World War I, Bryan eagerly embraced it and quickly became a major spokesman for the movement. With the national spotlight on Bryan, other issues of concern to fundamentalists, such as the virgin birth and premillenarianism, became subsumed in the evolution debate. Bryan spoke in behalf of evolution legislation pending in numerous states, mostly in the South and Midwest, and wrote regular newspaper columns, "Bible Talks," that appeared in more than a hundred newspapers and reached over twenty million readers. When the Tennessee case began to coalesce, he volunteered his services in what he believed would be a ringing endorsement of the mushrooming campaign to eliminate Darwin from the schools and restore old-time religion and morality.

Clarence Darrow, one of the most famous trial lawyers in the country, could not have more perfectly contrasted with Bryan if he had been cast by Hollywood. Darrow, joined by noted divorce lawyer Dudley Field Malone, served free of charge for the defense. Urbane, iconoclastic, agnostic, Darrow symbolized the cosmopolitan world that was so puzzled and frustrated by the Bryans of America. To the modernists, they symbolized not just the attack on educational freedom by an antiquated religion but also the "village" mentality responsible for prohibition, the Ku Klux Klan, and the 1920s' general temperament of what philosopher John Dewey called "illiberality."

As Bryan and Darrow converged on Dayton for what became popularly known as the Monkey Trial, the city eagerly prepared for its place in the limelight. The Progressive Dayton Club announced plans to spend five thousand dollars on advertising and to give visitors badges featuring monkeys with straw hats. Telegraph wires were strung to the courthouse, radio and additional phone equipment installed, and extra toilets provided. Sightseers poured in to witness the show. The circus atmosphere, along with the extraordinary media attention, threatened to overshadow the substance of the issues. But in contrast to our own contemporary news coverage of televangelists, reporters were less interested in the sex lives of key protagonists than in their theology.

Although the trial potentially encompassed a number of issues, including academic freedom and parental and states' rights (since it was viewed as a first step in challenging the Butler law in the U.S. Supreme Court), religion, or at least Bryan's followers' version of it, very quickly became the focus of the courtroom. Was Genesis or Darwin right? Or, in Bryan's terms, "Brother or Brute?" The heated exchange between the two key players included Darrow's "You insult every man of science and learning with your fool religion," and Bryan's "I am trying to protect the Word of God against the greatest agnostic in the United States." Darrow had planned to bring in a score of expert witnesses to prove the validity of evolution. The judge allowed them to present their views without the jury present to establish the evidence that would be used in an appeal. Although he blocked the experts' testimony in open court, it was summarized and reprinted in newspapers throughout the country, while Darrow, denied his expert witnesses, executed a tour de force and put Bryan on the witness stand as an authority on the Bible.

To present-day eyes, Darrow seems to have humiliated Bryan. In relentless questioning covering Jonah and the whale, the age of the universe, the history of the world's religions, and the origins of Cain's wife, Darrow exposed Bryan's historical and scientific ignorance. Pushing him about the age of the universe, he forced Bryan into the potentially most damning evidence: Bryan admitted that the "days" of creation referred to in the Bible might not mean days as modern people construed them. In effect, Bryan himself was straying from the strict interpretation of the Bible that was so central to his orthodoxy. Much of the reporting of the time concurred that Bryan had not made a good showing. Although Scopes was found guilty and fined a modest $100, the common interpretation was that the anti-evolutionists had been exposed as backward-thinking hicks. In H. L. Mencken's words, they were "morons," "hillbillies," and "yokels."

Historians have tended to agree that the trial damaged the fundamentalist camp. Not only were anti-evolutionists associated with antiquated ideas, but the extensive publicity given scientific explanations of Darwinian science undoubtedly made it easier for many Americans to question traditional religious belief. In addition to the negative light cast by the events in Dayton, the anti-evolution campaign suffered a major loss when Bryan died a few days after the trial. Fundamentalists persisted in their faith and continued the struggle to implement anti-evolution laws, but deprived of the charismatic Bryan, they had lost a central character in bringing the debate to the national public. However, the anti-evolutionist campaign may have been more successful than observers at the time thought. Although few states enacted statutory limitations on teaching Darwin (five laws of the thirty-seven introduced actually passed), local school boards throughout the country found ways to censor what went on in the schools' science classes. The campaign helped to set up a climate of opinion that discouraged many teachers from incorporating evolution into their lesson plans: a 1941 study of high school teachers found that one in three teachers feared teaching evolution.

The Scopes trial is thus significant on many levels. Despite the image of the roaring twenties and the media hype surrounding the trial, it suggests that religion was a deeply contested issue that mattered to millions of Americans. It reveals the unease that accompanied the challenge to traditional faiths and the eagerness to resolve the implications of modern science for religious faith. It is significant that one of the orations most warmly received by the courtroom audience was an impassioned speech by Malone, who demonstrated, not agnosticism, but rather the compatibility of evolution with religion. The trial is also important for the way in which it highlighted a polarization—not just in religion but in American culture itself. The presence of Bryan and Darrow set the contrast between devout and doubter, but also between country and city, between anti-modernist and modernist. Bryan represented the village mentality struggling to maintain traditional values in the face of vast social change. The anti-evolution drive had much in common with the prohibition, immigration restriction, and Ku Klux Klan movements. The spread of modern ideas forced tradition-minded Americans to turn defensively to the state to legislate morality, religion, and their cultural vision.

Many historians have adopted this polarized vision of country versus city, modernist versus antimodernist, but they did not invent it. Astute observers at the time, mostly intellectuals in revolt against the village mentality, cast the conflict precisely in these terms. Yet this polarized interpretation can be misleading. It oversimplifies a rural/urban dichotomy that ignores the presence of fundamentalists, prohibitionists, and Klansmen in the cities; it divides America into two neatly opposing forces and leaves out the diversity of the population and its religious and cultural ideas. Nonetheless, it is valuable for demonstrating that people living through the decade acutely felt the struggle between past and future, of the implications of living during a time of vast social transformation.

MODERNIZING RELIGION: MODERNISTS AND BUSINESSMEN

Consciousness of being on the cusp of a new era was especially demonstrated by religious modernists whom fundamentalists so vehemently opposed. The modernist movement grew out of the nineteenth-century Protestant liberalism that took a more optimistic view of humanity and the world than the Calvinist religious tradition. Liberalism emphasized God's immanence in all people and suggested that reason and experience were the sources of religious revelation. This view that God was everywhere broke down the strict separation between God and humanity, humanity and nature, and sacred and secular, and posited a continuity in the universe that de-emphasized the supernatural so crucial to fundamentalists. Adapting to new science and biblical criticism, liberals also broke with a literal interpretation of the Bible. Historian William R. Hutchison estimates that by 1920 half of the Protestant seminaries and periodicals and half of the pulpits, largely in urban centers outside the South, expressed liberal views. Self-conscious, self-styled "modernists" emerged among liberals in the early twentieth century, and in the 1920s, in part because of fundamentalists' attacks, grew strident and militant. Strikingly aware of a changing world and the need for religion to adapt to it, modernists felt that they were salvaging Christianity from an archaic orthodoxy that had robbed religion of its vitality. As Harry Emerson Fosdick, one of the major modernist figures, summed up the impact of new scientific ways of thinking: "The day is past when you can ask thoughtful men to hold religion in one compartment of their minds and their modern world view in another."

Modernists were no more monolithic than the fundamentalists. They varied in the degree to which they strayed from the orthodoxy that they had been raised in. Although Shailer Mathews of the University of Chicago School of Divinity was perhaps the most significant theologian, Harry Emerson Fosdick was the most popular preacher. Angered by fundamentalist efforts to exclude modernists from the churches, Fosdick attacked the fundamentalists head-on with a controversial 1922 article "Shall the Fundamentalists Win?" This in turn made Fosdick a favorite target of militant conservative Christians. Already well known, he catapulted to prominence when the fundamentalists within the Presbyterian Church effected his ouster from his New York pulpit at the First Presbyterian Church in 1924. This expulsion created much publicity in both the secular and the religious press. Fosdick, ordained as a Baptist, had been serving as a guest pastor in the New York church. His non-denominational bent was further exemplified in his next pastorate. Under the patronage of John D. Rockefeller, Jr., Fosdick agreed to become minister of the New York Park Avenue Baptist Church, with the stipulation that the church eliminate "all sectarian restrictions of membership." At Fosdick's insistence, the church later built a new edifice on Riverside Drive, which, although it had formal ties with the Baptists, operated as a nonsectarian Christian church.

This ecumenical arrangement was a fitting example of the modernist de-emphasis on creeds and denominations. Los Angeles minister Frank Dyer was instrumental in setting up the non-denominational Wilshire Boulevard Church in 1921: "We shall make it a church for all creeds, classes and parties. . . . The narrow-minded sectarian will not be happy with us but we believe that everyone else will be." Modernists were convinced that the credal specificity of denominations had damaged religion's appeal: "Organized, institutionalized, ritualized—religion has become for multitudes a stuffy and uninteresting affair." They further argued that the rigid, outdated "truths" of the fundamentalists, especially the literal interpretation of the Bible, kept the younger generation from religion, and that credal conflicts were distractions that, in Fosdick's words, deflected "the attention of people from the real problems of the generation." Like many modernists, Fosdick emphasized a pragmatic religion that could develop social consciousness and solve social problems.

In their quest to make religion relevant, Fosdick and other modernists also turned their attention to individual personal and spiritual adjustment. They implicitly and sometimes explicitly recognized that people shape religion to suit their needs, and that religion could have immensely therapeutic value for the modern individual. Fosdick helped to spearhead an expanded sense of the minister's role as counselor for personal as well as spiritual problems. The late 1920s witnessed the beginning of the incorporation of psychological training for pastors in seminaries. With this development, modernists paralleled some of the trends evolving in secular self-help which emphasized the development of "personality," which the modernists defined as the sum of the individual's distinctive qualities. Many modernists hoped to convey a gospel which could transform the individual from within in much the same way that contemporary psychologists hoped that their discipline could promote personal growth.

In constructing a meaningful religion, modernists centered on the example of the historic Jesus, emphasizing his moral and ethical teachings, a trend that had begun in the late nineteenth century. For many modernists, the divinity of Jesus was a moot point, since they believed in God's immanence in all people. Jesus was the perfect example of this universal immanence and divinity: "the unique expression of God as an individual." This sidestepping of the issue of divinity did not necessarily mean a downplaying of Jesus' significance. Among modernists there was much emphasis on returning to the "pure" religion of Jesus and jettisoning all the specific creeds that had evolved in the history of Christianity and had placed barriers between humanity and God.

Modernists, then, struggled to adapt traditional morality and religion to a newer mind-set, which Fosdick characterized as "plastic, pliable, fluid." Sensitive to the widespread sense of spiritual disorder, they hoped to help modern men and women "to find design in the universe . . . to believe that they were more than just a random collection of atoms." They believed, with Fosdick, that faith "has been involved in every step that humanity has taken away from a disordered existence, whimsical, without unity, sense, or reason, toward a meaningful universe seen steadily and seen whole."

While Fosdick and his colleagues attempted to construct a modernist theology, other ministers developed more practical ways to accommodate religion to a changing society. Robert Moats Miller relates that some churches resorted to such gimmicks as attractive female ushers and giveaway items to turn out the congregation. As sermon titles such as "Public Worship Increases Your Efficiency" and "Business Success and Religion Go Together" suggest, still other pastors incorporated modern business and advertising techniques to give their message the "relevance" and "pep" that would appeal to the busy "man of affairs."

The move toward more businesslike methods was strikingly evident in the shift away from the practice of hiring evangelists to come into communities to stage revivals. By the 1920s, door-to-door "visitation" campaigns had become popular. Less sensational and cheaper than revivals, the visitation system also lent itself to modern methods. The Reverend A. Earl Kernahan set up a national consulting office, the Directed Survey and Visitation Campaigns, in 1923. Small cities and towns hired his firm to conduct a survey and provide "prospect cards" for local churches to use. Kernahan's system was popular throughout the 1920s and helped to lend a tone of door-to-door salesmanship to the saving of souls.

The widespread use of radio was another example of the fusion of modern methods with a religious message. In the 1920s the networks began the practice of offering free time to church organizations. The National Broadcasting Company entrusted its religious programming to the liberal Federal Council of Churches, which meant that for the most part fundamentalists were denied free access to the airwaves. But churches outside the mainstream established their own stations. In addition to McPherson, for example, fundamentalist Paul Radner broadcast from Chicago with the call numbers WJBT: "Where Jesus Blesses Thousands," and Lutherans could turn to the Missouri Synod's radio KFUO, "The Gospel Voice," and hear Walter A. Maier address religious and social issues, including his critique of modernism. The use of technology, while it had far-reaching implications for the dissemination of religious ideas, did not necessarily transform the sacred message.

A striking modernization of religious ideas did appear in efforts to fuse spiritual and commercial values. Just as churches had copied business techniques, businessmen drew upon religious ideas. During the twenties, businessman Hubert Eaton transformed a failing enterprise in Los Angeles into the famous Forest Lawn Cemetery in part by astute business methods and advertising. But Eaton also had a message about death. Traditional religion had made funerals too somber and sad. He wanted to construct a cemetery with a beautiful parklike setting, with statuary and works of art that would be uplifting. His "Builder's Creed," which he wrote in 1917 as he began his work, proclaimed that "I shall endeavor to build Forest Lawn as different, as unlike other cemeteries as sunshine is unlike darkness, as eternal life is unlike death." In his vision, the burying of the dead became secondary to the hopeful atmosphere, to creating a place "where lovers new and old shall love to stroll and watch the sunsets." In his efforts to divest death of its unpleasantness, Eaton was contributing to its secularization.

Other businessmen turned their hand to reshaping religious values. Just as Eaton criticized traditional cemeteries, adman Bruce Barton attacked the churches for their mistaken image of Jesus. In the best-selling *The Man Nobody Knows* (1924), Barton chided the churches' image of a meek "sissified" Jesus who "went around for three years telling people not to do things." Barton offered Jesus, who "built the greatest organization of

all," as a model for the modern businessman. In constructing a
Jesus who would appeal to the red-blooded practical man of the
day, Barton sidestepped the issue of Jesus' divinity and concentrated on the human story of his mission and the methods he
used to become "successful." The Man Nobody Knows was a
secularized Jesus. Barton's book is easily lampooned as a crass
attempt to appropriate religion in the service of commercial success. Yet Barton's immense popularity suggests that he touched
a nerve in his criticism of the churches. His desire to valorize
business, to base even advertising on an ethical moral system
derived from Christianity, indicates a continued need for idealized purpose rooted in religious tradition.

In popular periodicals like *The Saturday Evening Post* and *Col-
lier's*, other authors took on the issue of "A Businessman's View
of Religion." With varying degrees of subtlety, they portrayed
religion as crucial to business success. Roger Babson claimed to
"know a dozen men who are drifting along, or plugging along,
not getting anywhere. If I could put into them the power of this
something which I call religion, they would go ahead twice as
fast, even ten times as fast." Echoing a theme Barton harped
on, popularizers of a practical religion also attacked traditional
Christianity as too feminized. Newspaper-syndicated poet Edgar
Guest explained that he was eager for his son to know "that he
can have his religion without being a mollycoddle. He can keep
his manhood and his faith side by side." Religion would not
keep him from playing football, swimming, hunting, or laughing.

In addition to criticizing a feminized religion, these authors
had little patience with traditional denominational and credal
distinctions, which popular religious commentator Frank Crane
described as "remnants of a former age that mean nothing
now." They also expressed little disposition to a literal interpretation of the Bible, which businessman Irving T. Bush characterized as having come to us "from ancient days of legends."
As with Babson, the tendency was to reduce religion to its lowest common denominator. As Bush put it: "I believe there is a
power which I am content to call God, and am convinced that
a recognition of the simple virtues of right and truth and kind-
ness lies at the base of the Power." These men reveal a desire

for faith, a hunger for it, but they stripped it of almost all its sacred content.

This desire to be idealistic, to have a higher purpose, yet to escape sentimentality and a sacred aura also pervaded one of the major male fraternal organizations, the Freemasons. In the early part of the 1920s, the Masons' membership, like that of other fraternities, boomed. Some of this growth can be attributed to the get-ahead mentality of the period and the expectation that membership in a prestigious fraternal organization could provide invaluable contacts. But another part of its appeal was its association with an idealism of fraternal goodwill and larger purpose that Masonic leaders were struggling to define in modern terms. In the nineteenth century, fraternal writers had emphasized the sacred quality of the organization. Religion permeated the fraternity's ritual and literature. By the 1920s, many Masonic leaders were self-consciously trying to modernize the order, with striking parallels to religious modernists. As one man expressed it in a 1925 letter to the editor of *The Masonic Outlook*:

> The religious sects and fraternal societies which are progressing are those which are being adapted to Twentieth Century living. The radio, the automobile, the modern newspaper, the air-plane, the liberalization of thought are changing our life. No institution can grow as it should which does not mould itself to the new conditions.

In molding the order to new conditions, Masonic modernizers downplayed the religion-based rituals, minimized heavily moralistic rhetoric, and fastened on the ubiquitous business slogan "service," which for them included a rhetoric of idealistic purpose and specific community service projects. "Service" offered Masons the opportunity to identify with a practical idealism; it became a means of secularizing the fraternity without losing its sense of high purpose.

While there is much evidence for the secularization of American culture in the 1920s, then, that secularization was a complex one. The fusion of business and religion certainly suggests the evisceration of the latter. But it is significant that although the sacred appears to have become an embarrassment for the urban, middle-class males attracted to organizations like Masonry, the alternatives to traditional religion were not blatant materialism and hedonism. As the idea of "service" indicates, as well as the popularity of books like *The Man Nobody Knows*, men were still eager for ideals and guidelines with which to order their lives. And many Americans—devout immigrant families, Pentecostals and fundamentalists, African American storefront congregations—continued to find those guidelines in an abiding, traditional faith. These diverse experiences suggest not so much a religious depression as a period of ferment, as Americans reinterpreted or reaffirmed religious ideas in their struggle to make sense of their modern world.

Whether we look at secular or sacred interpretations of American society in the 1920s, no easy generalizations emerge. Americans' response to change proved complex and ambivalent. Many people found comfort or meaning in reaffirming traditional values. The southern Agrarians and the fundamentalists met disruptive social change with a renewed commitment to absolutes—either in a literalist faith in the Bible or in the organicism of agrarian life. In contrast, many others found a certain exhilaration in the modern order. The Lost Generation and the modernists, despite their alienation, looked to new art forms and celebrated the spontaneity made possible by the erosion of the Victorian genteel culture. Modernists in religion, too, felt a sense of escape from the weight of archaic religious ideas and enthusiastically embraced the path of constructing new religious values appropriate and useful to modern times.

But even those most enthusiastic about the decline of the old order expressed clear anxiety about the contours of the new. The dilemma of the individual seeking autonomy in a society increasingly organized, mechanized, and routinized was repeated. The release from the constraints of the past brought new risks—the search for new meaning and purpose in a world where certainties had proved "relative." Intellectuals and artists explored and expressed this modern temper, while religious institutions and leaders offered a variety of solutions to the individual's search for meaning and security. The religious modernists proffered a revitalized religion to individuals looking for spiritual answers to modern questions. And in many urban churches—white and black, native-born and ethnic, Pentecostal and traditional—the institutions and their messages helped to create a sense of community and shared faith and values, thus meeting both a spiritual and a sociological need of their communicants.

Other themes unite the secular and sacred arenas. Both intellectuals and religious spokesmen conveyed a resentment about the influence of women in shaping the culture. Most white women artists were edged out of the developing artistic canon of the twentieth century, and African American women experienced a similar marginalization in relation to the Harlem Renaissance. Religious modernists complained about a feminized religion that had constructed a weak and sentimental Jesus, and spokesmen repeatedly called for a more virile religion that would appeal to the busy man of affairs. At the same time, in both Holiness and Pentecostal churches, as well as in more conventional denominations, challenges to women's influence in the ministry, missions, and other denominational concerns mounted.

Although perhaps too much could be made about these underlying anxieties concerning female power or influence, they are nonetheless suggestive. Despite popular imagery, the 1920s hardly saw a revolution in gender roles, but in many ways women were challenging conventional notions about their public role and their private lives, themes present in the work of writers like Flanner, Johnson, Taggard, Millay, and Stein. These gender issues are thoroughly "modern." Women's emergence in the public arenas of work and politics and their revisions in the private world of sexuality and the family have become ongoing issues that shaped twentieth-century culture.

Even more pronounced in the 1920s was the theme of ethnic and racial pluralism. Artists of the Harlem Renaissance self-consciously addressed questions of racial and American identity as they looked for a distinctive black art. Black churches were a major institutional framework for sustaining this black culture and identity, and movements like Garvey's UNIA suggest a clear resistance to white dominance. Among Jewish and Catholic religious leaders and intellectuals, we also see a struggle to sustain religious and ethnic identity while maintaining legitimacy in the broader culture. And social scientists like Robert Park and Franz Boas offered pioneering academic work that recognized the centrality of these issues for understanding the pluralistic society that America had become.

The ethnic and racial components of modern society stood at the center of some of the key conflicts and social movements that characterized the decade. Fears about rising secularism, changing sexual morality, declining community, and individual autonomy often merged with nativism and racism, as immigrants and African Americans became scapegoats for disruptive social change. As the following chapter suggests, the hysteria of the Red Scare, the drive to restrict immigration, the rise of the Ku Klux Klan, and the ongoing debate about prohibition all included resistance to ethnic and racial pluralism as a major motif in the struggle against modern trends in society and culture.

CONFORMITY AND

COMMUNITY

The Democratic Party's 1924 national convention was an especially contentious one. Fistfights broke out on the floor, and the resolutions committee remained deadlocked for days over one issue: should the party condemn the Ku Klux Klan? The controversy reflected the divisions within the party —Southerners and Westerners were most likely to resemble the Klan's membership of native-born, white Protestants, while the northern branch of the party increasingly included a significant number of ethnic, especially Catholic, voters who opposed the Klan and all it represented. After impassioned speeches on both sides, the convention reached a compromise of sorts; it passed by one vote a resolution that did not condemn the Klan by name but did affirm the party's commitment to the Constitution and its opposition to "any effort to arouse religious or racial dissension." The party then took 103 ballots to select its nominee for President, with the same conflict emerging. William Gibbs McAdoo had the strong support of the Klan, in part because he refused to criticize the order, in part because he supported prohibition. His opponent, Al Smith, represented everything the Klan abhorred: a Catholic from an Irish immigrant family who was supported by New York's political machine, Tammany Hall, Smith excoriated both the Klan and prohibition. Hopelessly deadlocked between these two men, the convention compromised on the lackluster John W. Davis, whom Calvin Coolidge easily defeated in the November elections.

Certainly many other concerns shaped the political controversies of the 1920s: the tariff, price supports for farmers, and, in the very beginning of the decade, U.S. membership in the League of Nations were hotly contested issues. But beneath these more traditional interests, as the 1924 Democratic convention suggests, lay a political climate shaped by deeply felt and highly disruptive cultural issues, as old-stock Protestant Americans sought to restore their hegemony in the face of a modern culture perceived to be dominated by immigrants, Catholics, and Jews. Although ethnicity provided the major focus for cultural conflict in the 1920s, the anxieties that prompted it had roots deeper than the perceived power of ethnic minorities. Crucial to these old-stock Americans' perception of the crisis of the 1920s was an implicit assumption about the past. They imagined a homogeneous society in which equality was real and democracy unchallenged. Native, Protestant, middle-class Americans dominated this world—politically, culturally, and economically. Above all, the society was harmonious, held together by shared values and assumptions.

This nostalgic, fictive vision contrasted sharply with the America of the 1920s. In the late nineteenth century, the increasingly national locus of economic power had shattered the relative isolation of what Robert Wiebe called "island communities" and undermined the sense of autonomy of the middle-class Americans who dominated them. Years of progressive reformers' agitation had helped to demonstrate how private power in the form of big business and political machines had usurped "respectable" citizens' authority over the economic and political system. There were challenges to the cultural values of island communities as well, a factor that had helped fuel the militancy of fundamentalists in their battle with modernism. With industrialization, urbanization, and immigration came greater pluralism. Mounting secularism and the influx of Jewish and Catholic immigrants threatened Protestantism and its hold over American culture. Conflicting standards concerning women's roles and sexual morality, coupled with leisure-time pursuits such as drinking and mass-culture entertainment, were still further evidence of diversification that challenged traditional values.

Native-born Protestants were not a monolithic mass, any more than the immigrants they castigated were. Class, gender, religion, and location were among the many variables that differentiated them. Not all responded to the transformation of American culture with anxiety and alarm. But for those who did, the alien, radical, Jew, and Catholic became a convenient scapegoat, a way of explaining the rise of modern ways that appeared to have eroded the idealized community of shared values. Through anti-radicalism, immigration restriction, prohibition, and the Ku Klux Klan, old-stock Americans sought to reassert their political and cultural hegemony and to reinstitute community.

IMMIGRATION RESTRICTION AND NATIVISM

THE DRIVE FOR RESTRICTION

Because consideration of cultural conflicts of the decade were so often cast in ethnic terms, the starting point for examining them must be patterns of nativism. They characterized the 1920s, and were in turn rooted in nineteenth-century attitudes toward immigrants. The term "melting pot" emerged in the early twentieth century as Americans sought to come to grips with the massive immigration of the decades following the Civil War. As sociologist Milton Gordon has pointed out, the celebration of the melting pot reflected faith in the capacity of American society to absorb immigrants, but in contrast to the term's imagery, its popular usage usually did not reflect an expectation of a melting of diverse peoples into a new American. To begin with, nonwhites were excluded from the concept altogether. Furthermore, the expectation of what would happen to diverse immigrant cultures resembled what Gordon has called Anglo-conformity. Immigrants were welcomed under the assumption that they would conform to the dominant English

Protestant culture. Many Americans in the nineteenth century, confident about their institutions and the power of the environment to transform individuals, had faith in this assimilative process. But equally potent was the other side of the coin: recurrent waves of intense nativism that linked xenophobia with nationalism. During times of internal crisis, immigrants were viewed as a threat to American institutions and society.

In the late nineteenth century, when immigration was dramatically expanding, conditions were ripe for nativist protest. Over five million people immigrated to the United States in the 1880s alone, and in contrast to earlier immigration, much of which dispersed throughout the country, these newcomers gravitated to ethnic enclaves in the cities, where their poverty and concentration gave them high visibility. These patterns of immigration, together with industrial disruptions, class conflict, economic depression, political corruption, urban squalor, and a widening of the gap between rich and poor, produced a profound sense of disorder among old-stock Americans. Many focused on the immigrant as a challenge to American culture and society. Some organized labor groups saw immigrants as economic competition; on the West Coast, this sentiment combined with a virulent racism that excoriated Chinese immigrants. Racism emerged in views of European immigration as well, especially after the public perception of a "new immigration"—a shift from Northwestern to Southern and Eastern Europe as the point of origin—coalesced and intensified ideas of "Nordic" superiority. Since the new immigration was heavily Catholic and Jewish, it stirred resentment among Protestants who already had a religious tradition of antipathy to these groups and who assumed that Americanism and Protestantism were interchangeable. Because of the high visibility of Irish American politicians, anti-Catholicism also fed anxieties about the immigrant vote. Political machines and the problems accompanying urban political corruption were easily attributed to the ignorant foreign vote. Indeed, nativists generally traced the crises of the cities to the presence of masses of unassimilated immigrants. Throughout the nineteenth century, observers worried about the face of the American metropolis: its corruption and chaos challenged traditional ideas of community, democracy, and order. In this view, immigrants were inextricably linked to the crisis of the cities. The foreign vote was only one of many distressing phenomena. Radicalism was another source of anxiety, especially in the tumultuous 1890s, when fear of anarchism unsettled the middle class and the business elite. In addition, some of the urban newcomers' patterns of leisure, which included drinking and Sunday recreation, underscored the public association of immigrants with saloons, vice, and immorality. All these factors led nativists to view immigrants as a multifaceted threat to the supposed order and homogeneity of American society.

As John Higham has shown, between the Civil War and World War I the patterns of nativism ebbed and flowed according to the intensity of Americans' anxiety about the state of their institutions. In 1882, Congress barred most Chinese immigration, and the first sustained effort to limit the entry of Europeans emerged with the Immigration Restriction League in 1894. Composed mostly of Boston patricians horrified by the threat to their culture and the challenge to their hegemony, the League embarked on a massive lobbying campaign to restrict immigration, and their promotion of a literacy test had the enthusiastic backing of organized labor and much of middle-class public opinion. It met with resistance as well. For many Americans, restricting immigration was a departure from honored principles, and they had faith in assimilative features, faith in education, faith in the environment, and faith in Americanization programs. Less idealistic, business groups such as the National Association of Manufacturers opposed immigration restriction because they sought to keep the sources of cheap labor flowing. Immigrants themselves lobbied hard against efforts to curtail immigration, with Jewish organizations emerging as leaders in the struggle, as they drew upon prominent Jews' links with the Republican Party to influence politicians. They were joined by the Foreign Language Press Association and the Liberal Immigration League in concerted efforts to stymie restriction. As nativists feared, immigrants did have political influence. Most votes on immigration legislation took place after elections because politicians, sensitive to immigrant voters, were chary of supporting the literacy test. Thus the literacy test repeatedly met defeat.

But the tide was turning, and World War I was the crucial factor. America's tense period of neutrality before it entered the conflict in 1917 exacerbated tensions over what was popularly called hyphenated Americans. German Americans' organized lobbying to influence U.S. foreign policy in favor of Germany became symbolic of the problem of dual loyalty among America's aliens. It was in this highly charged climate that in 1917 Congress finally enacted the literacy test over Woodrow Wilson's veto. Restriction became a moot point during the war since the hostilities themselves brought immigration to a virtual halt, but with war's end, the clamor for more drastic measures was renewed. Nativists' solution for reducing absolute numbers while at the same time prohibiting the most objectionable immigrants—Southern and Eastern Europeans—was the quota system, which discriminated against immigrants from countries of the "new" immigration. The renewed drive for more stringent restriction gathered strength during the war when nativism primarily centered on German Americans, who were portrayed with vicious and unrelenting hostility. A secondary but nonetheless important target was radicals, inevitably described as aliens, who opposed the war. The clear focus on war aims spared other immigrant groups from the nativist attack, but the war deepened American mistrust of "hyphenates," and led to aggressive campaigns to Americanize immigrants through propaganda, education, and exhortation. The call was for 100 percent Americans, characterized by an insistence upon unity, conformity, and obedience.

War's end did not shut off the currents of nationalism and nativism. Battles over the reconstruction of Europe and the League of Nations highlighted the rising ethnic consciousness of American immigrant groups. The Irish lobbied for Home Rule, the Poles for their native country's self-determination, and the Jews for Zion. This activism perpetuated anxieties about immigrant loyalties. Still more damaging, the Bolshevik Revolution in Russia, combined with labor unrest and economic depression in this country, deepened the widespread association of the immigrant with radicalism and threats to American security. The Red Scare that followed was of relatively short duration, but the hysteria had a long-term impact, including promoting a sense that immigrants carried the seeds of foreign radicalism.

Thus, when massive immigration, swelled by refugees from war-devastated Europe, began again in the spring of 1920 at the rate of 5,000 per day, restrictionists intensified their attacks, arguing that the literacy test should be replaced with more stringent restrictions. The first quota act, passed in 1921, was temporary; it set quotas for each country at 3 percent of its total U.S. population based on the 1910 census. The act was extended twice, and culminated in the National Origins Act, passed in 1924 with overwhelming support. In Congress, urban centers of immigrant concentration provided the only opponents of the bill, which was more drastic than the earlier legislation. Reducing the percentage from 3 to 2 percent, and using the census of 1890, not 1910, to determine the basis for each country's apportionment, it excluded Southern and Eastern Europeans more thoroughly. Moreover, the act broadened the exclusion of Asian immigrants to include the Japanese. Despite nativist pressure, Congress did not extend restrictions to immigrants from Latin America or Canada.

The drive to restrict immigration reflected an unrelenting campaign of hostility toward immigrants that characterized the early 1920s. Numerous organizations—business groups, labor unions, patriotic societies, patrician groups, and the Ku Klux Klan—lobbied for restriction, and extensive literature in favor of restriction appeared in newspapers and mass magazines. Nativism was pervasive, respectable, and comprehensive. Its expression in the 1920s echoed all the familiar strands—racism, antiradicalism, anti-Catholicism, and anti-Semitism—to offer something for every variety of fear and prejudice.

RACISM

The depth of racism in the 1920s and its importance for bringing about immigration restriction cannot be overstated. As we will see, African Americans, both stay-at-home Southerners and migrants to the North, experienced intense prejudice and discrimination. Immigrants, too, were victims of a highly conscious "race thinking." In the 1880s, elitist New England patricians celebrated Anglo-Saxon superiority and traced America's success in its English antecedents. By the twentieth century, these sentiments had coalesced into the "scientific racism" articulated most completely by Madison Grant in *The Passing of the Great Race* (1910). Although intellectuals began to distance themselves from scientific racism in this period, the idea continued to be promulgated in popular magazines like *The Saturday Evening Post*. Writers like Grant and Lothrop Stoddard in the 1920s drew upon the biological and social sciences to demonstrate the superiority of Northern Europeans, often called Nordics or Aryans. Sounding the alarm of race suicide for old-stock Americans, whose birth rate had fallen, they warned that without drastic measures, they would be taken over by the prolific inferior races who "swarmed" to these shores.

The most obvious example of the way in which racism affected immigration policy was the total exclusion of Japanese immigrants, who, unlike Europeans, were not even offered quotas. The history behind this exclusion dated to the mid-nineteenth century when anti-Asian sentiment on the West Coast had first focused on the Chinese. While the perception of the Chinese as "coolie" laborers who undermined the native worker featured prominently in the agitation against them, more generally the Chinese were vilified as a debased, corrupting race, and western politicians, trading on southern empathy for racial "problems," successfully campaigned to get Congress to pass an exclusion law. The law excluding Chinese immigrants for ten years passed in 1882 and later became permanent. Anti-Asian sentiment was further institutionalized in the 1917 immigration act which created a "barred zone" that prohibited Asian immigration except from Japan and the Philippines.

After the turn of the century, Japanese immigrants became the new focus of agitation on the West Coast. Japanese immigration had begun in earnest in the 1890s, but by 1920 there were still only 111,010 Japanese in this country, or one-tenth of 1 percent of the U.S. population. In California, the 71,952 Japanese represented 2 percent of the state's population. In contrast to European immigration on the East Coast, the Japanese represented a small number of the total population and were not associated with the poverty and disorder of eastern ethnic ghettos. Moreover, unlike European immigrants, they were politically impotent: naturalization laws were for freeborn whites, with people of African descent being specifically excepted after the Civil War. The first-generation Japanese (Issei) could not vote and the number of second-generation adults (Nisei) was quite small. But if the Japanese community presented no political threat, Californians still found grounds for alarm about the rising expectations of a racially abhorred group. Despite much discrimination, many Japanese had achieved a degree of mobility, and most were small businessmen or farmers. They achieved notable success in agriculture: in 1919, while owning 1 percent of the land, they produced 10 percent of the total value of California crops.

This success and the rising power of the nation of Japan were thorns in the side of nativists. It was not coincidental that the most vehement period of anti-Japanese agitation began in 1905 after Japan's victory over Russia triggered apprehension about Japan's military might and rejuvenated the fear of a yellow peril. The issue first came to a head in 1906 when San Francisco attempted to segregate Japanese schoolchildren. Japan protested, and the federal government mediated. Theodore Roosevelt put pressure on San Francisco to rescind its legislation and in return worked out the Gentlemen's Agreement whereby Japan would voluntarily limit its migrants to the United States. The federal government continued to attempt to restrain activities against the Japanese on the West Coast, but California, largely ignoring federal protests, passed an alien land law in 1913, which was beefed up by a referendum in 1920. By prohibiting noncitizens from owning land, California lawmakers hoped to put a stop to Japanese successes in agriculture, although loopholes in the law made it possible for Japanese farmers to continue on the land, a source of tremendous irritation to anti-Japanese agitators.

Concurrent with efforts to restrict the freedoms of the Japanese was the drive for Japanese exclusion. On the West Coast a variety of organizations promoted the movement, including the Oriental Exclusion League, the Native Sons of the Golden West, the California Federation of Labor, and the American Legion. In the 1920s they took their program to the rest of the nation, with the American Federation of Labor and the American Legion being most prominent on the national scene. The Hearst newspaper chain was vociferously anti-Japanese, and the drive for exclusion also appeared in national magazines, where authors pictured them as unassimilable, with racial characteristics that made them incapable of becoming good American citizens.

While the Japanese were subjected to the most virulent racism and experienced the most stringent restriction, other immigrants were identified as threats to Anglo-Saxon purity. Racial arguments figured heavily in the debates to limit Eastern and Southern Europeans. Jews, Italians, and "Slavs" were the primary targets of attack as inferior stock who would damage the vitality and institutions of American society. In addition, racism, coupled with fears of the economic competition and radicalism of Mexican immigrant workers, permeated the vigorous but unsuccessful campaign to add Mexican immigrants to the quota system. A prewar southwestern drive for restriction had been deflected by World War I and the focus on European and Asian immigrants, but after the passage of the National Origins Act, the American Federation of Labor, joined by various nativist groups, lobbied hard to bring Mexican immigrants under the quota. However, the power of agricultural and industrial interests who benefited from these easily exploited laborers outweighed the clamor for restriction, and Mexican migrants were the only group whose numbers would expand significantly in the 1920s. Although their immigration was not limited, nonetheless people of Mexican descent were victims of virulent discrimination and prejudice, and the 1924 establishment of the border patrol served as a harbinger of hostility toward Mexican immigrants that would escalate in the next decade.

POLITICS AND ANTI-CATHOLICISM

As pervasive as racism was in the nativist rhetoric of the decade, it was rarely divorced from the perception that old-stock Americans were losing power to the organized efforts of tightly knit groups of immigrants and their descendants. Political power proved a particularly potent theme that easily conflated with racist anxieties. Using dubious statistics on the fecundity of Japanese women, for example, nativists warned about the eventual presence of huge numbers of Nisei children who would eventually "swamp the white voters in the state." Similarly, the editor of *World's Work* explained: "The chief argument against the wholesale admission of unassimilable aliens is that it creates nationalistic and racial blocs which are constantly bringing pressure to bear upon law-making bodies in the interests of their particular nationalities, which do not think like Americans, but which retain indefinitely their European and Asiatic consciousness."

This anxiety about the political threat of immigrants had its roots in resentment about the power of urban political machines which began to flourish in the late nineteenth century, using as their base the votes of immigrants. The rise of Irish American and German American politicians gave high visibility to the threat of the foreign vote, but other disturbing examples were ethnic groups' opposition to prohibition and immigration restriction. Ethnic lobbying during the war years and during postwar European reconstruction further enhanced the perception of ethnic political aspirations and potential power. A Klansman summed up the resentment on the part of old-stock Americans: "Everybody knows that politicians nowadays cater to all kinds of 'elements' mostly selfish, some corrupt, and some definitely anti-American. They cater to the German vote, the Catholic vote, the Jewish vote, the Italian vote, the bootleg vote, the vice vote, and sometimes even to the violently criminal vote."

Although the concern about immigrants' political power was ubiquitous, it was especially evident in one of the major strands of nativism: anti-Catholicism, which had deep roots in English and American culture. Its first serious manifestation, which culminated in the Know-Nothing political movement, accompanied the immigration of Irish Catholics in the 1840s. After abating in the late 1890s, anti-Catholicism resurfaced in 1910, and by 1914 over sixty publications helped to fan anti-Catholicism into a potent political issue. To Catholics, the components of popular prejudice were depressingly familiar. Protestant antipathy to the church and salacious tales of immorality among priests and nuns proliferated. Anti-Catholics, insisting that Catholicism was incompatible with democracy, pictured both priests and Irish ward heelers as leading ignorant Catholics, sheeplike, to do the bidding of Rome, Tammany Hall, or both, and portrayed parochial schools as encouraging separatism and keeping their pupils from becoming loyal Americans. As John Higham has argued, these criticisms took on deeper meaning in the context of progressive reform. Indeed, noting that the two major purveyors of anti-Catholicism, former populist Tom Watson and socialist Wilbur Franklin Phelps, editor of the highly nativist magazine *The Menace*, shared a strong reform bent, Higham linked the prewar resurgence of anti-Catholicism to the failure of the progressive movement to fulfill its promises. Given the progressive era's theme of the evils of private power, and in particular the way in which it obstructed the pursuit of the general interest, it is not surprising that anti-Catholicism would appeal to some reformers. Just as many critics focused on monopolies as conspiratorial and detrimental to democracy and opportunity, anti-Catholic agitators viewed the Catholic Church as a secretive, monolithic, and powerful institution obstructing American progress and democracy. The political power of the Catholic Church and of Catholic voters became a convenient explanation for the failure of the political system to be responsive to the needs of ordinary, old-stock Americans.

After reaching a peak in 1914, anti-Catholicism faded during the war years, but with the armistice, the nativism the war helped to unleash included a strong dose of anti-Catholicism. The war also promoted anti-Catholic sentiment by underscoring the growing respectability and influence of Catholics: their organizations, especially the Knights of Columbus and the National Catholic War Council, were highly visible in the war effort. For those already inclined toward nativism, this heavily publicized demonstration of Catholic activism and influence on public policy undoubtedly served to deepen anti-Catholic sentiment. Traditionally suspicious that priests or politicians were organizing Catholics in order to subvert Protestant "American" control, nativists viewed the experiences of World War I as documenting the growing power of the enemy, and called for organization to repel the threat. The Klan's efforts in this direction are well known, but another, more respectable fraternity, the Masons, also sought to turn their order into a vehicle for promoting and organizing 100 percent Americanism. Masons especially concentrated on Catholics, explaining: "The Protestant has been practically ousted from political life, the city is Catholic-governed, and schools as well as municipal departments reflect the influence of the Church of Rome." In light of an older historiography that emphasized the urban/rural basis for cultural conflict in the 1920s, it is significant that both the Klan and the Masons had a strong urban component. Anti-Catholicism was certainly an expression of rural Protestant religious prejudice, but it also merged with anxiety about the Catholic challenge to old-stock political power in the cities.

Anti-Catholicism had many other manifestations in the 1920s, including job discrimination and a barrage of anti-Catholic literature. Not surprisingly, the most pervasive anti-Catholicism surfaced in local, state, and national politics. It not only disrupted the 1924 Democratic convention, but also emerged as a potent issue in the campaigns against Catholic governor Al Smith's bid for the presidency in 1924 and 1928, with critics insisting that Catholics, with their allegiance to the Pope, could not be loyal officeholders. Anti-Catholicism also played a vital part in the debate over immigration restriction and prohibition, but perhaps its most upsetting ramification for Catholics was the renewed efforts to regulate or eliminate private schools. Numerous states considered such legislation in the decade after World War I, with Oregon actually passing a prohibitive law, later declared unconstitutional by the Supreme Court. Catholics were too weak in Oregon to mount much effective opposition to the school referendum, but in other states, such as Michigan, they mobilized voters to oppose anti-Catholic legislation and politicians. For anti-Catholics, these defensive efforts were just further proof of the power of Catholics and their un-American influence on the political process.

ANTI-SEMITISM

If anti-Catholicism constituted an important part of the nativism that led to immigration restriction, anti-Semitism was even more pronounced. The alleged clannishness of Jews, together with their numerous voluntary associations, led them to be thought of as organized resisters to 100 percent Americanism. Anti-Semitism, like anti-Catholicism, has a long history. Nineteenth-century American Jews were inheritors of the medieval Shylock stereotype, as well as the epithet "Christ killer." The sporadic antipathy Jews encountered in America became pronounced in the 1890s, a period of intense nativism. Old-stock patricians resented upwardly mobile Jews, mostly of German origins, whose numbers included some spectacular successes like banker Joseph Seligman. Meanwhile, heavy immigration of poverty-stricken Eastern European Jews, with their "alien" religious rituals and customs and their "outlandish" Yiddish tongue, deepened suspicions that Jews would not assimilate to Protestant American culture. The most spectacular prewar manifestation was the 1914 lynching of Leo Frank, a Jewish manufacturer in Atlanta. Frank had been convicted of the murder of Mary Phegan, a fourteen-year-old employee, and his trial centered on what he was—a rich northern Jew—rather than evidence for the crime. Tom Watson, a former leader in the populist movement, used his newspaper, later to become virulently anti-Catholic, to whip up a furor over Frank and undoubtedly incited the vigilante act.

The Frank case was exceptional but symptomatic of a pervasive anti-Semitism. Deflected during World War I, hostility toward Jews rose dramatically in the next decade. As in the case of the 1890s, some of the hostility focused on resentment of Jewish economic and geographical mobility. Discrimination in social and civic clubs, hotels, resorts, and housing proliferated in the 1920s. College discrimination, especially among elite East

Coast institutions, added a new wrinkle, and those able to bypass educational quotas still met with extensive job discrimination.

These forms of anti-Semitism had serious repercussions for Jews by limiting the quality of life and aspiration. Other challenges centered on the pervasive sentiment that Jews were unworthy as Americans. This idea, part and parcel of the pattern of American nativism, in the Jewish case was furthered by the widespread association of Jews with Bolshevism, an idea given legitimacy by testimony in a Senate hearing to the effect that New York Jews had been the masterminds behind the Bolshevik Revolution. Burton Hendricks, one of the major popular propagandists of anti-Semitism, conflated the highly visible presence of Jews in the Socialist Party and labor unions with scientific racism to insist that the propensity for radicalism was inherent in the racial makeup of Eastern European Jews. As was the case with other ethnic groups, Jews were also accused of subverting the democratic process with the bloc vote.

In the immigration restriction debates, anti-Semitism figured heavily. With some justification, many Jews felt that the major thrust of the quota system was to eliminate Jewish immigration. Literature promoting immigration restriction in respectable magazines served as an important source of circulating anti-Semitism. While the major religious target of the Klan was Catholics, Jews came in for their share of abuse, cross burnings, and political opposition. As significant as these avenues for spreading anti-Semitism were, however, nothing surpassed the importance of Henry Ford's *Dearborn Independent*.

The *Dearborn Independent* began its attack on Jews in 1920 and continued, with some interruptions, through 1925. It had enormous circulation because Ford insisted that his dealers sell subscriptions and more or less imposed a sales quota. The text of the anti-Semitic attacks was the *Protocols of the Elders of Zion*, which purported to be a secret document written by a Jewish leader in 1897 detailing the age-old plan for Jews to destroy Christianity and dominate the world. Originally forged by the Czar's secret police, the protocols gained circulation in this country shortly after World War I. Various editions of the *Pro-*

tocols were published, but the key to circulating its ideas was the series begun in the *Dearborn Independent* called *The International Jew*. The writer, editor W. J. Cameron, not only summarized the gist of the *Protocols*, but in a series of articles, later brought together in book form, explicated their meaning for interpreting historical phenomena and contemporary events.

According to *The International Jew*, most nation-states were strongly influenced if not completely controlled by Jews. This honeycombing of influence allowed Jews, acting in concert all over the world, to determine international politics and economics. In their desire to bring about widespread disorder and thus undermine Gentile governments, the secret international government of the Jews was thus responsible for the Bolshevik Revolution and World War I. Jewish control of banking had resulted in a banking trust that had a stranglehold on the American people. The economic distress of farmers was traced to the Jewish effort to deprive landowners of their independence. Promoting high taxes and indebtedness, Jews "kept landownership in a state of unconditional subordination." The Jewish conspiracy also was invoked to account for changes in morality, which the *Dearborn Independent* linked directly to the commercialization of leisure. It argued that a Jewish theatrical trust "had reduced what was essentially an art to a time-clock, cash-register system, working with the mechanical precision of a well-managed factory. It suppressed individuality and initiative, killed off competition, drove out the independent manager and star . . . handled plays, theaters and actors like factory products, and now began a process of vulgarizing and commercializing everything connected with the theater." Similar arguments were made for the movies, the music industry, and sports.

Thus the *Dearborn Independent*, week after week, presented the Jewish conspiracy to destroy Christian civilization as Jews embarked on their relentless pursuit of power. And it presented it as a successful pursuit: Jews allegedly had already ascended to a dominant role in international affairs, economics, domestic politics, the media, and leisure, leaving old-stock Americans largely powerless. In publishing and distributing *The International Jew*, the *Dearborn Independent* did not create anti-

Semitism, but it reinforced popular mistrust of Jewish religion, culture, and influence. The gullible and intolerant, aware of a long tradition of conspiracy theories, could swallow the story whole. Even more sophisticated readers who doubted the existence of the Elders themselves could find in *The International Jew* evidence for the damage Jewish immigrants had done to American culture. If the major crime for nativists by Catholics was their political influence, by Jews it was their perceived cultural and economic power.

The *Dearborn Independent*, an important source for understanding the pervasive anti-Semitism of the decade, also provides insight into broader anxieties troubling many Americans in this period. As Leo Ribuffo has noted, the *Protocols* offered "a clue to the modern maze." The *Dearborn Independent* used them to explain complex patterns of modern life. The journal's reiterated alarm about Jewish monopolies and trusts spoke to the fears of many Americans about the decline in individual initiative, power, and independence. So did the attention to the transformation of the world of leisure, with the *Independent* pinpointing the Jewish-controlled mass media as a key source for explaining changing sexual, moral, and behavioral patterns. War, revolution, inflation, unemployment, jazz dancing, and provocative clothes were all part of a complex world over which individuals had seemingly little control. If *The International Jew* did not solve the problems, its easily understood conspiracy theory at least gave a coherence and explanatory mode which made them somehow more manageable.

The *Dearborn Independent*'s attack on the Jews thus encapsulates the issue of power that was crucial in early-twentieth-century America. By targeting Jews, it indicates the ethnic component of the cultural conflicts of the 1920s as white Anglo-Saxon Protestants struggled to maintain their hegemony in American society. By explicating all the disturbing symptoms that Jews were allegedly responsible for, the *Independent* also perfectly demonstrated the link between old-stock Americans' nativism and their anxieties about the loss of community, which they envisioned as a homogeneous world of shared values, local control, and individual autonomy.

RED SCARE

The Red Scare of 1919–20 was another manifestation of the drive for conformity and homogeneity that characterized the 1920s. The immediate explanation for the Red Scare was the success of the Bolshevik Revolution, which established the revolutionary regime headed by Lenin in what was to become the Soviet Union. The 1919 formation of two Communist Parties in this country, as well as a series of bombings aimed at political and business leaders, laid the groundwork for the fear that Bolshevik agents sought to foment revolution in the United States. These circumstances mushroomed into widespread hysteria over the prospect of imminent revolution, leading to a pervasive suspicion of radicals, immigrants, organized labor, and dissenters. Business leaders, public officials, voluntary associations, and the press encouraged the anxieties that led to a massive disregard for civil liberties and an overwhelming insistence upon conformity.

How could Americans jump from the existence of two weak, disorganized Communist Parties to the belief, as Senator Miles Poindexter expressed it, that "there is real danger that the government will fall"? To unravel the many-layered sources of the Red Scare, we begin with the immediate circumstances of 1919, a devastating year throughout the world. In this country, the rapid and unplanned demobilization had left the economy in disarray. Inflation was rampant: prices doubled between 1915 and 1920. Economic problems were exacerbated by the demobilization of servicemen who often returned to unemployment. It is not coincidental that men in uniform constituted a significant portion of the mobs that harassed radicals and immigrants in 1919. Not for the first time had hard times made people susceptible to the search for scapegoats.

Besides economic disruption throughout the year there was evidence of disorder. A series of bombings was alarming even if the intended targets went unscathed. It took flimsy evidence at best to convince the public that the bombs constituted part of a Bolshevik plot. The race riots that erupted in numerous cities during the summer of 1919 offered still further proof of instability. While many commentators sought to provide thoughtful explanations for the riots, one major speculation was that African Americans were being inspired and directed by Bolshevik agents.

Still another disturbing phenomenon was the strikes of 1919 —3,600 of them—involving over four million workers, with the most disruptive being the Seattle general strike, the steel strike, the coal strike, and the Boston police strike. The wave of strikes stemmed from the desire to sustain the gains made during the war in the face of employer hostility and to counter encroaching inflation. Most centered on bread-and-butter issues or the fight for union recognition, and in some cases the strikes were influenced by radical leaders. The first big confrontation, the Seattle general strike, showed the influence of a militant labor tradition in the Pacific Northwest, even though the radical Industrial Workers of the World (IWW) was not directly involved. The strike began as shipyard workers walked out to protest a wage cut. The city's Central Labor Council, which included a number of radically inclined leaders, called for a sympathy general strike, which Seattle's unionized workers enthusiastically embraced. Highly organized and peaceful, the strike shut down the city for five days. A history of labor conflict with the IWW, as well as the novelty of a general strike, the country's first, led Seattle newspapers and officials to portray it as an IWW-led Bolshevik plot. Negative public opinion, pressure from the national headquarters of the American Federation of Labor, and possibly the presence of federal troops brought an end to the strike, but not before it gained national notoriety as the first step in, as Mayor Ole Hanson termed it, "an attempted revolution which they expected to spread all over the United States."

The social disruptions of 1919 form only part of the explanation of why the American public became inflamed over the Bolshevik menace. For the Red Scare was not a spontaneous expression of public fear. Individuals and institutions promoted it. Eager to sell papers, the news media sensationalized events at every turn. Politicians like Mayor Hanson of Seattle traded on the public anxiety. In a flag-draped car, he presented himself as a warrior for 100 percent Americanism and later profited from his role in the stand against the Seattle strikers by resigning his office and setting off on a lucrative lecture tour. Attorney General A. Mitchell Palmer was another official who used the Red Scare for his own aggrandizement. His fervency may have been prompted in part by having been the target of one of the infamous 1919 bombings, but his presidential ambitions further fueled his intensity, as he pushed himself into the limelight as the nation's premier crusader against Bolshevism.

Voluntary associations also publicized the red menace. At the forefront were three organizations: the National Security League, the American Defense Association, and the National Civic Federation. Though small in membership, they had the backing of leading business elites such as Elbert H. Gary, T. Coleman Du Pont, J. P. Morgan, Jr., and John D. Rockefeller. These organizations embarked on massive publicity campaigns to arouse the public. Similarly, mass membership voluntary associations whipped up anxiety about the Bolshevik threat. The magazines and meetings of the Masons and the Knights of Columbus resonated with reports on the threat of Bolshevism. The middle-class members of these organizations were anxious about threats to property and the status quo, but their enthusiasm for the witch-hunt also reflected the dynamic of voluntary associations. Eager to build up membership, their leaders eagerly embraced causes that would engage their constituencies. The epitome of this process was the American Legion. In part a lobby of ex-servicemen, it also justified its organization as a defender of patriotism, with the Bolshevik threat giving the new organization a compelling rallying point.

The business leaders so eager to promote anxiety about Bolshevism had their own agenda. One was to find support for the repression of radical activity, especially the IWW. But the business community also sought to brand organized labor as "red." Typically, a spokesman for the coal operators reported that the coal strike was directed by Lenin and Trotsky. Thus the attention given to propagating the Red Scare became paired with the open-shop drive. With the willing help of the press, business leaders linked all strikes to the Bolshevik plot for an American revolution. In the process, they not only conflated Bolshevism with unions but, as Robert Murray noted in his study of the Red Scare, induced the public to "believe that almost every union man was opposed to the American way of life and was the unwitting, if not deliberate, dupe of dangerous radicals." This association had long-term results, for the Red Scare hyperbole contributed not only to crushing the strikes of 1919 but to crippling organized labor for over a decade.

The agendas of the business community, voluntary associations, politicians, and the press helped to persuade a susceptible public that the Bolshevik menace was a serious one. But the sources and nature of the Red Scare lay still deeper than the events of 1919. Yet another layer can be uncovered in the strident nationalism of the war years. The anxiety about hyphenated Americans, about loyalty and conformity, led to a frenzy of patriotic excess. The federal government promoted this 100 percent Americanism spirit. During the war, the Justice Department encouraged a volunteer network of spies, the American Protective League, whose 250,000 members searched for evidence of disloyalty and engaged in vigilante activity as well. The Committee on Public Information, eager to generate enthusiasm for the war, also whipped up a nationalistic furor. In addition to distributing propaganda promoting loyalty, it monitored foreign-language newspapers. Throughout the war its campaigns used publicity and persuasion as a means of assuring loyalty, and reveal a faith in voluntarism that was shaped by American traditions of limiting state coercive activity.

But while much of the federal effort in behalf of 100 percent Americanism flowed through volunteer channels, a coercive side did emerge. Accompanying the enmity for Germans was an abhorrence of radicals, whose critique of the war as a capitalistic plot led them to be viewed universally as pro-German conspirators. Hostility toward radicals had predated the war years, and had heated up as the Socialist Party gained strength in the teens. The 900,000 votes cast for Eugene Debs in the presidential election of 1912 represented only the most visible indication of radical dissent. More alarming to conservatives than the socialists were the Industrial Workers of the World, or as its members were called, the Wobblies. Aspiring to create one giant union of all workers, the Wobblies, with their revolutionary syndicalism and aggressive strike tactics, had made notable strides in organizing the West and had attained high visibility in a number of eastern strikes as well. The Wobblies' rhetoric of sabotage and violence was harsher than their actions, but their efforts, especially their successes in organizing the unorganized, frightened mainstream Americans.

In efforts to repress such radicalism, a number of states had passed criminal syndicalism laws to imprison members of organizations promoting violent revolution. Local business and state leaders had urged federal action as well. Provisions of the federal immigration legislation of 1917 and 1918 had been designed to rid America of alien radicals by making membership in a revolutionary organization grounds for deportation. Administrative complications, as well as the recalcitrance of the Secretary of Labor, William B. Wilson, forestalled extensive deportation, but the war brought another weapon to suppress dissent in the form of an old sedition act of 1798. In addition, the Selective Service Act provided punishment for those interfering with conscription, and the Espionage Act of 1917 offered still further statutory ammunition. Armed with the means to suppress dissent, the federal government jailed radical leaders, most notably Eugene Debs and anarchist Emma Goldman, conducted raids on IWW headquarters that all but destroyed the organization, and denied mailing privileges to a variety of left-wing and liberal newspapers. While the states and the federal government sought official means of assuring conformity, vigilantes pursued their own methods of harassment and physical abuse. Germans and radicals were the most frequent targets, but in many communities other citizens not deemed sufficiently fervent in their patriotism were likely to bear the brunt of being labeled a slacker or pro-German.

The war's abrupt end in 1918 did not stop the official and unofficial drives for 100 percent Americanism, but merely redirected their focus to radicals, especially alien radicals. The Red Scare patterns were very similar to wartime attempts to assure conformity. Here again, the most sensational episode of vigilantism concerned the IWW. On Armistice Day, October 1919, the

Centralia, Washington, American Legion's parade route went past the meeting hall of the local Industrial Workers of the World. Justifiably fearing an attack, IWW members in the hall were armed. As the parade marched by the hall for a second time, a few Legionnaires started toward the building and the Wobblies opened fire, killing two. Several Wobblies were arrested. Later a mob broke into the jail and removed Wesley Everest, whom they castrated and lynched. The lynching was condoned, while the Wobblies were arrested and convicted for murdering the Legionnaires, thus lending official sanction to vigilantes' attacks on radicals.

Officials throughout the country pursued various tactics to clamp down on dissent. In numerous cities and states legislators attempted to purify the schools by scrutinizing curricula and prescribing courses in civics that would promote loyalty. Teachers became the objects of loyalty oaths and investigations. Another vehicle for enforcing conformity was criminal syndicalism and red flag laws which proliferated in many states. The former provided for fines and imprisonment for anyone preaching overthrow of the government through unlawful means. Red flag laws provided stiff penalties for red flag demonstrations and resulted in the imprisonment of 300 people in the various states. Beside imprisonment, there were widespread limitations on free press and speech.

Other arrests stemmed from a series of raids on alleged radical headquarters. Some were conducted by state and local authorities, but the most spectacular were the Palmer Raids. Attorney General Palmer had repeatedly urged a peacetime sedition act that would make membership in a revolutionary organization a punishable offense. The Senate passed legislation, but it did not get through the House, leaving Palmer with deportation, based on the 1918 immigration act, as the key to ridding the country of radicals. These federal legal limitations meant that Palmer concentrated on immigrants, a factor that heightened public perception of the association between aliens and radicalism. In his highly publicized campaign against Bolshevism, Palmer created a new division of the Federal Bureau of Investigation to deal with radical activities, using it to collect information on left-wing and liberal organizations. In November he conducted dramatic raids on the Union of Russian Workers. Similar raids were carried out by local and state officials. Of the thousands arrested, 249 aliens were finally deported. In January a second series of raids on the two Communist Parties led to the indiscriminate arrest of 10,000 people.

Competing for sensationalism with the Palmer Raids were the escapades of New York State's Lusk Committee. Set up in the summer of 1919 to investigate sedition, the Lusk Committee not only held hearings but conducted raids, with dubious legal authority, on the Rand School, the Russian Soviet Bureau, and the IWW, to gather information and identify radicals. The committee's report fueled a highly intense public atmosphere which led to the refusal of the New York legislature to seat five elected socialist representatives from New York.

The excesses of the Palmer and Lusk raids and the action of the New York legislature eventually resulted in public criticism. Lawyers, judges, senators, and the Inter-Church World Church Movement condemned Palmer's methods after his second series of raids. Most impressively, Louis Post, Assistant Secretary of Labor, castigated Palmer in a congressional hearing originally designed to investigate Post. Palmer's credibility was also damaged by his confident warning that May Day 1920 would see widespread bombings and a general strike. The press responded with its usual sensationalism and warned the public of impending crisis. As May Day came and went without incident, Palmer became the ludicrous man who cried wolf. As Palmer was overreaching himself, the business community, with strikes broken and labor in disarray, and also alarmed by the disruptive quality of the Red Scare, began to back off from the Bolshevik threat as well. The economy improved, and "normalcy" began. The federal witch-hunt wound down and the hysteria of the great Red Scare faded away.

The short but intense Red Scare had far-reaching implications. By disrupting radical organizations, it permanently damaged the radical movement, with effects lasting well into the 1920s as states employed red flag and criminal syndicalism laws to stifle dissent, a practice the Supreme Court upheld. By branding organized labor as radical, the Red Scare contributed to the crippling of the union movement. The intense hysteria of 1919–20 was also a significant factor in the widespread support for the first immigration quota system, enacted in 1920. After the Red Scare faded, anti-radicalism took a backseat to other forms of nativism later in the decade, but did not dissipate altogether, as the case of Sacco and Vanzetti indicates. In 1920, when the nation was still in the grip of the Red Scare, two Italian anarchists were arrested for a robbery and murder in Braintree, Massachusetts. The evidence linking the two with the crime was sketchy and the conduct of the trial a travesty of American judicial procedure. The conviction stemmed less from the reliability of evidence and more from their status as immigrants, anarchists, and draft resisters. As Bartolomeo Vanzetti put it, "The jury were hating us" because it was a "time when there was a hysteria of resentment and hate against the people of our principles, against the foreigner, against slackers," a hysteria the prosecution inflamed. Their conviction became a cause célèbre for radicals and liberals, who kept the issue alive during the process of appeal. The most famous defender was Felix Frankfurter, later to be a Supreme Court Justice. In a lengthy document, he detailed the weakness of the prosecution's case and the prejudice of the judge, and linked all to prevailing patterns of discrimination. But despite the waning of the Red Scare, the sentiments that convicted them in the first place persisted. The efforts to obtain a new trial failed and they were executed in 1927.

The Red Scare was a manifestation of deeper problems that did not go away when the intensity of the scare had dissipated. One hundred percent Americanism remained a goal of old-stock Americans. One of the best analyses of the broader meaning of the antiradical hysteria in the context of the desire for national conformity is historian Stanley Coben's notion of the Red Scare as a revitalization movement. Drawing upon anthropologist Anthony F. C. Wallace's work, Coben argued that the Red Scare's "objective was to end the apparent erosion of American values and the disintegration of American culture." By deporting radical aliens and insisting upon a rigid conformity to cherished "beliefs, customs, symbols, and traditions," patriots hoped to revitalize the society, to "heal societal divisions and to tighten defenses against cultural changes."

PROHIBITION

Yet another movement associated with the 1920s that could be characterized as a revitalization movement was prohibition. Like the Red Scare, prohibition employed coercive means, the force of law, to impose cultural unity on an increasingly heterogeneous and complex society. The origins of the movement stretch back to the early nineteenth century. Riding on the wave of the evangelical revivalism of the Jacksonian period, the early temperance movement sought individual reform that would lead to spiritual and then social regeneration. While the movement encompassed a highly religious, millenarian spirit, it also reflected middle-class anxieties about the disorder of the period. The enfranchisement and rise of the common man, great geographical mobility, fledgling industrialization, and high alcohol consumption coalesced during a period when communal institutions such as churches were losing their ability to restrain behavior and maintain social cohesion. The emerging middle class used the temperance and evangelical movements to establish a culture of sobriety, restraint, and industry to strengthen the family, promote individual and community prosperity, and assure political and social righteousness.

The prohibition drive that culminated in the 1920s had much in common with the early temperance movement. It was an attempt to promote Protestant middle-class culture as a means of imposing order on a disorderly world. However, in the intervening years there had been changes. The focus of the movement had shifted from the regeneration of the individual drinker to the abolition of the saloon evil, which had become a metaphor for the dislocations accompanying industrialization, urbanization, and immigration. To the anxious old-stock middle class, the saloon fostered vice, prostitution, sexual excess, and crime. It robbed the poor of their wages, putting a burden on helpless women and children. As centers of ward politics, saloons formed a key part of the matrix of urban political corruption that was a constant concern of middle-class reformers. Moreover, the saloon was linked to the idea of a liquor trust, a symbol of monopoly that challenged the individualistic economic order.

Central to the focus on the saloon was its association with the home of immigrant culture. The anti-saloon movement was inseparable from the nativism and anti-Catholicism deeply embedded in nineteenth-century political culture. Religious and ethnic conflict had characterized much of local and state politics in late-nineteenth-century America in which Protestant evangelical "pietists" battled Catholics and other "liturgicals" for political power and cultural legitimacy. Pietists, in their evangelical enthusiasm for far-reaching reforms that would foster a virtuous society, promoted government action, as Paul Kleppner put it, "to enforce their value system and its social norms." Some of the battles hinged on the school issue. Pietists, fearful of the growing political and cultural influence of liturgicals, especially Catholics, and profoundly suspicious of their parochial schools, campaigned for laws which would require that instruction be in English, private schools be inspected, and, more drastically, attendance in public school be compulsory. Another heated issue was alcohol consumption. Pietists sought to regulate hours and conditions in saloons or to prohibit alcohol altogether, with the goal of bringing immigrant culture in line with Protestant behavior and values. By the twentieth century, this struggle became somewhat more secularized. While many prohibitionists were deeply religious and inspired by millennial hopes of a dry America, others conflated Protestantism with Americanism. The battle for prohibition as it shaped up in the twentieth century was an ethnic conflict. Feeling overwhelmed by immigrant masses whose religion, language, values—especially of sexual morality, drink, and leisure—seemed so much at odds with mainstream values, prohibitionists hoped to use law to coerce assimilation, to harness, as prohibition historian Norman Clark put it, "chaotic pluralism."

After decades of agitation, why was prohibition finally enacted into a national law in 1919? The Eighteenth Amendment's success stemmed in part from its relationship to the progressive reform movement of the early twentieth century. The campaign for prohibition benefited from the agitation for reform that had focused on the problems of economic concentration, political corruption, urban poverty, unassimilated immigrants, vice, and social disorder. Just as the progressive movement attracted support from a variety of sources, prohibition had a multifaceted appeal. It was supported by the nation's business leaders who felt that prohibition would help to control an unruly workforce and promote stability, efficiency, and industrial safety. The middle class was drawn in by nativism as well as the promise of social order and economy. Anti-Catholics viewed prohibition as a weapon against Catholics. Evangelical Christians saw prohibition as part of their millenarian hopes for a sober, Christian America. For many supporters, prohibition became a panacea, the key to social order and homogeneity. In contrast, professional progressive reformers, influenced by social science methods and relying upon scientific and statistical evidence which indicated that the saloon was a major contributor to social problems, viewed prohibition as part of a panoply of reforms, including child labor laws, factory legislation, and municipal reforms. Although the supporters of prohibition had somewhat different expectations and agendas, most shared a common ethnicity and the expectation that prohibition would re-create a socially ordered community through the establishment of Protestant middle-class values.

Supporters similarly shared a willingness to expand the power of the state to ensure homogeneity. Despite traditional beliefs in limited government, there was nothing new about the idea of using state power to impose conformity. The pietists in the nineteenth century had sought for decades to use the law to control behavior. This pietist tradition gathered strength from the progressive era reform drive, when many reformers had proposed a more powerful state to protect victims of industrialization. In this climate, prohibition could easily be viewed as a legitimate expansion of the interventionist state, where personal liberties took second place to the improved general social welfare that prohibition seemed to promise.

Prohibition, like other progressive era reforms, did not happen automatically. It resulted from the assiduous efforts of reformers working through voluntary associations, the most important of which were the Women's Christian Temperance Union (established in 1873) and the Anti-Saloon League (established in 1895). The title of the former suggests its nature, revealing the religious impulse behind prohibition, as well as the importance of women and their voluntary associations to the movement. Prohibition was closely linked to women's perceived role as moral guardians of the home and culture. Male drinking was seen as damaging women and children by impoverishing them. Equally serious, men's drinking led to sexual excess and thus made it more difficult for women to control their own bodies. Moreover, in the late nineteenth century there was mounting anxiety about venereal disease, which was widely linked in the public mind to excessive drinking. A typical scenario pictured intemperate husbands, their inhibitions destroyed, visiting prostitutes, often in saloons, contracting venereal disease, and then spreading it to their innocent wives and unborn children. Although the leadership of the WCTU was divided over the suitability of votes for women, the movements for sobriety and social purity undoubtedly promoted the cause of women's suffrage and vice versa. Through its dissemination of temperance propaganda and its agitation for prohibition laws, the WCTU was a key agency in bringing about middle-class enthusiasm for prohibition, but it was the Anti-Saloon League that brought political sophistication to the movement.

The League provides an excellent example of the organizational revolution of the late nineteenth century. Its leaders created their organization after a corporate, bureaucratic model that marshaled the strength of the Protestant churches in a political cause. It operated as a non-partisan political lobbying organization that used sophisticated techniques of propaganda and influence. Beginning with Ohio, it mobilized support in state after state from church congregations, leading citizens, and middle-class newspapers and magazines. It supported or opposed candidates of any party solely on the basis of their stand on prohibition, as well as agitating for prohibition legislation. By the turn of the century the Anti-Saloon League was clearly an organization to be reckoned with. Initially it scored successes through local option laws, then expanded to state laws: between 1906 and 1917 twenty-six states had passed some form of pro- hibition legislation. In 1913, the League began its drive for a national amendment. This amendment, viewed as the only means of bringing about a dry nation, would keep dry states dry; more important, it would bring states with high immigrant populations, unlikely to pass state laws, into the temperance column.

The reform climate, aided by the organizational techniques of the "drys," proved crucial to prohibition's success, but it was World War I that finally put the movement over the top. During the war, Congress passed a wartime prohibition act as part of an efficiency and conservation drive. Meanwhile, the campaign for a national amendment was abetted by the nationalistic spirit that engulfed the nation. Prohibition supporters promoted it as a patriotic measure that would contribute to making the world safe for democracy. They also traded on the association of Ger- mans with the brewery industry, implying that brewery interests that opposed prohibition did so out of loyalty to Germany. As the Anti-Saloon League put it: "German brewers in this country have rendered thousands of men inefficient and are thus crip- pling the Republic in its war on Prussian militarism." With this spirit, the amendment easily passed through Congress and was quickly ratified by the states. It became law on January 1920 through its enabling legislation, popularly called the Volstead Act. The Volstead Act, following the language of the amend- ment, forbade the manufacture, sale, and distribution of alcohol, but did not proscribe drinking or possession of alcohol. It also defined intoxicating beverages as anything with more than 0.5 percent alcoholic content, thereby making America bone dry, not merely temperate. The dry forces were jubilant. Evangelist Billy Sunday made a ritual of burning John Barleycorn, a cere- mony performed throughout the country.

Was prohibition put over on the majority by a small, well- organized, fanatical minority? Probably not. With prohibition touted as a solution to problems besetting American society, including unassimilated immigrants, many old-stock Americans, regardless of their drinking patterns, embraced the amendment as a measure to bring social order and assure middle-class Protestant culture's continued political and cultural dominance. It is not clear that the bulk of these supporters would have endorsed the definition of intoxicating beverages set out by the Volstead Act. Indeed, historians have noted a significant confusion in the public mind on the issue, suggesting that many may have assumed that beer and wine would be permitted under the terms of the amendment. Thus many of the supporters of prohibition, eager to eradicate the saloon evil and exert old-stock hegemony, may have been surprised by the final result.

Not surprisingly, immigrants and the working class opposed prohibition. Although generally supportive of moderation, many labor leaders characterized prohibition as class legislation and specifically damaging to workers in the brewery and restaurant businesses. Immigrants were resentful, with Catholics in particular outspoken in their hostility. However, neither labor nor Catholics were well organized in opposition. Breweries were the only nationally organized opposition and they brought too little too late to the campaign. Given the overwhelming critique of the saloon, national organization of anti-prohibition forces might well have been pointless. Large-scale opposition to the Anti-Saloon League's efforts would have placed opponents in the position of defending not merely alcohol consumption but the saloon itself. As Norman Clark put it: "Organized, disinterested support of the saloon in American life in the early 1900s would have been just as unthinkable as organized, disinterested support of child labor, or prostitution, or disease in the slums."

The battle for the amendment was won by the beginning of the decade, but the issue continued to be explosive, as the war over the future of the republic raged on. Throughout the 1920s, prohibition was a potent political topic, and candidates' stand on prohibition a key factor in elections. Those with urban immigrant constituencies were outspoken in their criticism of prohibition. Few people believed that repeal was possible. As one saying went: "There is as much chance of repealing the Eighteenth Amendment as there is for a hummingbird to fly to the

planet Mars with the Washington Monument tied to its tail."
But many hoped for modification of the Volstead Act. In some
states, more rebellious politicians called for repealing state laws
designed to facilitate cooperation between state and nation in
enforcement, and by 1927 only 18 of 48 states were appropri-
ating money for enforcement. Maryland never passed a state
law, while New York in 1923 became the first state to repeal its
mini Volstead Act. Significantly, it was Al Smith who signed the
repeal. Prohibition shaped many election campaigns, but it was
Smith's run for President in 1928 that was most symbolic of the
ways in which prohibition invaded the political arena throughout the decade. Smith's Catholicism was at least as important
as his stand as the nation's most preeminent wet, but prohibition was a key symbol in his campaign. Smith represented all
that ardent drys had hoped to overcome with prohibition. A
member of New York City's Tammany Hall, a devout Catholic,
and son of an Irish immigrant mother, he represented the rising
influence of immigrants and non-Protestants in modern America. He embodied an alien culture, in contrast to Herbert Hoover, the Republican nominee, who was an old-stock, self-made
man who paid homage to traditional values and supported prohibition. Hoover's smashing victory over Smith was as much
related to his representing Republican prosperity as anything
else, but many joyously interpreted Hoover's victory as a victory
for old America. The *St. Paul Pioneer Press* announced that
America is "not yet dominated by its great cities. Control of its
destinies still remains in the small communities and rural
regions, with their traditional conservatism and solid virtues . . .
Main Street is still the principal thoroughfare of the nation."

Just as political debates kept prohibition controversial, so did
the problem of enforcement. Ensuing generations' most persistent image of the 1920s is of bootleg gin, flappers, and up-
roarious parties. The decade's literature promoted a sense of a
widely flouted law. At Jay Gatsby's mansion on Long Island,
cocktail trays "floated" and "champagne was served in glasses
bigger than finger-bowls." But the Lost Generation aside, prohibition was not totally ineffectual. It did cut alcohol consumption, perhaps by as much as 30 percent, and was more effective

in the early years (1919–22). Drinking was curtailed primarily because prohibition had made it so expensive. Irving Fisher, a contemporary dry observer, investigated the price of bootleg alcohol in 1928 and found that since 1916 the cost of beer was up 600 percent, gin 520 percent, and whiskey 310 percent. A 1927 survey of social workers throughout the country confirmed the commonsense assumption that the price increases had led to a decline in alcohol consumption among workers. Another significant trend in alcohol consumption patterns was the shift from beer to hard liquor that came about because the latter was easier and cheaper to produce at home.

Despite the evidence that prohibition reduced drinking and changed drinking patterns, the law was flouted, especially in the latter half of the decade. The sources of illegal alcohol were numerous. Many wealthy or longsighted persons put down cellars in advance of prohibition, a perfectly legal practice. A much-cited example was the Yale Club in New York City, which had a fourteen-year liquor supply. Prescription and sacramental alcohol were permitted and apparently widely abused. Industrial alcohol, despite added denaturants, was doctored to make it potable. In rural areas, a long-standing practice of distilling "moonshine" whiskey continued unabated. And throughout the country, home stills multiplied, bringing the California grape industry a tremendous boom. Using an output system like early industrial manufacturers, bootleggers organized networks of home stills as part of their production and distribution system. And finally, smuggling through Canada and along the coasts brought in foreign whiskeys.

Why was enforcement not more successful? The sheer variety of sources of liquor was one problem. The connection of bootlegging with organized crime was another: prohibition did not create organized crime, but it helped it flourish. There were fortunes to be made from the illicit trade, and prohibition agents were not up against individual lawbreakers, but faced well-organized and well-manned gangs. Enforcement was also hampered by the widespread corruption of public officials. In cities prohibition was defied with the help of police and politicians, many of whom were on the take. Prohibition agents themselves were apparently easily corrupted, for the Prohibition Bureau was not staffed by the civil service, and low wages and poor screening made agents highly susceptible.

Prohibition's enforcement was further hampered by indifferent local officials and by severely limited funds. The Prohibition Bureau in 1922 had only 3,060 employees with a $6,750,000 budget. Despite widespread calls for more effective enforcement, the Anti-Saloon League did not press for greatly increased funds or more rigid enforcement because it feared it would weaken enthusiasm for the continuation of prohibition. League leaders expected that prohibition would take a generation to be successful. In the short run, they took satisfaction in prohibition as what Joseph Gusfield called a symbolic reform. Having the act on the books was almost as satisfying as enforcing the law. As Gusfield noted, if prohibition was "flouted by those who drank, it was clear whose law and whose culture was given dominant recognition as the legitimate and sanctioned mode of behavior."

Supporters of prohibition might take satisfaction in the symbolic value of having the law on the books and comfort in the expectation that with time their goals of single-standard morality would be achieved, but in the short run they could not have been blind to the implications of the widespread flouting of the law. Speakeasies, bootlegging, and the violence of organized crime deepened the disorder prohibition had aimed to resolve. Moreover, millions of Americans clearly did not share the view that drinking was sinful and resented efforts to regulate their behavior. Behind the violations of the law stood outspoken opposition. Controversy over the amendment and its enforcement infused the political debates of the decade, keeping the issue a highly charged one. As movements for appeal or modification began immediately, prohibitionists could not rest on their laurels. Prohibition, though accomplished in 1919, was an ongoing battle. A revealing 1923 letter to the editor in *The Outlook* expressed this perception perfectly. LuLu G. Birch, a schoolteacher, was distressed by the flagrant violation of prohibition, and reported her own students' cynicism about prohibition's impact on the country. "I have many acquaintances who feel an urge toward some sort of organization that will give them a chance to express dissatisfaction with the officials who fail utterly to support government. What is the private individual to do toward enforcing prohibition?" She called for a "non-political, non-sectarian, non-fanatical" movement to allow "earnest, courageous, and potent men and women" to "carry out their patriotic convictions."

THE KU KLUX KLAN

Although hardly nonpolitical, nonsectarian, or nonfanatical, one organization prepared to take on the battle to implement the multifaceted goals of the prohibition movement was the Ku Klux Klan. The Klan offered itself as an institution of "real" Americans designed to reestablish the waning influence of native white Protestants in American culture and politics. Klan rhetoric tapped anxieties about the organization of "enemies" of Americanism. The international Jew and the uppity black came into the Klan's purview of intolerance, but its greatest attention was focused on Catholic power. While nativism and racism were crucial to the Klan's rhetoric, it also identified the order as a militant wing of Protestantism. It was a vehicle for resisting encroaching secularization and, perhaps more important, for enforcing the Protestant moral code. Klansmen harped on fears about lax standards concerning prostitution, gambling, crime, and, above all, prohibition. Thus, law and order became one of the Klan's most potent symbols. In militantly resisting the new pluralism, the Klan rose to power on a rhetoric of restoring a vision of an older, more harmonious society of island communities. As one sympathetic observer of the Klan, who pictured the order as a reform organization, put it: "The Klan movement seems to be another expression of the general unrest and dissatisfaction with both local and national conditions—the high cost of living, social injustice and inequality, poor administration of justice, political corruption, hyphenism, disunity, unassimilated and conflicting thought and standards—which are distressing all thoughtful men."

The second Ku Klux Klan emerged in 1915 on Stone Mountain, Georgia, when sixteen men lit a cross to symbolize the new Klan. Colonel William Simmons fashioned this new fraternal order after the original Ku Klux Klan of the Reconstruction South. The Klan limped along until 1920, when two public relations specialists, Edward Young Clark and Elizabeth Tyler, who were experienced in promotion with the WCTU and war bond drives, cut a deal with Simmons in which they would provide the recruitment system in return for a share of the profits. The Klan's success is an example of the fine art of huckstering. But more, Clark and Tyler also seized upon issues that quickly drummed up enthusiasm for the order. They built upon the old Klan's emphasis on white supremacy to make the new Klan emblematic of 100 percent Americanism. Their organizational drive was ironically aided by the *New York World*'s 1920 exposé of the order and by a congressional hearing investigating the problem of vigilantism associated with the Klan. These events provided free publicity which led to even more initiations, some a thousand strong, in which recruits were naturalized as citizens of the realm through an impressive ceremony.

Because Klan rosters were secret, it is difficult to be certain of its numerical strength, but most estimates are that the Klan attracted over five million people during its heyday between 1920 and 1925. It was especially strong in the South, Southwest, and Midwest. It dominated politics in Indiana, Texas, Oklahoma, and Colorado, and was a potent political force in countless other states as well. Its membership tended to be drawn from a cross section of a community's occupations, with a strong following from the lower middle class. While the Klan was limited to adult males, its auxiliary, the Women of the Ku Klux Klan, encouraged newly enfranchised women to exercise their votes in behalf of 100 percent Americanism. Junior organizations tapped yet another market for Klandom, making the order a family affair. For many years, historians described the Klan as a rural movement set against the forces of urbanism, but as Kenneth Jackson has indicated, the Klan was a significant force in numerous cities, including Los Angeles, Chicago, Detroit, Denver, Atlanta, and Dallas. The Klan flourished in city and town, suggesting that the defensive traditionalism embodied in the Klan was not a simple matter of geography.

Although nativist ideology was central to its appeal, part of its phenomenal success stemmed from its variability. It offered many things to many people. In keeping with the huckstering impulse that drew many of the leaders and kleagles, men undoubtedly joined the Klan because it was good for business. Klansmen were expected to trade with one another. More traditional fraternal lodges operated in the same way, although the Klan in many communities was more overt. TWK (Trade with Klan) signs appeared in many office windows. More dramatically, Klansmen often engaged in well-disciplined boycotts against Catholics and Jews. Klan membership may also have been helpful in getting or keeping a job, and was often invaluable to politicians, or aspiring politicians. For women, as Kathleen Blee has argued, the Klan promised to enforce a morality aimed at abusive husbands and other sources of danger to pure womanhood. More surprisingly, the order offered some women a platform for political views which mingled nativism with support for women's rights and social reform.

Another facet of its appeal was the Klan's claim to be the militant arm of the Protestant church. Although not all Klansmen or Klanswomen were fundamentalists, they shared with fundamentalists a concern over "the weakened influence of Protestantism." Throughout the country the Klan played upon this theme, describing the order in religious terms with revivalistic fervor. No national denominations officially endorsed the Klan, but in local communities thousands of ministers supported it, drawn in by the Klan's religious rhetoric, its free membership for ministers, and its dramatic appearances in churches in which robed Klansmen would silently present donations to the church. The Klan's promise to promote Protestant religious and moral ideas had a far-flung appeal to many old-stock Americans alarmed by threats to their traditional religious values.

The Klan's fraternalism was another component behind the organization's drawing power. The early 1920s witnessed a general expansion of fraternal orders, and the growth of the Klan may be seen in part as a result of the general enthusiasm for joining. One of the most common methods for recruiting was to bring in leaders of other fraternities, especially the Masons. But the Klan's fraternalism was far more exciting and mysterious than that of Masonic lodges. The Masons may have had secrets, but the Klan was shrouded in secrecy, with guarded membership lists and hooded regalia. Moreover, Klan initiations often took place outdoors in remote sections of the countryside, with sentries posted to exclude outsiders. The highlight of the evening was the dramatic cross burning, repeated in countless communities throughout the country. The Klan also offered more traditional fraternal fare: parties, barbecues, and parades. It was fun to be a Klansman. And like other lodges, the Klan offered a sense of brotherhood with men of shared values. The women's and children's auxiliaries extended this community to one of families as well.

The Klan, however, was unique among fraternal orders in that the community it created was exclusively white, native, and Protestant, and saw its primary role as the active defense of Anglo-Saxon Americanism, of patriotism, and of law and order. In many communities, especially in the South, the Klan's activism took a violent path. What first excited concern about the rise of the Klan was its vigilantism. Reports of lynchings and beatings of Jews, Catholics, and African Americans by men in Klan regalia were ominous indications of the tenor of the new organization. While many of the Klan's victims were members of targeted minorities, they also included people suspected of crimes against morality, suggesting the breadth of Klan concern. The Klan did not induce violence in an unviolent society, but rather cloaked it in a mystique that may have increased its legitimacy. As Robert Moats Miller has argued, in its violence and its other characteristics, the Klan was not an aberration of American culture, but rather its reflection.

While vigilantism as a form of militancy was an important characteristic of the Klan, its entry into the political realm was far more significant. The Klan's political potential had been there from the start, but it gained an added boost after 1922, when Imperial Wizard Hiram Evans (who had ousted Klan founder Simmons in a palace coup) specifically sought to enhance the Klan's power by dominating local and state elections. Throughout the country the Klan became a potent political issue, disrupting communities and political parties. It dramatically entered the national arena when the battle over whether or not to condemn the Klan by name deadlocked the 1924 Democratic convention.

Some of the most intense Klan conflicts erupted in local politics. When kleagles entered a town their instructions were to seize upon a local controversy around which to generate Klan enthusiasm. The result was significant diversity in Klan rhetoric, activity, and style. Cities with large immigrant communities or recent black migrants were ripe for the appeal of the Klan and its promise to restore power to old-stock Protestant Americans. Not surprisingly, Chicago was a stronghold of Klan strength. Kenneth Jackson estimates that roughly 15 percent of the eligible population joined. The combined strength of the city's klaverns made it the largest Klan city in the country.

The scene of the bloody 1919 race riot that was symbolic of the social tensions accompanying massive southern black migration, Chicago was also a city of immigrants and their children. Its burgeoning population and industrial growth led to congestion and overcrowding, with native white residents resentful of incursions in their neighborhoods of African Americans and immigrants. Crime, prostitution, and violations of prohibition flourished. These problems were associated in the old-stock mind with immigrants and African Americans, as well as the corruption of political machines that seemed unresponsive to "100 percent Americans." Drawing heavily from those areas of neighborhoods in transition, the Klan in Chicago offered to redress the balance—to restore law and order and the dominance of white Protestant Americans by challenging the power of ethnic votes. The Klan was not successful in capturing Chicago politics. A strong ethnic political presence, the very thing that galvanized the Klan, was also what it made it difficult for the Klan to achieve success. Similar stories of Klan struggles against ethnic power appeared in other cities such as Detroit, Buffalo, New York, and Pittsburgh. Although the Klan was not successful politically in these communities, its presence indicates the nature of the ethnic identity and defensiveness that motivated Klan members.

The appeal to nativism also emerged in cities where the ethnic presence, while visible, did not exert significant power. This is evident in the Klan's success in Denver, Colorado. A stronghold of the Klan, Denver accounted for a significant amount of Colorado's Klan membership. Denver's population was heavily native, white, and Protestant, but there was sufficient ethnic presence to excite anxiety about 100 percent Americanism. Its small black population (5,000 out of 256,000) had established a branch of the National Association for the Advancement of Colored People in 1915 and after the war began efforts to challenge de facto segregation. The Jewish population (17,000) had expanded dramatically in the teens, with many concentrating in their own district, which stood out as exotic, alien, and "un-American." Both Jews and Italians were associated in the public mind with bootlegging and gambling. The greatest attention, however, focused on the city's 35,000 Catholics, 15,000 of whom were immigrants. None of these minority groups exerted any power in Denver, but their visibility and rising expectations, especially of Catholics and Jews, led Klansmen to believe, as one of their members explained, that the Klan was necessary because "the Catholics and Jews were taking over." While not the only factors in explaining the Klan's appeal to Denverites, anti-Catholicism, nativism, and racism were crucial to the order's success.

Anti-Catholicism constituted the most pervasive part of the Klan's nativism and emerged particularly clearly in its efforts to promote 100 percent Americanism in the nation's schools. Responding to a Klan campaign rife with anti-Catholicism, Oregon voters in 1922 turned out in record numbers to elect a Klansman as governor and to pass an initiative to make public school attendance mandatory for children between the ages of eight and eighteen, a not very veiled attack on the state's Catholic parochial institutions. Nationally, the Klan supported a federal department of education, which, it hoped, would enhance public education at the expense of private and would eventually be the vehicle for eliminating parochial schools altogether. Less ambitiously, the Klan backed state and local laws prohibiting the wearing of religious garb by public school teachers, and campaigned to introduce the mandatory reading of the Protestant Bible in the public schools. And in countless local communities the Klan took over local school boards, often dismissing Catholic principals and teachers. The schools became an important political battleground in which Klansmen and other nativists hoped to establish their vision of American ideals, which included political and social dominance by their own kind.

A broad antipathy to "un-American" forces, coupled with a strong desire for conformity and homogeneity, made many urban and rural old-stock Protestants susceptible to the Klan's rhetoric. But ethnic anxiety in itself does not explain the extraordinary appeal of the Klan. If Klansmen and Klanswomen looked back to a time in which white native Protestant hegemony flourished, they also looked to the "order" of island communities. They were experiencing changes that affected Americans everywhere: the economic transformations that were undermining individual and local autonomy and the belief that the political process was unresponsive to their needs. The sense of loss of power was deepened by the seemingly overwhelming challenges to Protestant morality represented by the new woman and the new morality. Equally important were the challenges to law and order. Murder, violence and robbery seemed endemic in many communities, a problem given deeper resonance by the idea of a national crime wave that the press sensationalized. The heart of the problem seemed to be prohibition, or rather, the flouting of prohibition that embodied the widespread disregard for law and order. In communities all over the country, the Klan offered itself as the solution to this crisis of morality and disorder.

This issue was not always divorced from ethnic ones, for in many instances anxiety about crime and immigrants coalesced. Thus, in Denver, the popular association of Italians and Jews with bootlegging and gambling inextricably tied nativism to concerns about law and order. However, throughout the Southwest, in Arkansas, Oklahoma, Texas, and Louisiana, historian Charles Alexander found communities in which ethnic issues were soft-pedaled, while concerns about prohibition enforcement were paramount. Leonard Moore has demonstrated that the Klan's moral crusade in Indiana was rarely linked to an immigrant or black community. Rather, the Klan turned its animosity toward community leaders who were thought to be indifferent to problems of law and order, especially enforcement of prohibition.

This concern about unresponsive leadership is significant for understanding the appeal of the Klan. In some communities, the Klan might direct its attention to officials who catered to the immigrant vote; in others, to officials who were unresponsive to moral problems. In either case, the Klan traded on a sense of powerlessness and promised through its militant activism to empower moral, Protestant native whites and to restore order, homogeneity, and "community" itself.

The complex themes of ethnicity, law and order, morality, and official unresponsiveness came together clearly in the activities of the KKK in El Paso, where it emerged in 1921 and quickly gained much support among the native white Protestant population. According to historian Shawn Lay, racism and nativism helped to make El Paso fertile ground for the Klan. While nineteenth-century El Paso had a tradition of relatively amicable relations between Mexicans and Anglos, by the 1920s several factors led to heightened racial tensions. New Anglo migrants who helped to swell the city's population to 77,000 in 1920 often hailed from the South and brought their patterns of racism and anti-Catholicism with them. Mexican migration, moreover, had expanded dramatically, in part because of the disruption of the Mexican Revolution, so that by 1920, 43 percent of El Paso's population was foreign-born. Fear about unassimilated immigrants in their midst was increased by World War I's hysteria over disloyal hyphenates. Resentment of the political influence of alien Catholic voters who helped keep machine politicians in office had led to successful agitation for a constitutional amendment excluding aliens from the franchise, which went into effect in 1921. Mexican voting did indeed decline, but it continued to be an issue throughout the 1920s.

Another issue linked in the public mind with the Mexican population of El Paso was the contentious issue of prohibition.

El Paso had been sharply divided over the Eighteenth Amendment. Mexicans, businessmen, city officials, and older settlers had opposed repeated attempts to enact local prohibition laws, much to the dismay of the ardent supporters of the Eighteenth Amendment. Opponents believed that prohibition itself caused increased lawlessness. Others felt that lax law enforcement was at the root of widespread crime and sought a crackdown on bootlegging and vice. As a means of cleaning up El Paso, they were particularly eager to institute an early closing of the bridge to Juárez, an "entertainment city." While proponents of law and order and Protestant morality focused on Mexicans as the perpetrators of crime and disorder, they also targeted the city's business and political leadership. The latter, until recently, had been dependent upon the Mexican vote, and continued to be viewed as corrupt and feeding on graft related to the vice industry. Similarly, businessmen were not interested in a moral cleanup which might damage the city's economic base. They were particularly alarmed that closing the bridge might bring retaliation from Mexico in the form of a tax-free zone situated across the border from El Paso, which would damage El Paso's retail merchants. Thus, there were tensions between Anglos and Mexicans, but also divisions within the Anglo community itself.

The Klan played upon these anxieties and tensions. Because it met with strong resistance from local leaders, it kept a low profile in politics. It achieved a few victories, most notably in controlling the school board for a short time, but despite these successes, the Klan's political fortunes quickly waned, as opposition mounted and it faced internal problems. Although the Klan's influence was short-lived, the experience of El Paso is important for delineating the appeal of the organization in the nation at large. The Klan in El Paso incorporated much of what made the Klan attractive in a variety of communities. It linked nativism, racism, and anti-Catholicism with themes of morality, prohibition, and law and order. Another important element was resentment against public authorities not eager to promote the Klan's vision of Protestant morality and community. In El Paso there was a split within the old-stock white Protestant community. Anti-Klan forces may have been influenced by sheer political considerations—they wanted to stay in power—but they also reflected a secular, cosmopolitan business culture that was at odds with the El Paso Klan's more traditional antimodern moralism.

The year 1924 was a triumphant one for the Klan: it was at the height of its power. Yet even in places where the Klan dominated local or even state governments, its political successes rarely resulted in sustained reforms. Klan political inexperience or opportunism made it difficult to deliver on promises made. The cavalier behavior of politicians backed by the "invisible government" of the Klan disconcerted those who had hoped for a more responsive government. The sense that the Klan was not delivering—whether law and order, responsible government, Protestant old-stock domination, or a moral community—may have been one factor that led to the Klan's decline, which was evident by 1925.

Internal conflicts among Klan leaders, eager for power and profits, were another important source of the order's demise. The disruption caused by power plays between local and national headquarters and within individual klaverns undoubtedly disaffected many Klansmen. So did the scandals that exposed corruption and hypocrisy. The most spectacular featured D. C. Stephenson, the Grand Dragon of Indiana, who had a national reputation. In 1925, Stephenson abducted and assaulted his secretary, Madge Oberholtzer, who later died. In a dramatic trial, Stephenson was convicted of murder. When he was denied pardon, he released his Klan files, which exposed numerous Klan politicians' malfeasance and led to widespread indictments. In addition to scandal, the Klan was hurt by the social and political disruption that followed in its wake. By disturbing traditional political alignments, it disgruntled professional politicians who had to cope with this explosive element in local, state, and national politics. Further damage to the Klan's public image came from the realization that the Klan was exacerbating the social disorder it promised to combat. In communities where there was sufficient ethnic presence to oppose the Klan, there was often a prolonged and highly charged atmosphere of discord.

Boycotts and counterboycotts disrupted the commercial life of communities. Riots, often the result of Klan parades or vigilantism, represented another serious problem.

As the Klan's strength ebbed, the intense spirit of 100 percent Americanism that had gripped the country also declined. By 1926 the passions unleashed by the war and the Red Scare had abated somewhat. The passage of time was one factor; the enactment of the 1924 National Origins Act, another. With restriction enacted, nativism, racism, anti-Semitism, and anti-Catholicism, although still persistent, lost their force. The 1928 presidential candidacy of Catholic Al Smith momentarily brought back the intense battles and briefly revived the Klan. But although the election revealed the ongoing anxiety about America's pluralism, by the end of the decade the ethnic conflicts that had so dominated politics in the early 1920s were fading and would be largely displaced by the economic crisis of the Great Depression.

While the Depression defused the campaigns of old-stock Americans against the incursion of out-groups with alien values, they were waning before the Depression. The fate of prohibition is an indication of these developments. Apologists for the amendment insisted throughout the decade that the "noble experiment" could and would work. For others, the conviction deepened that prohibition was a horrific mistake. It is not surprising that immigrant groups protested and criticized. It was, after all, their culture and leisure-time pursuits that had been the focus of the prohibition drive. But opponents and critics also came from the urban middle class, which had formed an important part of the support for the amendment. Prohibition became the butt of humor magazines like the old *Life*. Its cartoons harped on the theme that was to become widespread: prohibition had created a nation of spies, of nosy busybodies, empowered by the state to infringe on personal liberties. As its supporters took up further causes such as anti-evolution, anti-smoking and anti-jazz, prohibition became tainted with priggish fanaticism. As the decade progressed, many contemporary observers increasingly viewed prohibition, the Klan, and anti-evolution as all of a piece—movements of ignorant ruralites against progressive city dwellers. By the time prohibition was repealed in 1933, a clear fissure had developed within the middle class. Urban and rural old-stock men and women had been linked in the campaign for prohibition by their shared ethnicity and shared values. By the end of the decade, many in the urban middle class began to abandon the more traditional values of their past. They were becoming part of a consumer culture which placed less value on restraint and sobriety. Thus the pluralism that prohibition had hoped to contain multiplied despite the amendment and eventually eroded support for prohibition.

The struggle for repeal began almost as soon as the Eighteenth Amendment was ratified. The most important repeal organization was the Association Against the Prohibition Amendment (AAPA), founded in 1920. Its leaders, elite, wealthy men such as New York senator James Wadsworth and the Du Pont brothers, were eventually joined by many prominent former prohibitionists such as William Randolph Hearst and John D. Rockefeller. Like many early supporters of prohibition, they were dismayed by the widespread flouting of the law and convinced that it was leading to a breakdown in the social order. As we have seen, they objected to the expanded federal power represented by prohibition. Stressing not only individual rights but also states' rights, they insisted that the Eighteenth Amendment violated the spirit of the Constitution and American traditions.

The AAPA pragmatically, but unsuccessfully, put most of its early efforts into agitation for modification of the Volstead Act to permit the sale of light beer and wine. Reorganized in 1928, and spurred on by the way in which 1928 elections spotlighted the issue, the AAPA began more aggressive, organized tactics to promote repeal. The emergence of a strong national women's organization, composed of elite, respectable women, contributed dramatically to the politics of repeal by challenging prohibition's status as a women's movement. It further demonstrates how far public sentiment had traveled since 1918. A good example of the increasing respectability of antiprohibition sentiment was the fate of the Washington State Women's Christian Temperance Union. As Joseph Gusfield has noted, in 1910 the organization had attracted "the wives of prominent physicians, lawyers, and men of commerce," but in 1930 "it could list only the wives of morticians, chiropractors, tradesmen, and ministers of minor distinction." In Washington, and doubtless elsewhere, prohibitionists declined in community and social status, as enthusiasm for prohibition became identified with marginality and provincialism.

When the ratification of the Twenty-first Amendment came before the electorate, the votes were in favor of repeal: 72.9 percent of people voting in thirty-nine state referendums supported repeal. These votes came from rural areas as well as cities. The AAPA and the Women's Organization for National Prohibition Reform were crucial in articulating repeal sentiment, and getting the ball rolling for setting up referenda. But as in the case of the Eighteenth Amendment, the Twenty-first's rapid success was made possible by external events: the stock market crash and the Depression. Just as prohibition's supporters had used economic arguments to make their case, advocates of repeal insisted that it would bring in federal tax revenues and jobs that would help to offset, if not reverse, the economic collapse. The Depression itself, then, provided the final blow to prohibition.

The Depression also facilitated repeal by bringing the Democrats to power after twelve years as a minority party. The Democratic Party's new urban liberalism, which had been an important component of Franklin D. Roosevelt's election, had been gathering strength in the 1920s. The issues that helped to bring together a coalition of the urban middle class and immigrants had included prohibition. Al Smith's campaign consolidated the identification of the Democratic Party as the party of repeal. Despite Roosevelt's caution about the danger of being labeled wet, the Democratic convention of 1932 overwhelmingly embraced repeal and called upon its candidate to do so as well.

Prohibition's end thus encompasses two aspects of the failure of old-stock Americans to rein in the chaotic pluralism, to restore island communities of shared moral values. One was the split within the old-stock middle class which reveals the changing nature of American culture as it became more modern and more consumer-oriented. The other was the continuing political influence of ethnic voters which was perfectly symbolized in the transformation of the Democratic Party.

To emphasize the failure of prohibition and the decline of the Klan is not to argue that the cultural conflicts of the 1920s were surface phenomena whose importance ended as the decade came to a close and the Depression began. The spirit of 100 percent Americanism, with its emphasis on conformity and the suppression of dissent, had long-term implications. It hampered the labor movement, crippled radicalism, and set limits on freedom of speech and the press. Moreover, the anxiety about personal and community autonomy that underlay much of the discontent in the 1920s continued into the Depression years. As Alan Brinkley has noted in his study of the success of the 1930s populist protest movements led by Huey Long and Father Coughlin, an important element in their appeal was the sense of declining community and loss of control in the face of the continuing integration and consolidation of the American economy and society. And while nativism played a much less significant role in the protest movements of the Depression years, anti-Semitism was an important component of Coughlin's rhetoric.

Even though nativism declined significantly in the 1930s, the National Origins Act of 1924 had institutionalized nativism by permanently transforming American immigration policy. Obviously it affected men and women denied the possibility of immigration, most seriously the refugees from Hitler's Germany, most of whom found America's shores closed in the 1930s. But immigration restriction and the constant barrage of racist and nativist hostility of the early 1920s also profoundly affected immigrants and their children already in this country. For them, and for African Americans, the old-stock drive for conformity and community represented attacks on their culture, religion, and ethnicity. Repeatedly their stake in American society, their right to be American citizens, was denied. Historians have compiled a rich literature of the old-stock Americans' cultural offensive in the 1920s, but the ideas and experiences of the targets of the drive for cultural conformity and political hegemony have been less well documented. The following chapter takes up that task.

PLURALISM AND COMMUNITY

VI

A merican historians are familiar with the 1925 photograph of 50,000 members of the Ku Klux Klan marching down Pennsylvania Avenue in Washington, D.C. Depicting them with their hoods off, brandishing American flags against the backdrop of the Capitol dome, the photo is a graphic representation of the boldness of the Klan in the 1920s. However, little known or remembered is another march the previous year in the same place and with similar symbolic intent. On September 21, 1924, carrying papal banners and U.S. flags, 100,000 men from all over the country marched as representatives of the Catholic Holy Name Society. At the conclusion of their procession, they listened to a speech by President Calvin Coolidge extolling religious liberty, which they interpreted as a veiled attack on the Cardinal Klan. And when they were addressed by Boston's William Cardinal O'Connell, who "flung the challenge to those who would question the loyalty of Catholics to America," the "entire assemblage," waving small American flags, "rose to its feet spontaneously and cheered so enthusiastically that it temporarily halted the address . . ." The obscurity of the earlier march points to a gap in our knowledge of the cultural, ethnic, and religious conflicts of the 1920s that this chapter seeks to correct by examining the efforts of Catholics, Jews,

Japanese, and African Americans to define their position in society in the context of the decade's rampant nativism. As they articulated their vision of pluralism, leaders for these groups became representatives of a modern society in the process of sorting out the implications of religious, ethnic, and racial diversity.

For disparate groups of minority outsiders, the 1920s were a period of community building and definition vis-à-vis the mainstream, as many individuals sought to construct an "American" identity that did not entail abandoning their racial, ethnic, or religious distinctiveness. Both African Americans and Mexican immigrants became increasingly urban. War-generated opportunities helped to swell the numbers of rural African Americans in the South who headed to southern and especially northern cities. Almost half a million Mexicans, prompted in part by the disorder of the Mexican Revolution, and unaffected by immigration restriction legislation, migrated north during the decade. Despite the image of Mexicans as agricultural workers, in the 1920s almost half were urban dwellers who concentrated in the Southwest and to some extent the Midwest. For both groups, participation in the urban industrial order meant new opportunities, despite the persistence of racial discrimination and economic marginalization. It also meant significant cultural and social adjustments. Not the least of their problems was tension between "old settlers"—the native-born of Mexican descent and African Americans already established in the cities—and newcomers. In both cases, kinship networks, churches, newspapers, and voluntary associations made individual adjustment and the process of establishing new, expanded communities smoother. The food, religion, and music that African Americans brought with them contributed to a new version of a distinctive African American urban culture. At the same time that migrants established a strong sense of racial community and identity, their rising expectations and a growing middle class also heightened their desire to explore their relationship to the white mainstream and to achieve the rights of American citizenship. In the Mexican American case, shared language, culture, and discrimination, as well as the expectation of return migration, gave urban communities strong internal cohesion. Although many in

the small second generation and middle class were strongly attracted to mainstream American culture, the community as a
whole maintained deep attachments to and identification with
Mexico.

In contrast to Mexicans, for another immigrant group in the
West, the Japanese, the 1920s were not a period of expansion
but consolidation. Japanese immigration, although not officially
excluded until 1924, had been sharply curtailed by the 1908
Gentlemen's Agreement. The community thus remained small
and dependent on natural increase for its growth. Many families
had weathered the hardships of the first generation to achieve
modest financial gains, especially in agricultural production and
distribution. This was also a period in which the second generation began to enter high school and college. As they came into
adulthood, the children, who, unlike their parents, were citizens
and native English speakers, struggled with the issue of their
dual American and Japanese identity. But like Mexican immigrants, the Japanese community had few options which would
permit the integration that could vitiate strong ethnic identity.
Various forms of legal discrimination, as well as de facto racial
segregation, widespread on the West Coast, kept the Japanese
community turned inward; throughout the interwar years, its
members sustained a strong sense of their Japanese culture and
identity.

In the long run, the National Origins Act undoubtedly worked
to weaken strong European ethnic communities. The vitality of
the community depended in part on the constant infusion of
newcomers to sustain a strong culture. Over time, the absence
of new immigrants softened the edges of ethnic communities.
In addition, the nature of ethnic enclaves was being transformed
by the emergence of significant numbers of second and third
generations, whose ties to the old country were less profound
and whose education, language, and citizenship gave them an
American identity. And unlike the Japanese and Mexican second generation, their white skins made incorporation into the
mainstream more feasible. Nonetheless, there is strong evidence for a continuing ethnic identity. As Lizabeth Cohen has
demonstrated, in Chicago European immigrant communities,

shaped by ethnic stores, mutual-aid societies, and banks, resisted the encroachments of chain stores and other institutions of national culture. Similarly, in the early days of radio some stations broadcast "nationality hours" and others programmed for ethnic audiences; even movies were viewed in an ethnic setting, with neighborhood theaters including ethnic live entertainment and providing a meeting ground for the community.

Ethnic ties also transcended the boundaries of the old ethnic ghettos. The modest economic mobility of second-generation European immigrants led to movement out of the areas of first settlement. This dispersal did not necessarily mean a merging with mainstream America. Jews, for example, in part because of patterns of residential discrimination and in part by choice, congregated in new communities. Although upwardly mobile and ready to cast off the immigrant past, members of the second generation often sought to maintain their ethnic identity, which they reinforced by creating Americanized forms of traditional institutions. For other immigrant groups, relocation often meant shedding the congestion and harsh poverty of the immigrant ghetto, but not the sense of ethnic kinship.

As African Americans and immigrants and their children maintained and created distinctive cultures and communities, they were influenced by mainstream American culture, but were also contributing to its transformation. As we have seen, African Americans and immigrants influenced the contours of urban mass culture and leisure. The persistence of their ethnic and racial communities created the urban mosaic that would be a hallmark of modern America's cultural pluralism.

Demographic factors—migration and the maturation of second and third generations—were central to this refashioning of ethnic and racial identity. Ethnic leadership also played a significant role. Leaders of voluntary associations, politicians, and entrepreneurs had a vested interest in promoting strong group identity. Their success and status depended on it. At the same time, these same leaders often served as bridges to Americanization by interpreting mainstream society and institutions. Many who achieved middle-class status assiduously promoted "respectable behavior" that they felt would help win the group's legitimacy. As they gave speeches, wrote editorials, and stumped for votes, they articulated an ethnic or racial identity within the American mainstream.

As they defined their group's identity in the 1920s, they encountered the wall of nativism and racism described in the previous chapter. Attacks on their legitimacy led many leaders to redouble efforts to defend their rights and establish their "Americanness." The National Association for the Advancement of Colored People (NAACP), B'nai B'rith, the National Catholic Welfare Council, and other groups stepped up their activities. They lobbied local, state, and federal legislators to protest discriminatory laws and to promote those that would further their members' interests, and dispensed reams of literature that trumpeted their version of Americanism. In contrast to nativists, many minority groups insisted upon pluralism. They demonstrated their loyalty to American society, militantly expressed ethnic, religious, or racial pride, and insisted upon their right to all the benefits of citizenship. Nativists were correct in their perception that many minorities were "organized," but wrong in thinking that that represented a challenge to American institutions. On the contrary, they were trying to make a home for themselves within the system. There were exceptions, of course, but by and large leaders of most groups evinced a strong faith in liberal institutions and a belief that a diverse society could operate harmoniously and equitably if racism, anti-Semitism, and anti-Catholicism could be eliminated.

African Americans, Japanese, Catholics, and Jews were four groups subject to scurrilous attacks, targeted by the Klan, and with the exception of African Americans, affected by immigration restriction. To varying degrees they were victims of discrimination in jobs, housing, and education. And in varying degrees of militancy and organization, leaders among all four groups protested nativism and racism. The remainder of the chapter focuses on their efforts to counter prejudice and discrimination and to construct a dual identity that would give them legitimacy.

This emphasis should not obscure the fact that for many minorities their relationship to the mainstream was probably not a pressing concern. Ethnic "leaders" often represented a small

middle-class constituency, and even if democratically elected—
as fraternal order officials and politicians were—they did not
necessarily reflect the needs and aspirations of their respective groups. In contrast to an often self-selected leadership, for
poor, working-class people—which the vast majority of Catholics, Jews, African Americans, and Japanese were—making a living and maintaining their families were paramount. Since they
often lived in ethnic enclaves in which old-country ways or black
southern traditions persisted, they lived much of their lives in
isolation from old-stock Americans. Moreover, for many, the
most probable source of discord in their daily lives was not their
relationship to the mainstream but rather to other ethnic
groups, with whom they competed for jobs and housing. Thus
in Chicago recent immigrants resented black encroachment in
their neighborhoods and resisted with force and violence. In
New York, as historian Ronald Bayor has shown, there was persistent tension among the Irish, Jews, and Italians, a situation
that would escalate dramatically during the Depression. Conflict
also emerged within religious groups. Differences between Orthodox, Conservative, and Reform Jews were deep; many Italian
and Polish Catholics resented the domination of the church by
the Irish. Although minority groups shared a basis for complaint,
they did not have a shared consciousness.

Members of these communities thus lived with many tensions
and resentments that were largely divorced from the mainstream. Nonetheless, in the face of the structural changes in
their communities and the relentless nativism and racism of
the 1920s, many Catholics, Jews, African Americans, and Japanese had to come to grips with what W.E.B. Du Bois termed
"twoness":

One ever feels his twoness—an American, a Negro; two
souls, two thoughts, two unreconciled strivings; two warring
ideals in one dark body, whose dogged strength alone keeps
it from being torn asunder. The history of the American
Negro is the history of this strife—this longing to attain self-
conscious manhood, to merge his double self into a better
and truer self. In this merging he wishes neither of the older

selves to be lost. He would not Africanize America, for America has too much to teach the world and Africa. He would not bleach his Negro soul in a flood of white Americanism, for he knows the Negro blood has a message for the world. He simply wishes to make it possible for a man to be both a Negro and an American, without being cursed and spit upon by his fellows, without having the doors of Opportunity closed roughly in his face.

Although Du Bois was speaking of black Americans' dilemma, which slavery made unique, this eloquent statement of dual identity was appropriate for immigrant groups as well. It spoke to many men's and women's desire to participate in American society, while maintaining their racial, ethnic, or religious identity. It expressed a faith that one could be an American without losing an essential part of oneself, and moreover, that American democracy would benefit from diversity. There is no evidence to suggest that immigrant spokespersons were directly influenced by the ideas of Horace Kallen or Randolph Bourne, but like these leading proponents of cultural pluralism, ethnic leaders challenged the nativists, and in varying degrees, articulated religious, ethnic, and racial pluralism.

Within minority groups, pluralism was not without its complications. Individuals differed as to what balance there could or should be between group identity and American identity. This question could produce turmoil for the individual, but it also divided communities, and was often linked to other divisions as well. Generation served as an important determinant; first-generation immigrants were obviously more closely linked to the old country than their children were and far more likely to insist upon the preeminence of ethnic survival. Old settler/new settler conflicts often divided communities. Class was yet another factor in shaping response to mainstream society. Middle-class, upwardly mobile people, usually the second generation, were closest to the material promise of American life. With much at stake, they were the most likely to be on the side that embraced American identity most enthusiastically. Differences over the proper balance between "American" and group identity thus led to varying responses to the nativism of the

1920s and often led to group and institutional confrontations. My major concern, however, is to discuss those who protested nativism and racism most emphatically. Many differences surfaced between Catholics, Jews, blacks, and Japanese, but a common thread of ethnic pride and insistence upon their Americanism pervades much of the struggle to legitimate their place in a pluralistic society.

CATHOLICS, JEWS, AND JAPANESE

Catholics, Jews, and Japanese were all immigrant outsiders in a culture that celebrated its Anglo-Saxon Protestant origins: all grappled with the question of legitimacy and identity and insisted that group pride and distinctiveness were compatible with American institutions and culture. Members of these groups, like those in the mainstream, also turned to institutions for defense and power. These similarities justify considering them together, but their differences are instructive as well. The discrimination these three groups encountered followed a rough hierarchy. As a clearly defined racial group, the Japanese experienced the most. Catholics, particularly those of Northern and Western European descent, the least. There were also noticeable differences between institutional responses to nativism. Catholics had an advantage in that the hierarchical nature of their church permitted a well-organized defense. The Jewish community was characterized by a much greater diversity of leadership and institutions. Its organizational response was less unified, but nonetheless Jews were militant in their resistance to anti-Semitism. The Japanese response was constrained by their small numbers and the cautiousness their precarious position on the West Coast induced. These divergent patterns suggest not just the pluralism of modern American culture but the complexity of its ethnic and racial mix.

CATHOLICS

The postwar period witnessed a strong effort on the part of the Catholic hierarchy to minimize ethnic differences within the church and to promote a clear American Catholic identity. Prompted in part by a need to coordinate their war effort and demonstrate patriotism, the church leadership encouraged Americanization. This new direction was accompanied by a new organization of the hierarchy, the National Catholic Welfare Council (NCWC), which was established in 1919 to bring unity and national direction to American Catholicism. The NCWC's commitment to Americanization reflects several layers of anxiety concerning the high proportion of immigrants within the church. On one level, leaders hoped that their efforts would strengthen immigrant loyalty to the church by deflecting the appeals of radicalism and Protestant proselytizers. On another level, in the nationalistic climate of World War I and the Red Scare years, church leaders desired to demonstrate Catholic loyalty in order to defuse anti-Catholic sentiment. And, finally, as the rhetoric of those spokesmen eager to link Catholicism and Americanism indicates, many leaders were themselves infected with the nationalistic spirit that demanded conformity to American values. With these underlying concerns, the NCWC spearheaded programs for Catholic immigrants that would promote an understanding of good citizenship and its duties. One method was programs of education in English and citizenship, but the hierarchy also tried to phase out strong ethnic identity by decreeing an end to new national or ethnic (as opposed to geographical) parishes and encouraging the use of English in the parochial schools.

Not all Catholics agreed. With an estimated 85 percent of America's almost twenty million Catholics descended from immigrants who had arrived after 1820, the church in the 1920s was still an immigrant church whose ranks included Germans, Irish, Poles, Italians, Bohemians, Mexicans, and African Americans. Poles were among the most vociferous opponents of the new direction of the hierarchy, and struggled with some success to maintain an ethnic cast to their parishes, including the use of their native language in church and schools. They thus remained at odds with the hierarchy over the issue and maintained a degree of Polish identity and separatism.

Italians also remained somewhat apart from the Northern

European–dominated Catholic mainstream. American clergy had traditionally worried about the "Italian problem." They often took a condescending view of Italians as ignorant peasants, suspect because they came from a country with strong antipapal sentiments. But the major problem the Italians presented was "leakage"—or apostasy. Italian Catholics, while deeply religious, were often indifferent to the institutional church. Southern Italians' Catholicism, which included a blend of folk religion and superstition, was marked by festive street processions honoring saints and patrons. To them, the American church seemed cold and unappealing. Unlike Poles, they did not support church building programs or send their children in large numbers to parochial schools. But, like the Poles, they persisted in their own ways and hung on to national parishes during the 1920s.

Mexican immigrants faced somewhat similar problems. They, too, were less enamored of the institutional church and had religious customs that were significantly different from American Catholicism. When Mexican migration increased during the 1920s, the church responded by creating new national parishes for them, especially in the new areas of urban migration, Los Angeles and Chicago. The clergy opted for national parishes for Mexicans to ensure that they maintained their faith while the gradual process of Americanization took place. But Mexican separation was not altogether voluntary. Along with African Americans, Mexicans were subject to racism within the church, and in many communities they experienced de facto segregation.

Although ethnicity was a source of tension that segmented the church, there was one arena in which Catholics could unite. They all resented the resurgence of anti-Catholicism. The failure of the Democratic Party to condemn the Klan in 1924 created much dismay, as did the virulent anti-Catholicism of the campaigns against Al Smith in 1924 and 1928. Many Catholics resented the "Anglo-Saxon" Protestant bias of the immigration act of 1924 and considered it an insult to Catholic immigrants; more widespread was the sense that prohibition was anti-Catholic in intent, especially when some states attempted to proscribe sacramental wine. Other moral reforms, such as Sunday closing laws, were taken as evidence of bigotry, as were the sporadic attempts to eliminate Columbus Day as a holiday. Perhaps more upsetting to Catholics were the renewed efforts to regulate or eliminate parochial schools. Proposed state laws and the vigorous campaign to establish a federal department of education kept Catholics in a constant state of alarm about threats to their faith and challenges to their citizenship. In addition, Catholics often faced job discrimination. In the late nineteenth century "Irish Need Not Apply" signs were common. Discrimination had lessened, but in the 1920s Catholics still encountered hiring practices that excluded them. Teachers in the public schools in areas where Catholics were in the minority were especially vulnerable.

The group that was most militant in its campaign to counter the effects of anti-Catholicism was composed of the elite, the English-speaking "assimilated" Catholics who dominated church leadership.* Of Irish and Northern European descent, they were distancing themselves from the poverty and separatism of immigrant culture and seeking legitimacy within American society. For this group, the twenties mark the period of growing militancy, institutional and political power, and increasing group self-consciousness. While numerous factors contributed to this process, anti-Catholicism itself, by creating a need for unity, galvanized Catholics to organize to promote their vision of a pluralistic America in which Catholic faith and rights would be legitimated.

JEWS

Jews also challenged the pervasive drive for homogeneity by insisting on their rights. Concentrated in America's largest cities —New York in 1925 contained 40 percent of the 3.8 million Jews in the United States—Jews formed diverse, complex com-

---

* The term "assimilated" here refers to Milton Gordon's "behavioral assimilation," which is basically adapting to American cultural patterns, as opposed to "structural assimilation," which "refers to the entrance of the immigrants and their descendants into the social cliques, organizations, institutional activities, and general civic life of the receiving society."

munities. The most obvious cleavage among them was between old and new immigrants. By the 1880s, Jews from German-speaking countries had been in America long enough for many of them to achieve a striking degree of economic mobility. Most viewed themselves as thoroughly Americanized and embraced Reform Judaism, a self-consciously modernized form of Judaism that dispensed with many traditional laws and rituals. The late-nineteenth-century influx of Eastern European Jews transformed the Jewish community, especially in cities of high Jewish concentration such as Chicago and New York. They were far from homogeneous, as the hundreds of *landsmanshaft* congregations—synagogues that brought together people from the same European towns—attest. Although the Eastern European Jewish community was itself divided, the sharpest conflicts were with the earlier settlers, the German Jews. The Yiddish-speaking, Orthodox, working-class Eastern European Jews were contemptuous of the German Jews' sensitivity to the Gentile world and condemned both their Reform Judaism and their elitism. German Jews, for their part, were alarmed that the separatism and "foreignness" of the Eastern Europeans would bring all Jews into disfavor. Like the Catholic hierarchy, German Jews embarked on charitable activities and Americanization programs, both from a sense of communal responsibility and from anxiety about anti-Semitism.

More than the newcomers' foreignness troubled German Jews, however. Class conflict divided the two groups as working-class Eastern Europeans often found employment with German Jews. Some of the bitterest garment industry strikes in the early twentieth century pitted Jewish factory owners against Jewish workers. The new immigrants also included a rich variety of radicals—anarchists, bundists, and socialists of many stripes—who were at odds not only with each other but also with the Orthodox Judaism that most Eastern European Jews embraced. Radicalism was distressful to German Jews, many of whom were staunch Republicans who shared other prosperous Americans' horror of challenges to capitalism. Moreover, the radical taint of New York's Lower East Side contributed to anti-Semitism, and was thus all the more objectionable to German Jews. Still another disagreement among Jews emerged after 1917 when the British Balfour Declaration, which seemed to promise a Jewish state in Palestine, ignited hopes for a Jewish homeland. American Zionists were divided over ideology and tactics, but Zionism also set off bitter debates with non-Zionists. The division was roughly parallel to the old and new immigrant dividing line, since most Zionists were Eastern Europeans.

A final component in the complexity of the Jewish community was the emergence in the 1920s of a second generation of Eastern European Jews. As historian Deborah Dash Moore has shown, it was this group, along with relatively acculturated members of the first generation, who physically transformed the geography of Jewish New York. By the 1920s, the Jewish population of the Lower East Side had been diminished as Jews migrated to the outer boroughs of the Bronx and Brooklyn. This dispersal did not mean a merging with mainstream America. In part because of residential discrimination, in part out of choice, Jews congregated in new communities. The second generation, although upwardly mobile and ready to cast off their past, nonetheless often sought to maintain their ethnic identity. They were assisted by numerous leaders who helped to create Americanized forms of Jewish institutions. The existence of these Americanized Eastern European Jews eventually helped to soften the conflict between old and new Jews, but in the 1920s divisions were still apparent and they were reflected in the way in which Jews responded to anti-Semitism.

Jews were plagued with a variety of indications that American society viewed them as second-class citizens at best, and highly undesirable persons at worst. Discrimination in social and civic clubs, hotels, and resorts, which had first emerged in the 1870s, deepened in the 1920s. Housing continued to be a problem for Jews seeking residential mobility. College discrimination created yet another barrier. Aspirations for upward mobility, as well as the intellectual enthusiasm of second-generation Eastern European Jews, had led to exceptional rates of college attendance. By 1918–19, they were heavily enrolled in institutions located in cities with a substantial Jewish population. School administrators, faculty, and students, eager to maintain their Anglo-

Saxon Protestant elite cast, were hostile to what was popularly called an "invasion." They criticized Jews for being overzealous grinds, who not only engendered difficult competition but challenged the student culture's view of the nature of college life and behavior. In the 1920s, Harvard University and other private institutions primarily in New England and New York instituted a variety of admission rules that limited Jewish enrollments. The problem was also evident in postgraduate programs which limited Jews' admission to medical and law schools.

Those able to bypass institutional restrictions still met with economic discrimination. The corporate world was largely closed to Jews. Private professional practice was no solution. Doctors, for example, frequently had difficulty obtaining privileges in private hospitals. At the opposite end of the economic spectrum, Jewish newspapers frequently noted the discrimination faced by Jewish girls who tried to break into the rapidly expanding clerical market. But the problem went beyond young women. In the private sector, the non-Jewish white-collar workplace remained largely closed to Jews until after World War II.

Other challenges centered on the pervasive sentiment that Jews were racially inferior and generally unworthy to be Americans. The widespread attempts in the 1920s to introduce the Protestant Bible and religious instruction in the public schools, and to pass Sunday-closing laws, while not necessarily overtly anti-Semitic in intent, reminded Jews that America was a Protestant country. They were alarmed (as Catholics were) by these legislative campaigns that ignored the constitutional separation of church and state and discounted Jewish Americans. The drive to restrict immigration, accompanied as it was by racist insistence on "Nordic" supremacy and explicit anti-Semitism outraged Jews, as did the insults emanating from the Klan and the *Dearborn Independent.*

JAPANESE

In 1920, 111,000 Japanese lived in the United States, mostly on the West Coast. Two-thirds were in California. Their late-nineteenth-century pattern of immigration was similar to that of many other immigrant groups in that it consisted primarily of male "sojourners" who expected to work for a few years, save money, and then return to Japan. The 1908 gentleman's agreement severely limited immigration of laborers, but did enable wives of settlers to come to America. This exception produced the picture-bride phenomenon, whereby women in Japan married men by proxy. A shocking practice to Americans, it was in keeping with the Japanese tradition of arranged marriages. These marriages were part of a broader shift of permanent settlement on the part of Japanese immigrants: by 1910 there was a clear pattern of family formation and a transition from itinerant labor to farming. In the 1920s, the agricultural sector was the most significant for Japanese, followed by small retail establishments, often linked to agriculture, and then by personal service. From the poverty of early immigrant days, many had carved out a modest success, sustained by long hours of work by all members of the family and cooperative ventures organized by Japanese.

The Japanese immigrants lived in tightly knit ethnic communities, buttressed by a variety of institutional supports such as Japanese-language newspapers and a multitude of voluntary organizations, including trade associations, athletic clubs, religious institutions, and *kenjenkai*, associations based on prefecture origins. This network of associations, similar to other immigrant groups' organizational life, functioned to foster self-help, while maintaining ties with the old country and traditions. Most immigrant groups struggled to retain bonds with the old country, but the Japanese did so more intensely. Because of the naturalization act of 1790, which prohibited naturalization of immigrants who were not freeborn whites, the Issei, or first generation, could not become citizens. This status made it especially important to maintain links with Japan and its culture. It also made them nervous about their children's rights. Fearing that it might be necessary to return to Japan someday, they maintained dual citizenship for their children, the Nisei. In 1926, 84 percent of Nisei were registered in Japan; by 1940, the figure was still high at 50 percent.

As with all immigrant communities, there was tension between the second and the first generation. Both Issei and Nisei had an acute sense that a problem existed, that a gulf separated parent from child. Indeed, a common topic in Japanese periodicals was the "second-generation problem." Demographics exacerbated the generation gap. Issei parents began family formation relatively late in life, which resulted in a significant age disparity between generations. Moreover, because immigration was virtually halted in 1908, few young immigrants offset the growing gap between Issei and Nisei. Equally significant in creating a sense of generational difference was the fact that Nisei had the citizenship their parents were denied. Legal distinction took on heightened significance with the West Coast discriminatory laws against aliens ineligible for citizenship that forced the Issei to put property in the names of their children. Despite these generational tensions, Japanese communities remained tightly knit.

Communal solidarity was not altogether a matter of choice, however. Even more so than religion or ethnicity, race drew very tight boundaries. Japanese in West Coast cities paid high rents for substandard housing. Their move to better neighborhoods was stymied by informal housing restrictions that effectively excluded Japanese from "desirable" white neighborhoods. When they did buy into white communities they risked harassment and threats. Segregation extended to many public and private facilities: municipal golf courses in Los Angeles, for example, were closed to aliens ineligible for citizenship. Swimming pools were off-limits to Japanese, although the YMCA's policy permitted national groups to swim separately on designated days. In most rural areas there was de facto, and in a few cases legal, school segregation. The American Federation of Labor excluded the Japanese. And, as the Nisei were to discover as they pursued higher education, strict patterns of occupational discrimination kept even educated, Americanized Japanese from participating in most middle-class vocations.

Japanese experienced day-to-day discrimination, but there were also recurring periods of severe anti-Japanese agitation. The first serious crisis emerged over the 1906 San Francisco school segregation case. The gentlemen's agreement in 1908 by which Japan voluntarily agreed to limit emigration did not appease the rabid anti-Japanese agitators who next fastened on the alien land laws, which prohibited aliens ineligible for citizenship from owning land, as a means of containing the "yellow peril." California passed its first law in 1912 and strengthened it in 1920. Although many Japanese found loopholes, the legislation was nonetheless damaging and demoralizing. Other issues that ignited anti-Japanese sentiment included the picture-bride practice, which Japan stopped in 1921 in the face of mounting opposition, and Japanese-language schools, which were the subject of successful referendum campaigns that brought them under strict state regulation. And finally, the 1924 exclusion of Japanese provided the final insult to Japanese in America.

DEFINING IDENTITY AND
AMERICANISM

How did Catholics, Jews, and Japanese respond to the racism and nativism they encountered? Although the nature and intensity of discrimination varied for individuals, the perception of one man about Catholics, that "in some way or another we are all handicapped," applied to all three and often led to deep personal struggles over identity. This was particularly true for the second generation. Pulled by their parents toward the old country, they were nonetheless eager to be Americans, to cast off their immigrant roots. They were embarrassed by their parents' foreign ways and humiliated by the mainstream's refusal to accept them. In the face of this rejection, for example, some second-generation Eastern European Jews took the path of denying their Jewishness. The 1920s witnessed the first period in which many Jews began to anglicize their names to obscure their origins. Although it was impossible for the Japanese to cast aside what Robert Park called the "racial uniform," many Nisei tried to divorce themselves from their culture. At one point or another, most of the high school and college Nisei interviewed for a Stanford University Race Relations Survey in the mid-1920s expressed indifference to or rejection of their Japanese roots. Susie Yamamoto, who was so intent on learning American ways that she went to work for an American family against her mother's wishes, reported that she was often embarrassed by certain Japanese. "I have gone to [movie] shows quite frequently, but if I go with Japanese I want them to be well Americanized. I have been in groups with older Japanese but then people look at us and I feel uncomfortable."

Perhaps more common than an attempt to reject their ancestry was the second generation's dismay that they were not accepted by the mainstream nor could they share their parents' identity. In the Stanford interviews, Nisei children reported on generational conflicts in which they contrasted their American identity with that of their parents. Teru Miyamoto complained that her mother is "always fussing about something that I do." When her mother said that Japanese girls "don't do that," she replied, "But we are in America and we ought to have the American ideas and do as Americans do." Parents' desire that their children retain their Japanese identity conflicted with the Nisei desire to be "Americans." But if parents were part of their problem, the more severe dilemma was white America's rejection of Nisei. Citizenship was no protection against endemic discrimination. Often the situation led to a sense of having no clear identity. K.M., a Nisei girl, summed up the dilemma by invoking Philip Nolan, "the man without a country," explaining: "We can neither claim Japan nor America as a true fatherland. We are not Japanese in custom nor in education. We are not Americans in color." The bitterness of these young students stemmed in part from the depth of their belief in American ideology, especially those tenets of equality and democracy which so clearly did not operate in their case.

The meaning of American identity was repeatedly addressed by Catholic, Jewish, and Japanese leadership. The Catholic hierarchy, for example, insisted upon Americanization and tried to minimize ethnic identity. But while church leaders encouraged immigrants to learn English and embrace "American" principles, most chafed against programs designed to homogenize the culture in the image of Anglo-Saxon Protestantism. They insisted that society recognize immigrant contributions, and denied that immigrants could not make good Americans. Bishop

Joseph Schrembs of Toledo, addressing the Slovak Catholic Federation in 1921, offered a definition of American identity that often surfaced among his co-religionists: "National aspirations constitute Americanism. We are the blend of all the peoples of the world, and I think we are much the better for that. Americanism is not a matter of birth, Americanism is a matter of faith, of consecration to the ideals of America." Catholic leaders were accepting of ethnic differences as long as they did not hinder immigrants' commitment to their new country or their church. The major focus of the hierarchy in this period, however, was not ethnic defense, but rather Catholic rights. There was no institutional opposition, for example, to immigration restriction. The essence of the pluralism they promoted was the legitimacy of religious diversity.

Jewish leaders were divided over how much pluralism was compatible with Americanism. Many Reform German Jews tended toward a vision of Judaism as yet another denomination among diverse American religions. They were bothered by notions of a Jewish people or nation. Eagerly promoting Americanization for newer immigrants, they were critical of Yiddish as part of a ghetto culture that kept their co-religionists separate from America and encouraged anti-Semitism. The Reform newspaper *The Israelite*, in a 1922 definition of its general policy, rededicated itself to "advocating American Judaism as the religion for American Jews and Americanization in nationality and in all else. If we do not wish to be regarded as aliens, we must in habits and customs conform to those of the best people about us, whatever their faith, as far as we can without sacrificing any religious principle." Even more so than the Catholic hierarchy, most Reform Jews embraced religious pluralism exclusively.

But at the other end of the spectrum were those who celebrated Jewish cultural and ethnic distinctiveness and deeply resented demands for conformity. Many explicitly defended Yiddish and other aspects of immigrant culture, insisting that they were compatible with an American identity. A typical editorial in the *California Jewish Review* made an eloquent appeal for cultural pluralism, not just religious pluralism, when the author insisted that it is "most unreasonable to ask the Jews who possess a rich heritage of culture to disregard and forget it," and concluded:

> We may well attempt to legislate the hyphen out of existence, we may place a taboo upon our native culture, but nothing will be accomplished openly for the need and the yearning will still be there. . . . Judaism is one of the large ingredients in the mixture out of which shall come the American culture which will have all the finest elements of the oriental as well as the occidental.

Another important arena in which Jews insisted upon cultural pluralism was in the support for Zionism. For many Reform Jews, Zionism connoted the specter of dual loyalties, and they emphatically opposed it as un-American and conducive to anti-Semitism. But after World War I, various forms of Zionism became popular, not just among Eastern European Jews, who were its most devoted enthusiasts, but also among more Americanized Jews. Louis D. Brandeis, elevated to the Supreme Court in 1916, its first Jew, was perhaps the most important leader of American Zionism in the years following the Balfour Declaration, and provided American Jews with a vision of Zionism that was compatible with American identity. Historian Melvin Urofsky has argued that Brandeis was a quintessential progressive and his Zionism reflected his political and social ideology. He believed that when Jews built up Palestine as a Jewish homeland, they would also be furthering the ideals that Jews and the mainstream shared: "The highest Jewish ideals are essentially American in a very important particular. It is Democracy that Zionism represents. It is Social Justice which Zionism represents, and every bit of that is the American ideal of the twentieth century." Not all Zionists endorsed Brandeis' vision, and ideological and tactical divisions would lead to a major rift in the Zionist Organization of America in 1922. But Brandeis' explication of the link between Zionism and Americanism did make it easier for many Americanized Jews to support creating a Jewish state, and to insist that Jews could maintain their loyalty to a sense of Jewish peoplehood without in any way limiting their claims to be Americans.

The Japanese Issei, who because of the very young age of the Nisei, were virtually the only leaders in the West Coast Japanese community, also struggled with the problem of accommodating Japanese identity to American society. In the face of their insecure position, Issei leaders urged their countrymen to acculturate to mainstream society. While strongly encouraging the maintenance of Japanese ideals, language, and customs, they also promoted the idea of *gaimenteki doka*, or highly visible but limited acculturation. Historian Yuji Ichioka has observed that Issei leaders urged Japanese to adopt American clothing, homes, and holidays. They justified the adaptation by drawing upon traditional ideas about the family. In Japanese adoptions, "no matter how trying his situation, an adopted person was compelled to make himself acceptable to his new family." They must do the same in the United States, permitting their family (Japan) to "preserve its face in the international arena." But while the impetus to adapt to American society—at least in public—stemmed in part from Japanese cultural values, it also indicates a survival strategy. The Issei hoped that *gaimenteki doka* would defuse anti-Japanese sentiment.

A significant number of Issei leaders embraced this tactic as a means of coping with the hostility of mainstream society. In the tightly knit, well-organized Japanese communities, they attempted to use social pressure to coerce Japanese into acceptable behavior patterns. Leaders also were eager to demonstrate commitment to Americanization programs, a tactic also pursued by Catholics and Jews. Spearheaded during the enforced patriotism of the war years, the Americanization efforts usually operated under the auspices of the Japanese Associations. They offered English classes, translated pamphlets, and taught civics. In their approach to their language schools, the Japanese also indicated their willingness to Americanize. These schools began at the turn of the century and were designed to teach children the Japanese language and customs to in effect keep children Japanese, with the expectation that they would return to Japan. By 1911, however, the schools' focus began to shift. Issei leaders still believed that the schools were necessary to teach language and culture, but they also insisted that public school attendance was crucial. In part, the shift reflected a recognition that the Japanese were permanent settlers. Since their children would not be moving to Japan, they needed skills that would serve them in this country. In 1912 Kamada Masayoshi, for example, arguing that children should be trained to be citizens, explained that the schools could "produce individuals who will be able to stand up for the rights and privileges of the Japanese people among Americans."

Leaders of all three groups shared this insistence about privilege. Part of their justification for the pluralism they demanded was the contributions their people had made to America. But they also invoked a definition of Americanism that emphasized the political and social values of democracy, equality, and liberty. The latter, especially religious liberty, was a sacred element in the panoply of principles that Catholics and Jews enshrined. As one Knight of Columbus expressed it on the Fourth of July: "Catholics, perhaps more than any other group of people, realize the untold value of liberty and freedom—especially the liberty and freedom to practice their religion untrammeled by governmental interference." Reflecting their deep anxiety about the fate of refugees from Eastern Europe if the United States restricted immigration, Jews also defined Americanism to include the idea of a haven for the oppressed. Further, they inveighed against those spokesmen of Americanism who proposed immigration restriction, prohibition, and blue laws. Japanese spokesmen also challenged the mainstream to live up to its own ideals. Kiichi Kanzaki, general secretary of the Japanese Association of America, testifying before a U.S. congressional hearing held in California on Japanese immigration in 1921, lashed out at the hypocrisy of white Americans, urging them to "crush all barriers of prejudice, both social and racial," and demonstrate "genuine Americanism" by granting the Japanese "the full privilege of American citizenship."

Thus endorsing the nation's most cherished patriotic symbols, leaders turned the rhetoric of nativists on its head, insisting that it was they, not the superpatriots, who endorsed American principles and values. The Cincinnati *Israelite*, for example, approvingly recounted a particularly dramatic Klan confrontation in Far Rockaway, New York. At a ceremony to honor war dead, a gold star mother insisted that a wreath from the Klan "be removed because her son had not died for the tenets of its faith." When American Legionnaires attempted to remove the wreath, a scrimmage ensued. The wreath was removed and peace restored. But when Rabbi Isaac Landman began his speech, a young man interrupted him, shouting that his brother's name was on the monument and that he wanted the wreath put back. Landman's response was to point at the disrupter and exclaim:

> I tell you that neither your brother nor any of those other boys whom we honor today died that America should be torn by racial hatred and religious conflict. The very whisper of an Americanism judging its citizens by the place of their origin or by their affiliations is a desecration of these honored dead and of the flag which will daily float over their monument.

The audience cheered. Landman's comment summed up nicely what Catholic, Jewish, and Japanese leaders shared: the desire to widen the parameters of Americanism. Within limits, leaders urged accommodation to the mainstream. Catholics and Jews were similar to nativists in their nationalistic, unquestioning enthusiasm for American ideas, institutions, and history. Issei spokesmen encouraged adaptation to the main contours of the culture. But in important ways, leaders of these groups also represented a challenge. They opposed the assumptions of nativists that American society belonged exclusively to native-born white Protestants. As Rabbi Steven Wise expressed it: "Let us have an end of the spirit which limits the possession of America to any group of Americans." Taken together, these minority group leaders reflected an insistence that American society was based upon and strengthened by its ethnic, racial, and religious diversity.

It was one thing to articulate cultural pluralism and the rights of minority groups, another to implement them. Individuals were hard pressed to stake their claims, and their frustration sometimes led to sporadic acts of violence. An unnamed seventeen-year-old Nisei boy reported that he fought back when called "Jap": "To the countless kids whose noses I have punched, I will add, 'The pleasure was all mine.' " An oral history account by Leon Mark Raab gives insight into some Los Angeles Jews' tactics in literally fighting the Klan. Raab recalled that he and other members of his B'nai B'rith lodge met a group of Klansmen at Western and Slauson avenues. "Our gang was about eighteen to twenty in number and we went down with clubs." He reported that "we beat them within an inch of their lives. We accepted the challenge: they said we Jews only knew one thing, and that was not to fight. So we showed them we could fight, too." Scattered references in Catholic newspapers refer to "scuffles" between Catholics and anti-Catholic agitators, such as the one in which soldiers in Aberdeen, Maryland, threw eggs at a speaker who declared that "no Catholic could be a good citizen." Tragically, one Catholic died in a 1920 riot in Michigan touched off by an anti-Catholic lecturer who claimed that Catholic soldiers had been slackers. There were also numerous riots linked to Klan activity, including one in South Bend, Indiana, where a march to Klan headquarters by 500 anti-Klan demonstrators, mostly Notre Dame students, resulted in a riot.

CLAIMING AMERICANISM: THE INSTITUTIONAL RESPONSE

Grass-roots responses to prejudice and discrimination are hard to document, but minority leaders' activities are far more accessible. Like the nativists, minority group leaders turned to organizations to stake their claims as part of American society. Of the three groups, Catholics' response was the best-coordinated and reflected most clearly the ways in which American politics was being transformed by interest group agitation and the use of modern techniques to influence public opinion. In the words of Archbishop Michael Curley of Baltimore, Catholics recognized that "the watchword is organization." Implicit in such an analysis was a perception of a changing social order in which individual efforts could no longer be effective. An editorial in the *Brooklyn Tablet*, entitled simply "Organization," noted:

> Big business and secret societies have grasped this striking truth. Fanaticism, too, has put it to successful use. The Jews have just used it conclusively against a Mr. Ford. Must we, who ought to be first, be the last to see the light? Will intense parochialism and provincialism, good in them-selves—and perhaps good nationally before shining bands of steel and gleaming wires had made 110,000,000 people as one—hold us back much longer?

Reflecting both specific Catholic concerns and the broader so-ciety's organizational revolution, Catholic organizations prolif-erated in the 1920s. In addition to pursuing systematic anti-defamation activities, they turned to symbolic means to demonstrate their loyalty and their unity. Public parades and rallies in which Catholics sought to display their numerical strength and their patriotism became commonplace, as they physically asserted their right to American public space.

Many Catholic leaders felt it unwise to use the church or its voluntary associations openly in partisan politics because of pos-sible backlash, but they did attempt to marshal their organiza-tional strength to protect their rights. On the state level, for example, a variety of lay groups established legislative commit-tees to serve as lobbies in state legislatures. The major organi-zations, such as the Ancient Order of Hibernians, the German Central Union, the Catholic Federation of Charities, the Cath-olic Education Association, the Knights of Columbus, the Holy Name Society, embarked on letter-writing campaigns on issues concerning their church. Numerous groups lobbied Congress in behalf of Irish independence and against U.S. policy in Mexico, which was deemed sympathetic to anticlerical forces there. Catholic women's groups in particular challenged legislative pro-posals to ease restrictions on birth control and divorce. Although these issues were important, the major focus of Catholic polit-ical attention was to ensure their right to maintain parochial schools in the face of attacks on the state and national level.

These efforts at political agitation and organization are significant for understanding the dynamics of religious and political conflict in the 1920s. In effect, the fears stirred up by anti-Catholic agitators became a self-fulfilling prophecy. Convinced that Catholics were a dangerously well-organized force in American life, anti-Catholic groups campaigned against them, focusing especially on their educational system. This, in turn, led Catholics to exert a greater degree of organized political power, precisely the development that so terrified their opponents. Anti-Catholic agitation, in short, served to promote Catholic militancy and political activism. Nowhere is this ironic link between the dynamics of anti-Catholicism and enhanced Catholic organization more evident than in the formation of the permanent National Catholic Welfare Council in 1919.

In their studies of the NCWC, historians Elizabeth McKeown and Joseph McShane have noted that it represented "a profound new Catholic understanding of the exigencies of power in American life." With the hierarchy believing that their opponents were well organized, a key consideration in its establishment of the NCWC was the desire to counterorganize by setting up a national agency in Washington, D.C., to lobby on behalf of Catholic interests. Although many categories of legislation captured the attention of the NCWC, the most important and pressing were laws concerning education. The council kept watch on local legislation, especially the Oregon case (see Chapter V), as well as a similar referendum in Michigan, but its major concern was the 1920s campaign to establish a federal department of education.

What emerges most strikingly from the NCWC's activity in connection with the education bill is the way that Catholic officials were learning the ropes of lobbying in the nation's capital. Their efforts indicate that by 1919 Catholics were already influential and confident enough to risk a potential anti-Catholic backlash by establishing a national agency. Moreover, the way in which their tactics mirror other voluntary associations' lobbying efforts in this period also suggests the extent to which Catholics were becoming structurally integrated into American politics. Indeed, it indicates their political coming-of-age. They were not only arguing the case for religious pluralism, they were creating a national institution to implement it—an institution that still exists as the United States Catholic Conference, self-described as the "national-level action arm of the Catholic Church in the United States."

Jews, like Catholics, often called for "organization." Rabbi Leon Harrison of St. Louis, noting in 1922 that "every race is jealously guarding its own interests," insisted that Jews do the same. "And to fight effectively for justice, for complete democratic rights in this democratic land, you must organize, you must unite." Compared with Catholics, however, the enthusiasm for "organization" was slight. German Jews felt that open organization and agitation would just give credence to fantasies about the international, organized Jew. Another factor was that without a hierarchy to insist upon conformity and unity, there could be no Jewish version of the NCWC. And indeed, deep cleavages expressed in a variety of competing institutions kept Jews at odds with one another. Two major organizations that professed to speak for Jews in the United States were the American Jewish Committee and the American Jewish Congress. For many years Gentiles had accepted the American Jewish Committee as the representative Jewish institution. Founded in 1906, it was a self-appointed group of prominent, highly assimilated, mostly Reform Jews of New York City. Louis Marshall was their leading spokesman, but other important members included Cyrus Adler, Oscar Straus, and Julius Rosenwald. The American Jewish Committee was tireless in its efforts on behalf of European and American Jews. In its campaigns to promote antidiscrimination legislation and to fight immigration restriction, the committee for the most part exerted quiet, subtle pressure. Its successes stemmed from the individual prominence of its members, who included leading bankers and merchants, many of whom were influential in the Republican Party. Members of the American Jewish Committee, like most assimilated German Jews, abhorred political agitation and rarely turned to mass agitation. They were particularly horrified at the notion of a Jewish vote and repeatedly denied its existence.

Eastern European Jews who wanted a more representative

body to speak for American Jewry challenged the American Jewish Committee and formed the American Jewish Congress to offer a more inclusive, democratic organization. Founded in 1918, discontinued briefly and then reconstituted in 1920, the congress was never very strong in the 1920s. However, it limped along with Rabbi Stephen S. Wise as its leader, offering itself as an alternative to the American Jewish Committee and appealing primarily to Eastern European Jews with Zionist leanings. Its rhetoric was far more aggressive than that of the American Jewish Committee and it was far more likely to call for Jews to organize.

Another contender for the representative institution of Jews was B'nai B'rith. National in scope, with lodges throughout the country, it could claim far-flung membership. But B'nai B'rith was largely a middle-class organization that had only recently begun to admit Eastern European Jews to its ranks. Moreover, it had a strong midwestern bias, and its leaders were often in conflict with the New York–centered American Jewish Committee over methods and leadership, the institutional rivalry that permeated almost all of Jewish organizational life. But although Jewish organizations were not united, they nonetheless struggled to counter anti-Semitism by attacking Henry Ford's anti-Semitic *Dearborn Independent*, fighting immigration restriction, and opposing the Ku Klux Klan.

The bulk of anti-defamation efforts were undertaken by the Anti-Defamation League of B'nai B'rith. Most of the work was done through local correspondents, prominent men, who contacted individuals and institutions responsible for perpetuating negative images of Jews in the media and in public institutions. Not surprisingly, the attacks of the *Dearborn Independent* sparked a major campaign. On the local level, lodges sponsored good fellowship nights, to which the community was welcomed, and Gentile speakers joined Jews in condemning Ford. Although there is no way of knowing how much influence the Anti-Defamation League activities had on Gentiles, it is clear that they offered Jews an opportunity to vent their anger, express their communal identity, and assert the compatibility of Jewishness and Americanness.

The main thrust of antidefamation efforts was publicity and

persuasion, but other Jewish defense activity centered on lobbying. The most important legislative concern was immigration restriction, where divisions that existed among Jews surfaced with a vengeance. Many old-settler Jews actually favored some form of restriction because they feared the threat of the recent unassimilated immigrants. As Rabbi Marco Newmark put it, explaining why he favored immigration restriction as long as it did not single out Jews as a class: "There was no Jewish problem until the Jews came here in great numbers." With few exceptions, however, the Jewish press condemned the quota system, and many explicitly insisted that the proposed legislation was anti-Semitic. Acting for the American Jewish Committee, Louis Marshall used influential German Jews' position within the Republican Party to apply political pressure and appeared before congressional committees. Profoundly disturbed by the way in which other Jews and Jewish organizations made immigration restriction seem exclusively a Jewish issue, Marshall tried to keep protest firmly in the hands of the American Jewish Committee and attempted to discourage other organizations from appearing at congressional hearings.

Despite Marshall's objections, other Jewish organizations did protest. Many lodges and local organizations, such as the Sioux Falls chapter of Hadassah, a Zionist women's group, sent Congress resolutions of protest against the bill as un-American. Moreover, a variety of groups appeared at congressional hearings, including the American Jewish Congress and workers' organizations such as the United Hebrew Trades Association and the radical Workmen's Circle. Despite Marshall's fears, spokespersons for these organizations rarely referred to the specific threat immigration restriction had for Jews; rather they spoke of the problem as an American one, with the quota system being un-American in the way in which it discriminated against specific groups.

The divisions between conservative and more militant Jews also emerged in the protests against the Ku Klux Klan. The American Jewish Committee counseled caution. As Louis Marshall put it: "The moment that the Jews take the lead in fighting the Klan you may rest assured that the immediate effect will be to increase the numbers of the Klan." Marshall and Stephen

Wise, of the American Jewish Congress, locked horns on this issue when Wise repeatedly spoke out at Jewish mass meetings staged to demonstrate against the Klan. Jews held meetings such as the town forum sponsored by the *Jewish Tribune* in New York in 1924, where speakers condemned "Fordism, Nordism and Klanism" and urged the political parties to include planks in their platforms condemning the Klan.

The fight against the Klan also led to some political activism. Here, predictably, elite Jewish leaders, similar to Catholics, reiterated that Jews as a body should not become involved in partisan politics. Attempts to vote as a bloc would merely encourage anti-Semitism. Most Jewish newspapers agreed in theory that a "Jewish vote" did not and should not exist; nonetheless, the Klan's anti-Semitism led many to become embroiled in partisan issues. This was strikingly evident in the Detroit city elections of 1925, which were dominated by a Klan drive to control the city. Promoting J. W. Smith for mayor on an anti-Klan plank, the *Detroit Jewish Chronicle* ran editorials in support of him and featured numerous ads for Smith and other "Men Who Don't Wear Masks."

The Klan issue also led Jews to become involved in national campaigns. The elite German Jews had traditionally aligned with the Republican Party and several prominent Jews had attempted unsuccessfully to get a plank in the party's 1924 platform condemning the Klan. Marshall opposed this activity, but did join with other Jews in urging Coolidge (unsuccessfully) to condemn the Klan. Many Jewish newspapers were critical of their leaders for failing to extract concessions from the Republicans. Others criticized Coolidge, and endorsed either the Democrat John Davis or the Progressive Party's Robert La Follette because they condemned the Klan. This rejection of the Republican Party was not exclusively related to the Klan issue. Like other urban minorities, Eastern European Jews were shifting toward the Democratic Party in this period, attracted by the emerging urban liberalism personified by men like Al Smith. The controversy over the Klan was one more indication of the cleavage between the German Jewish leadership and Jews of Eastern European descent.

The divisions among Jews help to explain their failure to construct a united front, but their primary importance is that they illuminate the difficult choices facing minorities in American society as they struggled to strike a balance between accommodation to the mainstream and maintenance of ethnic identity. The divisions on the issue of anti-Semitism, however, should not be overstated. The protests of both groups may have had only minimal success, but they served an important function nonetheless. They provided Jews with an opportunity to express pride in their Jewishness while at the same time articulating their essential Americanness. German and Eastern European Jews were not very far apart in their desire to be American, although the latter were more eager to assert Jewish culture. When the process of Americanization was drawing the second generation away from its heritage, anti-Semitism, by forcing Jews to defend themselves, may ironically have assisted them in strengthening their Jewish identity.

In contrast to Jews and Catholics, the Japanese were in an unenviable position. Small in numbers, with few adults eligible to vote, their community had little power or influence. Issei leaders were indignant over prejudice and insistent upon Japanese rights, but their powerless position left them few opportunities for effective action. They were not passive, however. Like other minorities, they turned to organization in self-protection. The major institutional defense was through the Japanese Association, which had been founded in 1908. Its efforts took several directions, but its major thrust was to challenge laws that threatened Japanese rights. Turning to the courts, it focused on a crucial barrier, the naturalization law that denied Issei citizenship. In the face of the political climate, the Japanese recognized that a change in the federal law was unlikely, so they opted for testing it in court (they were unsuccessful). They also challenged the legality of the alien land laws. Two of the regional Japanese Associations took up the task of coordinating the attack, raising money, and hiring an attorney, Louis Marshall, whose concerns for minority rights went beyond Jews. But here again, legal approaches had limited success; the Supreme Court upheld the land laws and ruled that three of the strategies the Japanese had used to circumvent the laws were illegal.

Japanese viewed the 1924 act which excluded Japanese immigrants as highly insulting. Unlike the Jews, they did not organize protests against exclusion; there were no mass meetings or petitions. At committee hearings, few Japanese criticized the general notion of restricting immigration, while others applauded it, reflecting the belief that restriction would bring an end to anti-Japanese agitation that affected those already settled. But the Japanese were not altogether complacent. They used the hearings to protest discrimination against them, especially the inability of Issei to become naturalized citizens. They also criticized the racism of excluding Japanese immigrants rather than using the quota system applied to European immigrants.

By mid-decade, exclusion, coupled with the failure to overturn the alien land laws, had left the Japanese community shocked and demoralized. Not surprisingly, a 1925 poll of Issei indicated that few excluded the possibility of returning to Japan. In a 1924 interview conducted by the Stanford University Race Relations Survey, J. Hirai, Jr., a successful Hollywood nurseryman, explained: "I think maybe someday I will go back to Japan. . . . As long as I live here I abide by the American laws, the laws protect me, I pay the taxes, but then I am just a dog. You have no laws for dogs, do you? I like to live where I can be man with man. Here all I get is the money I make. I think someday I will go back to Japan." Relatively few Issei left, however. Instead, they persisted in a hostile environment, always fearful that new laws could impinge upon their fragile economic security and marginalize them still more. They turned still further inward, binding themselves to their ethnic communities, and placing their hopes for the future on their children.

At first glance it is surprising that the Nisei were not more active in defending their rights and insisting upon the validity of racial pluralism in American society. Throughout the 1920s there had been periodic attempts to establish defense organizations among Nisei. But despite the assault on Japanese rights in the early 1920s, these organizations met with little success, primarily because the Nisei were too young. As journalist Bill Hosokawa put it, teenage Nisei "were more preoccupied with baseball and church socials than their political obligations." By the end of the decade, however, some stirrings of Nisei activism emerged. James Yoshinori Sakamoto, founder of the Seattle *Japanese American Courier*, spearheaded the efforts to reinvigorate a defunct defense organization, the seattle Progressive Citizens League. Along with other cities' local organizations, it eventually affiliated with the National Japanese American Citizens League, which held its first convention in 1930. The founding of the JACL was marked by a telling dispute over the use of the name "Japanese" in the title of the organization, which was solved by allowing the local branches to decide for themselves whether or not to use the word "Japanese." That some Nisei were unwilling to include the descriptive adjective indicates the depth of the rejection of their Japanese roots. Once formed, the JACL did not pursue the political activism that people like Sakamoto hoped for, a realistic decision, given the small number of Japanese citizens on the West Coast. It did give some attention to continuing the legal battles that the Issei had begun, with a small measure of success. Its primary focus, however, was to counter the stigma of dual loyalty attached to the Nisei.

The JACL became a propaganda machine for demonstrating the superpatriotism of the Nisei. In its eager accommodation to mainstream America, the JACL was to some extent following the lead of Issei leaders whose strategy had been to demonstrate that the Japanese were assimilable. But most JACL leaders went beyond encouraging public forms of acculturation. Largely rejecting the Japanese language and customs, they insisted that they were American to the core. Their efforts to accommodate, which increased as the danger of war between the United States and Japan grew, were no more successful than their parents'. Up against deep-seated racism, with no political power, in 1942 after Pearl Harbor the Japanese were defenseless against the hysteria that led to the incarceration of 110,000 people of Japanese descent in American concentration camps.

The Japanese, as an immigrant group, had experiences that paralleled those of Catholics and Jews, and turned, albeit in limited ways, to organizations for defense. Like the others, the Japanese also struggled over identity. The Nisei especially had a clear sense that legitimacy, to use Werner Sollors's terminology, stemmed not from descent, but from consent. They defined

American identity in terms of contributions and allegiance to society, freely and gladly offered. But race and racism, and the issues of descent, were major factors that distinguished the Japanese situation. The challenges they faced were far more institutionalized and endemic, and their access to means of redressing their rights more limited. In this, their experience paralleled that of African Americans more than other immigrant groups.

AFRICAN AMERICANS

As Protestant, native-born citizens and English speakers, African Americans differed significantly from immigrants. But racism, which canceled the potential benefits of their American birth, placed them in a separate social and economic category. Certainly African Americans shared with the Japanese the impact of pervasive and institutionalized racism. In contrast to the Japanese, however, African Americans' ancestors had been involuntary migrants, slaves. The legacy of slavery—the caste system that kept African Americans in subordinate economic and social positions both North and South—made them an especially disadvantaged group, with limited mobility and opportunity. But however great the differences between immigrants and African Americans there were also parallels. Like immigrants, African Americans faced the problem of twoness—how to achieve their legitimate rights without denying their roots, their race. And, like other groups, African Americans differed in their approach to white society. Although there were many nuances, the sharpest dividing line was one of class, with the elite African Americans being far more eager to carve out a place within the existing mainstream. But while African Americans were divided, they shared rising expectations and heightened militancy that led black observers in the postwar years to celebrate the "New Negro."

One recent historian of black urban America called a chapter on the 1920s "Progress and Poverty," a fitting title. Certainly most African Americans continued to be at the bottom of the economic ladder and the circumstances of southern blacks were truly abysmal. Despite the hardships, for urban blacks the decade began with a sense of excitement about the possibilities for a better life and fuller participation in American society. Their hopes were tied to the recognition that World War I and the mass migration of southern blacks to northern cities had brought about tremendous changes for black America.

When the United States entered the war, most black leaders —ministers, newspaper editors, and organization officials— viewed the conflict as an opportunity for African Americans to prove their loyalty and establish their claims to equity. Many African Americans were eager to display their support for the war. They contributed to conservation programs and Liberty Bond drives, and served far out of proportion to their numbers in the military. Those who supported the war were influenced not just by Woodrow Wilson's rhetoric of a war to preserve democracy but also by their community leaders, who believed that African Americans' wartime service would further their struggle to win their rights. But African Americans soon found that they had to fight even for the right to serve. They were frustrated not only by the segregation of black troops but also by the lack of African American officers and by the military's unwillingness to use blacks in combat. Organizations like the National Association for the Advancement of Colored People scored minor successes: some black squadrons did see combat and acquitted themselves spectacularly, and there was a black officers' training program. Despite the fact that their treatment during the war was for the most part disillusioning, as it ended African Americans still were optimistic that by virtue of the strength gained by fighting, they would be better able to demand equal citizenship.

Rising expectations also stemmed from migration. In 1914, the vast majority of African Americans still lived in poverty in the rural South. Migration to southern and northern cities began before World War I, but the war years turned the trickle into a flood. During the years 1916–18, 450,000 African Americans streamed into Chicago, New York, Pittsburgh, and other cities. The migration subsided briefly and then continued into the 1920s, when 750,000 made the trek north. This was part of a national rural-to-urban pattern in the early twentieth century. Some African Americans migrated because of a desire to leave the South. The years 1914 and 1915 were particularly bad, as crops were ruined by boll weevils and floods, natural disasters that exacerbated an already fragile economic situation. Blacks in the South were tenants and sharecroppers, easily exploited by white landlords. They were subject to peonage, the chain gang, lynching, and Jim Crow. In 1918 alone 63 African Americans had been lynched.

But it was not the push of the South so much as the pull of the North that explains the timing and the volume of the great migration. For during the war years, the North held out the promise of jobs. The war had cut into the supply of factory workers by shutting down immigration and drawing off workers for military service. A decreasing worker pool in the midst of increased war orders gave employers reason to look to a source of domestic labor they had not tapped—southern African Americans. Some firms sent agents to the South to promote migration. But southern African Americans also found out about opportunities up north through word of mouth and through northern black newspapers like the *Chicago Defender*. Beyond economic opportunity, African Americans also hoped that the North would bring them and their children better education and a more decent life.

With these hopes, African Americans moved north. Migration and resettlement were disorienting and disruptive; migrants had to find jobs and housing, get used to an urban economy, and adapt to the demands of modern industry. The process was made easier for many because of the patterns of chain migration, by which one member of the family left first to prepare the way for others to follow. Migration clubs sprang up and led to whole communities moving together. These internal migrants re-created their communities in cities, forming their own churches, buying southern-style food, listening to blues performers sing songs about migration, and patronizing businesses run by their former neighbors. Thus they combined the comfort of the familiar with the excitement of the new possibilities urban life promised.

The Urban League, with branches in all the major migrant cities, tried to help migrants adjust to their new environment. Primarily a black organization, financed by white philanthropists and corporations, it sought to assist the newcomers with housing and employment. But it also tried to assimilate migrants to northern middle-class culture, and in doing so it revealed a rift in the new black communities. As with the German Jews, these old settlers were sympathetic to the plight of migrants fleeing the South, but they were also embarrassed by them. They considered them uneducated peasants whose uncouth ways were likely to damage the precarious status of those African Americans already established in the North.

Tensions within the black community aside, most African Americans expected that in the long term the migration would prove beneficial. The burgeoning black population in northern cities had led to the growth of a middle class which seemed to represent the potential of the race. Industrial jobs offered mobility for the rest of the black population. But the war's end brought changes: African Americans were laid off when whites returned. And since they were at the bottom of the industrial ladder, they were most hurt by the depression of 1920–21; for the rest of the decade in most cities, black employment was precarious and opportunities limited. The dirtiest, hardest industrial jobs were the ones African Americans could obtain. Women were excluded from the industrial workforce almost completely and were left with the "traditional" job of domestic service. The majority of unions were hostile and tolerated black organization only when it helped white workers. African Americans' participation as strikebreakers—often the only jobs open to them—intensified animosity.

Economic problems were compounded by a housing crisis. In most cities, there was severe housing pressure, which was especially acute for the migrating African Americans, who were forced into a black belt where rents were exorbitant and neighborhoods severely overcrowded. African Americans who attempted to buy in white areas were subject to harassment and violence. In Chicago in 1919 their houses were routinely bombed, with much of the violence coming from white ethnic groups, resentful of black encroachment and eager to protect their status as white. Escape from Jim Crow also proved illusory. De facto residential segregation, bolstered by housing covenants, was standard. Schools might be legally integrated, but neighborhood segregation led to schools being heavily black, and these schools tended to be in crowded, older buildings where blacks received a poorer education. And in the twenties, northern cities saw other forms of discrimination tighten up as restaurants, theaters, and swimming pools excluded African Americans.

With all these shortcomings, the North was still undoubtedly better than the South, with its peonage and lynching. At least in the North, African Americans could escape the day-to-day monitoring of their lives and create a vibrant cultural life in the cities. That the North seemed better than the South was shown by the continuation of migration throughout the twenties, even though jobs in the North had dried up and the black press had stopped encouraging Southerners to head North. Urban migrants experienced tremendous hardship, but many still felt they had made the right decision.

In the long term, African Americans would recognize the limits to the promise of the North, but they also had more immediate evidence that their expectation that war service and migration might bring significant change was flawed. The year 1919 proved to be a brutal one. The numbers of lynchings in the South were up—eleven men were burned at the stake—and in the North cities exploded in race riots. In 1917, East St. Louis had been the scene of a bitter and destructive riot that killed forty African Americans. What was striking about 1919 was that violence broke out in several cities within a short period of time. Chicago had the major one, but riots also erupted in Knoxville, Omaha, Washington, D.C., Longview, Texas, and other cities. Each riot had its own etiology, but the roots of conflict were in white denial of rising black expectations. Thus, in Chicago whites resented black competition for jobs, their encroachment into white neighborhoods, and their political influence—tensions that were ignited over the murder of a black youth who had drifted while swimming into the white section of Lake Michigan.

THE "NEW NEGRO"

Although the riots were usually begun by white mobs that invaded black sections of a city, they were also characterized by black resistance. African Americans took the battle into white areas and fought back, a significant departure from nineteenth-century urban riots. Observers did not have far to look to explain the new spirit of resistance. They attributed it to the war experience and the exodus from the South. Black newspapers and magazines delighted in the sense of the new militancy. The *Kansas City Call*, for example, divined a lesson from the recent riots:

> That the Negro MEANS to be as merciless in repelling attacks upon him as the attackers. THE NEW NEGRO, unlike the old time Negro, "does not fear the face of clay," and the white man will learn in time that he has in this new type of Negro a foeman worthy of his steel. The time for cringeing [sic] is over. If we are driven to defend our lives, our homes, our rights either by responsible or irresponsible mobs, let us do it MAN FASHION.

This notion of the New Negro appeared repeatedly and implied a rejection of the "Old Negro," which entailed casting off stereotypical images of the accommodating Uncle Tom and the nurturing mammy. It also meant a rejection of the ideas of Booker T. Washington, the former slave who became principal of Tuskegee Institute and the undisputed leader of black America in the late nineteenth century. His message to African Americans was to be patient, to accept, at least temporarily, segregation and disenfranchisement. Before seeking these goals, they must prove their worth through concentrating on economic self-help and self-improvement. When preaching his gospel of self-help, he also minimized the extent and impact of racial discrimination on African Americans. His attitude of counseling patience and moderation won him the ear of white philanthropists and southern leaders who found his language of accommodation reassuring. Acknowledged as a leader by both blacks and whites, he had immense patronage and power that was particularly evident in his ability to influence black public appointments and philanthropy.

Challenges to Washington's leadership and ideas began to surface after the turn of the century. Foremost among his critics was W.E.B. Du Bois. The Harvard-educated Du Bois was dismayed by Washington's exclusive emphasis on manual training, a tendency he felt would keep African Americans in their place at the bottom of American society. He called instead for the creation of a talented tenth—an educated elite—who would pursue a liberal arts education and would form the basis for racial uplift. There was more at stake than pedagogical differences here. Du Bois insisted that African Americans had the capabilities to be educated, and moreover, to be equal citizens. Thus he decried Washington's apparent willingness to acquiesce passively in discrimination and disenfranchisement. In 1905, Du Bois implemented the first organized challenge to Washington by spearheading the Niagara Movement, an all-black effort that called for vigorous assertion of black rights.

The conflict between Du Bois and Booker T. Washington divided African American leadership for over a decade. Washington's death in 1915 softened the edges of the controversy somewhat, and by the end of the war Du Bois sympathizers were in the ascendant. But while there were both rising expectations and militancy in the postwar years, African Americans were not of a single mind in their approach to the problems they encountered in white-dominated America. There was not just one New Negro, but many.

The Harlem Renaissance discussed in Chapter IV was the intellectual version of the New Negro. In their insistence on racial pride and distinctiveness, writers and artists served as powerful militant voices. A key institutional vehicle for the New Negro was the National Association for the Advancement of Colored People, the major African American defense organization, which white and black reformers had founded in 1910 to promote equal rights. From the beginning, the NAACP concentrated on a legalistic approach of lobbying and protest through the courts. Before the war it was a small, northern-based organization. Not surprisingly, the war years brought heightened activity and membership. In 1919 the organization boasted 310 branches with 91,203 members, in contrast to 1917, with 80 branches and 9,282 members. And, significantly, the expansion included southern cities, which like the North witnessed a surge of militancy in this period. By 1919, there were more southern members than northern. Besides expanded membership, the early postwar years saw a shift to predominantly black leadership, marked by James Weldon Johnson's 1920 appointment as the first Field Secretary. White philanthropy continued to be important to the organization, but with 90 percent of the membership black, a significant proportion of its contributions came from African Americans.

NAACP members came from an elite middle- and upper-class group that was educated and prosperous, yet excluded from the privileges their attainments called for. Their marginal status made them especially sensitive to discrimination and inequality. Thus much of the institution's focus was on fighting discrimination in housing, schools, and transportation. In the North, this meant struggling against the increasing trend toward legal and de facto segregation. In the South, the new militancy had to be tempered by the realities of race relations. In 1919 in Charleston, South Carolina, for example, the newly founded NAACP began a well-coordinated plan to get black teachers hired in black schools in that city. Their work, including a petition signed by 5,000 African Americans, was successful. Southern tactics were to eke out better conditions within the segregated South. These early efforts usually met with white backlash, and by the end of decade the organization's membership in the South had fallen off and militancy, such as it was, largely stilled.

While struggling with segregation, the NAACP also tackled a major problem of southern African Americans—disenfranchisement. Black leaders were hopeful about the potential of black votes for improving African Americans' circumstances. They urged northern African Americans to vote independently, to insist upon candidates who would be responsive to them in their struggle to fight Jim Crow and other forms of discrimination. This enthusiasm for the franchise never led the NAACP to organize the black urban electorate, however. And even if it had sought such political organization, the black electorate's unwavering loyalty to the party of Lincoln made it unlikely that African Americans could rally behind a third party or have significant clout within the Democratic or Republican Party. Instead of attempting to organize the votes of northern African Americans, the NAACP used the courts to challenge disenfranchisement in the South. It achieved a major victory when the case it supported that challenged the southern states' use of the grandfather clause, which limited suffrage to men whose grandfathers could vote, was favorably decided by the Supreme Court in 1915. After this success, the NAACP began a campaign to break down the white primary system, which effectively excluded African Americans from a voice in the solid Democratic South. Begun in 1923, the battle against the white primary would not succeed until the 1940s.

The means that the NAACP used to challenge discrimination was reflective of its members' status. As Nancy Weiss has shown, its efforts exhibited the hallmarks of the progressive movement. It used careful investigations and publicity, similar to the muckrakers' approach, to expose an evil. And it tried legal tinkering—court cases and expanded suffrage—to achieve democracy. As Du Bois put it in 1920: "The NAACP is a union of American citizens of all colors and races who believe that Democracy in America is a failure if it proscribes Negroes, as such, politically, economically, or socially." The black leaders in the NAACP, like progressives, clearly believed in the promise of American life, in the system, and wanted to expand that promise to African Americans.

Because of its elite membership and focus on legal issues, some historians have criticized the bourgeois nature of the NAACP. There is no question that its members were far from the poor, ill-educated blacks. But although they did not specifically tackle the economic problems of the black masses, they were hardly indifferent to them. One of their most persistently pursued goals was to end lynching. The anti-lynching campaign had begun in the late nineteenth century when Ida B. Wells and later the National Association of Colored Women relentlessly agitated against the gruesome practice. After the war women worked primarily within the male-led NAACP campaign, which included careful investigation and documentation of reported lynchings. A major concern was to prove with statistical evidence that rape of white women was rarely the incident that sparked lynching. The organization distributed reams of publicity on lynching to the press, chambers of commerce, and government officers. In addition to arousing public sentiment, it sought legal redress as well: a federal anti-lynching law. In 1920, it obtained an antilynching plank from the Republican Party, and in 1922, the House, by a vote of 230–119, passed the Dyer bill, which would fine counties in which lynching occurred, with some of the proceeds to go to the victim's survivors. Although the bill was defeated in the Senate, the NAACP lobbied continually throughout the 1920s and 1930s for its passage. The legal campaign was unsuccessful, but the NAACP did take credit for the decline in lynching after their campaign began.

By the end of the decade, the NAACP could list few concrete accomplishments in its legal battle for civil rights. That the militancy and optimism which had opened the twenties had been dissipated was reflected in serious membership loss. By 1930, it could claim only 30,000 members. But even at the height of its strength in the early 1920s, when the organization had more than 90,000 members, its membership had rested on a narrow base. Although sympathetic to the black masses, the NAACP held aloof from them and made no concerted attempt to organize them. Moreover, although the NAACP provides a prime example of middle-class African Americans' vision of how to deal with the race problem, it was not the only one. The middle class itself was far from uniform in its thinking. Many middle-class African Americans focused on the economic frontier and, along with their newspapers, promoted the idea of black business. They called for racial solidarity and economic self-help, which often translated into a campaign to "buy black." This emphasis on boosting African American business occasionally led to conflict. In Milwaukee, the NAACP split into two branches, with one wishing to use the organization "to protect and enhance the local interests of the expanding business and professional elite" and the other seeking to pursue the more traditional NAACP program. Middle-class African Americans in the North also divided over whether or not to support separate black institutions, for the jobs they offered and the services they provided. While the NAACP was fighting the encroachment of legalized segregation, other African American leaders were supporting segregated institutions because social services were so desperately needed that they believed all-black facilities, even unequal ones, were better than none at all.

Black students and educators represent another elite who chose to express the New Negro spirit. A series of conflicts emerged during the 1920s in all-black colleges and universities between the administration on the one hand and students and faculty on the other. Black faculty at Fisk and Howard, for example, criticized a white administration that was too accommodating to white philanthropists. They also called for curricular changes that included courses in what we would now call black studies. Faculty were also exercised over the issue of academic standards. They wanted to phase out the emphasis on industrial training that still existed in numerous institutions, but they met resistance from administrations sensitive to white criticism of how colleges were educating African Americans above their station.

While black faculty were chafing against white presidents and trustees, students complained about ROTC, compulsory chapel, curfews, and dress and behavior codes. At first glance, their complaints seem indistinguishable from the controversies that galvanized white students at the same time: there was a general push for greater personal freedom on campuses throughout the country. But black students, especially in places like Fisk where the behavior code was exceptionally rigid, interpreted the stringent moral rules as an indication that administrators viewed them as untrustworthy and racially inferior. Students at Fisk, Howard, and Hampton also protested the tradition of students singing spirituals and plantation melodies to segregated audiences. Their discontent often led to student strikes, which leaders interpreted as part of a broader movement of blacks away from a submissive past. The strikes, in conjunction with faculty protests, led to changes that helped to mold African American institutions of higher learning to reflect the model of the "New Negro."

The voices of the Harlem Renaissance, the NAACP, students and professors, and other middle-class African Americans were the voices of rising expectation. They reflected the hope that twoness could be resolved—that they could be both American and black, without sacrificing either. In the struggle to achieve that goal, the black middle classes were militant in their rhetoric about defending their rights, but their militancy was tempered by their class position. They protested, but their protest, accompanied by a degree of accommodation, remained firmly within the system.

RADICAL ''NEW NEGROES'':
A. PHILIP RANDOLPH AND MARCUS GARVEY

Other black voices speaking more directly to and for the masses of poor African Americans channeled their protests outside the system. During and immediately after the war years there was a small but significant group of socialist and communist African Americans who offered a far more militant vision of the New Negro. Among the most radical was Cyril Briggs, who edited *The Crusader* and in 1917 founded the African Blood Brotherhood, a communist-oriented organization determined to forge a link between the liberation of Africa and the liberation of African Americans. The best-known radical of this period was socialist A. Philip Randolph, who along with Chandler Owen edited *The Messenger*, which they subtitled "The Only Radical Negro Magazine in America." A militant proponent of the New Negro's resistance to white domination, Randolph was highly critical of W.E.B. Du Bois and the NAACP, which he characterized as a bourgeois institution, far too eager to curry black acceptance by white America. Randolph criticized the

NAACP's focus on legal tactics in defense of African Americans, especially its campaign for an antilynching law. For Randolph, the long-range remedy to problems like lynching was socialism, and the short-term solution unionization. Initially he supported radical unions such as the IWW and castigated the conservative AFL. His radicalism was evident in his notion that organized black workers could paralyze industry through general strikes, and thus achieve redress from racial injustices. But with time, Randolph tempered his beliefs. The magazine began printing stories boosting black business and glorifying the black businessman, and Randolph also sought to work with the AFL. A student of the history of *The Messenger* insists that Randolph remained a socialist, but that the extraordinary impediments to reaching blacks with the socialist message of class consciousness or even of unionization led him to a more moderate stance.

The 1920s were an especially inhospitable time for black radicalism. After 1919, organized conservative labor was in disarray, and radical labor largely crushed. The American Federation of Labor continued its long-standing unwillingness to organize African Americans, which encouraged black workers' hostility to unions and a willingness to break strikes. Many of their leaders endorsed black resistance to unions. They defended strikebreaking as legitimate: with jobs hard to get and no support from racist unions, why show solidarity with white workers? Randolph discovered the barriers to unionization firsthand when he began to organize the Brotherhood of Sleeping Car Porters in 1925. The AFL refused to give the union a charter until 1936, and he not only had a long struggle with the Pullman Company over recognition of the union, but also had to fight indifference on the part of black porters and hostility from much of the black press. In the long term, the BSCP became a successful union. But neither socialism nor unions were a significant vehicle for African American militancy in this decade, for race consciousness preceded class consciousness. Although few rallied around socialism, this did not signify contentment with the system, for the masses responded enthusiastically to Marcus Garvey, who mounted a challenge to both mainstream America and more conservative African American leaders in the 1920s.

Of all the efforts to organize African Americans in the 1920s, only one was successful in capturing the imagination of large numbers. No one knows for sure how many members Marcus Garvey's Universal Negro Improvement Association enrolled. Garvey's claim of four million was undoubtedly exaggerated. But the 25,000 people who turned out in Madison Square Garden to hear Garvey speak as part of his 1920 UNIA convention indicated that the organization clearly had tremendous appeal. It was an international organization, with members in Garvey's homeland Jamaica and elsewhere, but the bulk of Garvey's support was American. Although hostile observers at the time claimed that Garvey appealed only to the most ignorant, unskilled blacks, historian Judith Stein has indicated that the Garvey message also attracted skilled workers and some businessmen in branches in cities all over the country, North and South. It became the largest mass movement of African Americans to date.

On the surface, the UNIA was another black fraternal organization with all the usual accoutrements of exotic titles and impressive uniforms and ceremonies. Like many other fraternal orders, the UNIA offered insurance and death benefits. It also had a woman's auxiliary, which helped to spread the appeal of the UNIA and provided a significant avenue of influence for women. Part of the attraction of the organization, then, was its familiar context of fraternalism, which had an established appeal in the African American community.

But despite its traditional format, the UNIA had a radical message of militant black pride and nationalism that was at the heart of its attraction for the black masses. An integral part of Garvey's insistence on racial pride was his glorification of the African past. He repeatedly reminded blacks that Africa had a powerful and cultured civilization that predated European development:

> When Europe was inhabited by a race of cannibals, a race of savages, naked men, heathens and pagans, Africa was peopled with a race of cultured black men, who were masters in art, science and literature; men who were cultured

and refined; men, who, it was said, were like the gods. . . .
Black men, you were once great; you shall be great again.
Lose not courage, lose not faith, go forward. The thing to
do is get organized.

More than symbolizing blacks' proud past, Africa represented
the hope of the future. Garvey, in contrast to leaders like Du
Bois, was profoundly cynical about white American society: "Political, social and industrial America will never become so con-
verted as to be willing to share up equitably between black and
white." He placed no hopes in the campaigns against discrimination and segregation, and indeed often criticized civil rights
leaders for wanting to be white. And not until after the UNIA
had ceased to be a vital institution did Garvey try to organize
blacks as voters within the American political system. Rather
than seek any form of integration, he placed his hope on the
potential political power of blacks in Africa. Despite the popular
terminology of "back to Africa," the UNIA did not encourage
a massive return to the homeland. Although Garvey anticipated
some migration, he concentrated on the idea that a strong African empire, freed of colonial rule, would be the protector of
blacks throughout the world. Conscious of the efforts of Irish
nationalists and Zionists, he envisioned the UNIA as the agency
of national liberation and planned not only to free Africa from
colonial rule but to bring it forward into the twentieth century
with American know-how. As Robert Hill has noted, the separatism of Garvey's black nationalism did not totally reject
Western civilization. He expected to fashion the new Africa on
Western models, to create a parallel civilization: "There are
more than two hundred million Negroes in Africa with a continent that is large and resourceful. Let him build there, let him
build his own nations, let him build his own civilization, let him
show the world a duplicate in Africa of what exist[s] in Europe."
   Political power through Africa was only part of Garvey's plan.
Through his Black Star Navigation Line and his Negro Factories
Corporation he planned to fashion a separate black economic
infrastructure. Here, too, his belief that African Americans
could expect nothing of whites led him to argue that they must

create their own institutions. The UNIA's Negro Factories Corporation succeeded in establishing several enterprises, such as a restaurant, a millinery store, a tailor shop, a chain of cooperative stores, and a publishing house. Far more visible was the Black Star Line. Established in 1919, over a period of three years the line bought four ships, with each purchase accompanied by tremendous publicity, which helped it to sell 155,510 shares to 40,000 people and bring in three-quarters of a million dollars. But 1919 proved an inauspicious time to start a shipping line. A highly competitive and difficult industry, it required more capital and experience than the UNIA possessed. Another type of investment might have been wiser, but a shipping line had tremendous symbolic value: ships were traditionally associated with national power, and the idea that these ships would be part of a broad program of establishing black power and pride added to the excitement the project generated. Despite African Americans' enthusiasm for the venture, the Black Star Line failed dismally. All of the ships bought were unwise purchases; the inexperienced UNIA was duped by shipowners; incompetence and even malfeasance within the organization further plagued the line. By 1922, it had suspended operations and Garvey had been indicted for mail fraud. Meanwhile, Garvey's negotiations with Liberia had faltered and many leaders had deserted the UNIA.

Other factors contributed to a general decline in the UNIA. One was a shift in Garvey's tactics. By 1921, Garvey's cynicism about black opportunity in white America had deepened, and he began to emphasize not just racial pride but also racial purity and a strict separation between blacks and whites. Following the logic of this, he began to seek white supremacists' assistance in backing the activities of the UNIA. He frequently expressed open admiration for white racists because of their honesty and lack of hypocrisy, and for this reason he refused to condemn the Klan. Viewing Klansmen as no worse than other whites, Garvey was apparently willing to work with them, and in 1922 he went to Atlanta to meet with KKK Imperial Giant Edward Young Clarke, presumably to find out if he could get support for UNIA plans from the Klan.

The Klan meeting was a tactical mistake, for it brought down a shower of criticism from the black press and most black leaders. Even before this episode, Garvey had not been popular with most African American leaders. Undoubtedly critics W.E.B. Du Bois and A. Philip Randolph, among others, were envious of Garvey's ability to attract such large numbers when their results had been much more modest. Garvey also embodied the tension existing between the masses and the elite African Americans who controlled the black press and organizations. He routinely criticized them as a light-skinned aristocracy who worked with whites and in fact, in their pursuit of integration, sought to be white, and thus did not have the interests of most African Americans at heart. And conversely, Du Bois, Randolph, and others characterized Garvey as an ignorant demagogue whose followers were illiterate peasants. Nativism entered the picture as well. In Harlem there was much tension over the influx of West Indians and many of the barbs directed at Garvey emphasized his Jamaican origins.

But while class and personality figured in the controversy, important ideological differences also played a pivotal role. Randolph, who was perhaps Garvey's most unrelenting critic, was dismayed by the influential Garvey's hostility toward unions. Moreover, Randolph repeatedly attacked Garvey as a charlatan whose simplistic solutions deflected African Americans from more radical critiques of the system. Leftists like Randolph had different agendas than the NAACP leadership, but they shared a commitment to establishing social equality and to fighting discrimination, segregation, and violence against blacks. Garvey's nationalism and his emphasis on racial purity were alarming enough. But when he denigrated the goal of social equality and condoned the epitome of African Americans' enemies, other leaders viewed Garvey as a dangerous traitor who was merely duping the black masses and intensifying racial discord.

In addition to criticizing Garvey in their newspapers, black leaders also worked behind the scenes to undermine Garvey's power. In 1923, eight black leaders—including two NAACP officials and Chandler Owen, Randolph's partner at *The Messenger*—sent a letter to the Attorney General urging that Garvey's trial for mail fraud be expedited and that he be deported. Whether or not the letter was effective, the case did come to trial shortly thereafter and Garvey was convicted in 1923 and imprisoned in 1927. Although the UNIA survived Garvey's imprisonment, it never achieved the success of the early years, and Garvey ceased to be a "black Moses."

Garvey's plans for independent black economic and political power came to naught. His importance lies not in the tangible achievements of the UNIA. Rather, Garvey is significant because he offered African Americans an opportunity to align themselves with a charismatic leader who articulated both racial pride and cynicism about white America. Compared with most middle-class African American leaders, Garvey was a radical. Unlike Randolph, his radicalism did not encompass rejection of capitalism and its institutions. His plans for Africa and his Black Star Line indicate that he expected to model separate black institutions on the structure of white ones. What was radical about Garvey was his racial separatism that led him to seek power for African Americans outside the structure of white-dominated America. At least in the early stages of the UNIA, Garvey brooked no accommodation to the white world. He offered New Negroes a way of solving the problem of twoness by denying its premises. Thus fundamental differences separated Garvey and black elites who struggled to legitimate and implement racial pluralism in America. But one tenuous thread—besides race—linked the diverse components of the black community. Students and professors, NAACP members, Du Bois, Randolph, and Garvey, and countless other African Americans began the decade of the 1920s with rising expectations that led to militant expression of black discontent. The New Negro in the 1920s made few tangible gains vis-à-vis the mainstream, but did succeed in rallying African Americans to an articulation of racial pride and confidence.

Catholics, Jews, Japanese, and African Americans had widely varied experiences and expectations that reflected their different races, cultures, and specific historical circumstances. There was never any substantial effort to come together in a unified assault on discrimination. Interethnic and racial prejudice, as well as a sort of parochial tribalism that kept leaders centered on their own problems, precluded cooperation. Although they did not act together, they had a common link. Subjected in varying degrees to virulent prejudice and discrimination, in the 1920s their leaders struggled to find ways to challenge the prevailing conformity of 100 percent Americanism. In carving out a response to anti-Semitism, anti-Catholicism, racism, and nativism, leaders invariably defined their relationship to mainstream society.

Despite internal dissension, most leaders could agree in their insistence on their right to enjoy equality and citizenship. The vulnerable Japanese, with their small numbers and total lack of political power, were the least militant and organized in self-defense. Catholics, with their already strong political presence and the hierarchy of the Catholic church behind them, were the most consistently aggressive, well organized, and successful. With varying degrees of militancy, leaders of all four groups articulated a definition of Americanism that considered diversity legitimate. Each group stressed its contributions to American society and celebrated those aspects of American culture consistent with the protection of minorities—i.e., democracy, equality, and liberty. By insisting upon the legitimacy of pluralism, ethnic leaders expressed group pride and solidarity while at the same time challenging the Anglo-conformity assumptions of most mainstream Americans. This insistence, accompanied as it was by militant rhetoric and lobbying activities on the part of African Americans, Catholics, and Jews, undoubtedly contributed to the deepening of cultural conflict with mainstream society. In the minds of nativists, this militancy reinforced the picture of uppity African Americans forgetting their place and organized Catholics and Jews exerting illegitimate power at the expense of "real" Americans.

Old-stock Americans were correct in their assessment that their exclusive claim to political power and cultural influence was being challenged by minority voters and minority organizations, but the challenges they offered in this period were narrowly construed. Certainly socialists among African Americans and, to a greater extent, Jews dissented from prevailing economic and political institutions. And Marcus Garvey's insistence on black separatism was in effect a rejection of white society. But for the vast majority of minority group leaders, dissent proved quite limited. They were critical of nativists' emphasis on conformity and the denial of rights of minorities, but beyond that they generally expressed faith in the American system. Thus along with the strong element of protest in their insistence on their rights in American society, minority leaders in the 1920s promoted accommodation to prevailing American institutions.

This is not to suggest that ethnic, racial, or religious minorities had no impact in shaping the contours of American society. Although they did not challenge the political system per se, they affected its direction. As the twentieth century progressed, ethnic voters, especially European immigrants, had more influence on public policy. By participating in the Democratic Party, for example, they helped to shape the new urban liberalism, with its expanded state and social services. Perhaps more significant than their impact on politics was the way in which minorities challenged the cultural hegemony of old-stock Protestant Americans. By enshrining diversity, their leaders sought to broaden the definition of what it meant to be American. Less consciously, immigrants and African Americans helped to expand the definition of cultural and social standards. Ethnic, racial, and religious pluralism, along with secularization, urbanization, and the evolution of a consumer culture, was one part of a process that was eroding the power of old-stock Americans' moral and religious code. In place of the idealized homogeneity of island communities was a multiplicity of cultural and behavioral standards that was to become the hallmark of modern America.

EPILOGUE

Just as the end of World War I helped to frame the beginning of the decade, the stock market crash of October 1929 seemed to herald the demise of the 1920s. The crash not only served as a powerful marker, but also symbolized the failure of a key trend in the 1920s: the get-rich-quick mentality that catapulted many Americans into a speculative frenzy. This spirit emerged first in the Florida land boom during the first half of the decade. After the war, enterprising developers began touting Florida as the American Riviera. They subdivided almost sixty miles of coast south of Palm Beach into fifty-foot lots, built hotels and resorts, and dredged and filled to create new cities like Coral Gables. There, the developer embellished his creation with canals and gondolas to enhance the sense of a Mediterranean paradise of sun and sand. As part of an imaginative advertising campaign, he brought in William Jennings Bryan to offer a sort of sermon on the wonders of the Florida climate while seated on a raft in a lagoon. Songwriter Irving Berlin contributed to the magic with his song "When the Moon Shines in Coral Gables." All the boosterism and advertising worked and people flocked to Florida to invest in the miracle.

Miami's population more than doubled and became, as Frederick Lewis Allen described it, "one frenzied real-estate exchange." Buyers were apparently so eager that they obstructed traffic, prompting the city to pass an ordinance prohibiting people from selling land or even opening a map while on a city street. There and elsewhere in Florida, investors put down a mere 10 percent and paid fantastic prices with the expectation of selling at a hefty profit within a matter of weeks or months. The scramble to invest reached its peak in 1925, but eventually, as with all bubbles, the boom collapsed and prices began to plummet, leaving investors with huge debts on highly depreciated land. As prices began to slide, a natural disaster compounded the man-made one; a hurricane roared through the area in September 1926, killing 400 people and wreaking widespread havoc. Individuals defaulted and banks failed. Although major investors went on to develop the state at a more gradual pace, the Florida frenzy was over.

Just as this bubble popped, another, even more exciting one was developing. The stock market boom began as early as 1925, but it was in 1928 that the dramatic surge in prices and volume took off. Before that point, prices bore some relationship to the productivity and dividends of the company issuing the stock, but increasingly after 1928, investors were speculating in profits to be made in selling securities. With this, John Kenneth Galbraith argues, "the mass escape into make-believe, so much a part of the true speculative orgy, started in earnest."

Although not everyone participated in the craze, it seemed that everyone, encouraged by the awestruck media, followed the progress of the spiraling prices. It was news when General Motors stock rose 75 points in two months. People marveled at the profits to be made. The Radio Corporation of America offered the most spectacular example, rising in 1928 from 85 to 420 points, and by September 1929 cresting at 505 points. An individual who bought RCA stock on January 1, 1928, and sold in September 1929 would have made a profit of 530 percent. Expectation of this sort of gain led to frenetic buying that was fueled by the practice of purchasing on margin: putting a small amount of cash (10 percent) down and financing the rest of the sale through broker loans. By late 1929, these loans had topped $7 billion. There was no regulation of brokerage houses; inside trading and other irregularities were widespread. Nor were there any specific regulations to keep banks from rashly speculating with depositors' money or from underwriting broker loans. Non-banking sources, corporations like Bethlehem Steel and Chrysler, also backed broker loans, thus becoming deeply enmeshed in the fortunes of the market.

In hindsight, a crash of some sort would seem to be inevitable. Although a few warning signs flickered before then, October 24, 1929, marked the first dramatic slide; by noon, $9 billion had been lost in an unprecedented trading of 13 million shares. After a slight rally, on Monday the 29th the market plunged more disastrously. Sixteen million shares changed hands in tumultuous trading that left the ticker lagging several hours behind in recording the transactions. The *Times* industrial index fell 43 points, wiping out the gains of the entire preceding year. Investors, brokers, bankers—and the nation—were stunned.

The shock continued in the next year. Although Herbert Hoover insisted that "the fundamental business of the country, that is production and distribution of commodities, is on a sound and prosperous basis," economic indicators suggested otherwise. Bank failures more than doubled to almost 1,600 in 1930. Unemployment escalated dramatically to 5 million people (by 1932 that number would reach 13 million), and both prices and production fell. In 1930, the GNP had dropped by almost 14 percent; by 1933 it was less than a third of what it had been in 1929, and would not show significant, permanent improvement until the end of the thirties.

The crash provides a partial explanation for the sharp onset of the Depression. Despite the image of a democratization of wealth that pictured both the banker and his chauffeur as stock investors, only about a million and a half of the country's 120 million people participated in the market. But they were an important minority. When the wealthy cut their consumption and corporations retrenched to weather their losses, together they contributed to falling consumer demand, decreasing production, and increasing unemployment, a process repeated in a downward spiral.

The crash might have resulted in a relatively short downturn, but despite Hoover's insistence that the fundamentals were in good shape, the general aura of prosperity of the 1920s had masked numerous weaknesses. In the pro-business climate of the 1920s, the strong resistance to federal regulation had left a corporate and banking structure with many weak links and highly susceptible to a domino-like collapse. Moreover, despite very real gains in productivity and wealth, growth had been uneven. A number of sectors in the economy—especially textiles, bituminous coal, and agriculture—had faltered well before the stock market debacle. Additionally, as the nation shifted to a consumer economy, the demand for iron and steel began to fall, and chemicals, appliances, and food processing began to take their place. The crash caught the economy in the midst of this transition and made recovery more difficult because newer industries had not developed enough strength to bounce back quickly.

A structural weakness of a different kind was the unequal distribution of income in the 1920s: 5 percent of the country's families received a third of all income. This not only made consumption by the wealthy—the very people most affected by the crash—crucial to economic health. It also suggests that average Americans—especially workers and farmers—did not share enough in the prosperity of the country to keep buying the goods that rolled off America's productive assembly lines. Before the crash, there were signs of a falling-off in automobile purchases, and home construction had leveled off as early as 1925. After the crash, "underconsumption" accelerated as unemployment escalated, further reducing the ability of workers to consume.

Another source for the severity of the Depression came from the solutions adopted to stem the crisis. Economists—even now—do not agree on causes or cures of depression, but in the 1920s the state of economic knowledge was surprisingly primitive. The monetary policy followed by the Federal Reserve Board served to exacerbate the problem of declining demand for goods and services by allowing the supply of money and credit to contract. Herbert Hoover, following prevailing economic advice, called for a balanced budget and government retrenchment—a program that undoubtedly made matters worse by removing the prospect of government spending as a spur to confidence and investment. Hoover was not the do-nothing President that his critics have portrayed; nonetheless, his faith in volunteeristic approaches to economic planning and his abhorrence of an interventionist federal government did limit his ability to act constructively in the crisis. Hoover was further constrained by his firm belief that the causes of the Depression lay outside the country.

Although Hoover's assumption of causation was simplistic, he was correct in understanding the importance of the international nature of the crisis. Western European economies were tightly tied to that of the United States, which after World War I had become the world's creditor, so that instability abroad affected the United States. For example, a crisis in London banking was one of the factors that precipitated the panic in the American stock market. A more systemic problem stemmed from the crises that plagued European nations throughout the 1920s as they struggled to recover from the war, pay their debts, and, in the case of Germany, their war reparations. America's high tariff policy contributed to their difficulties in discharging their debts by making it difficult to export their products to the United States as a way of redressing an unfavorable balance of trade. They turned instead to loans from private U.S. sources, but when the stock market collapsed the sources for loans dried up. The result was a deepening crisis of loan defaults and decreased demand for U.S. products, thus exacerbating the weakness in the American economy, which in turn contributed to destabilization abroad, and helped to prolong the national and international crisis.

It is hard not to picture the crash as a fault line running between the prosperity of the New Era and the economic collapse that characterized the 1930s. Following a period of humdrum and conservative politics that had dampened the reform spirit, the thirties were enlivened by the energetic administration of Franklin D. Roosevelt. His New Deal programs of extensive federal social services and increased regulation of the economy seemed the fruition of much of what progressive reformers had envisioned. The ebbing of the conservative tide was also evident in a changing climate for labor. After the reversals of the 1920s, the 1930s witnessed militant strikes, a burgeoning labor movement, and unprecedented recognition of the rights of labor unions by the federal government. This labor militancy was part of what encouraged many intellectuals once again to be optimistic about social change and political activism. Also inspired by what they viewed as the remarkable progress of the Soviet Union, many writers and artists, while not abandoning the potent theme of the alienated individual in modern society, became much more concerned with issues of social conscience and class conflict. The wave of interest in documentaries further spoke to a new tone of social realism and seriousness that made Fitzgerald's flappers seem frivolous.

The tone of the two decades suggests a sharp dissonance. Bathtub gin gave way to breadlines. The image of the ticker-tape welcome for aviator hero Charles A. Lindbergh was superseded by representations of a new American icon: the haunting portraits of forgotten men and women like the famous "Migrant Mother" that the photographer Dorothea Lange captured. The "era of wonderful nonsense," as one popular historian called the 1920s, seemed to many to give way, almost inevitably, to retribution for the decade's sins of excess: the grim and harsh Great Depression.

As this book has indicated, this view of the roaring twenties is in many ways a false one that obscures the considerable tensions surrounding social and cultural change that permeated the period. It distorts the lives of most ordinary Americans and in particular negates the experiences of poor people, of African Americans and ethnic minorities. The image perpetuates a notion of extremes, contrasting the "decadence" of the twenties with the despair of the next ten years. Although the differences between the decades are indeed striking, there are strong continuities as well that defy convenient periodization.

To a great extent, the sources of the Depression are to be found in specific economic developments of the preceding period. In addition, the international nature of the Depression brings into sharp relief the interdependence of the world economy and is a compelling example of the developments that had for many decades been transforming economic life in the United States. Corporations and other large bureaucratic structures had been integrating the nation into a web of interdependence, bringing about a decline in local and individual autonomy, and an environment in which remote decisions and events could have far-reaching, rippling effects. In this context, the Great Depression represents not a break from the past, but rather an almost logical consequence of the organization and complexity of a modern economy.

In the 1920s, as Americans grappled with the implications of this more "organized" society, social tensions emerged that reflected a nostalgia for rugged individualism, for a harmonious society undisturbed by class tensions or ethnic diversity. As we have seen, the nativism of the decade stemmed in part from the search for scapegoats to explain disruptive forces that were unseating traditional forms of community. Although nativism in the 1930s was not as virulent as in the preceding period, it nonetheless persisted, with Father Coughlin, the demagogic "radio priest," the most notable exemplar. Using a rhetoric laced with an appeal to tradition and community, Coughlin repeatedly invoked the disappearance of the small merchant who had been swamped by the octopus of giant corporations and chain stores, a problem intensified with the economic collapse. In offering his explanation for the Depression, Coughlin emphasized a stereotype made familiar by the *Dearborn Independent*—the villainous international Jewish banker—and helped to keep alive a popular anti-Semitism that was also evident in the refusal by Congress to modify the National Origins Act to permit the entry of Jewish refugees from Hitler's Germany. Hostility to Mexican immigrants deepened in the 1930s as well. Fears of competition in a scarce job market, anxiety about the radicalism of foreign workers, and a desire to keep welfare rolls down led to the large-scale deportation of immigrants and sometimes citizens back to Mexico with little attention to the niceties of legal procedures or civil rights. Discrimination against African Americans constituted another continuity with the 1920s. Lowest on the economic totem pole, they experienced devastating poverty in both the South and the North during the Depression. Although New Deal programs helped many African Americans weather some of the hardships of the period, the New Deal's emphasis on reform did not encompass a drive to topple the country's racial caste system.

The efforts of minorities to stake their claims to recognition and power that were so evident in the 1920s also persisted in the next decade. As the Democratic Party's identification with urban liberalism and social reform sharpened, European ethnic voters became extremely important to the New Deal coalition. Although African Americans were not yet important players in the party, the 1930s marked the shift of black voters from the Republicans to the Democrats, a development that had long-range implications for black political influence. The recognition of the country's pluralism was also evident in the changing face of organized labor. In contrast to the restrictive policies of the American Federation of Labor, the fledgling Congress of Industrial Organizations, founded in 1935, acknowledged the necessity of organizing a diverse workforce. In tackling the mass production industries, it incorporated ethnic workers, African Americans, and women into its organization drives. Particularly for European ethnics, the more inclusive stance of organized labor, as well as the changed constituency of the Democratic Party, helped diminish their sense of marginality and legitimate their claims to equal citizenship.

The presence of women in the Congress of Industrial Organizations, even though their numbers were limited, points to another continuation with the 1920s. Women's participation in the workforce continued to climb, despite intense public hostility to working women that had been exacerbated by the economic crisis and the fear that working women robbed men of employment. Women were also active participants in the New Deal, finding new opportunities in an expanding federal bureaucracy and helping to shape the New Deal's social welfare policy. In the final analysis, although we can chart women's "progress," including the increased use and availability of birth control, changes were still, as they had been in the 1920s, within narrow limits. Discrimination and the ideology about women's roles that underwrote it continued unabated.

Women's involvement in the New Deal underlines the return in politics to a social reform agenda, at first glance a sharp contrast with the 1920s. The federal government expanded in unprecedented ways. New regulatory agencies such as the Federal Deposit Insurance Corporation indicated a federal government more involved in the economy to protect the interests of ordinary Americans. Legislation like the 1935 Social Security Act signaled the beginnings of a modest welfare state that acknowledged federal responsibility for the well-being of its citizens. Despite these innovations, the New Deal was powerfully affected by New Era themes. Ideas about individualism and local democracy, as well as hostility to federal bureaucracy and power, remained very potent. The legacy of the Red Scare also ran deep and encouraged the association of government activism with foreign radicalism. Traditional ideology, thus buttressed, was a powerful influence that helped to keep the New Deal constrained and to maintain the structure of corporate power.

The New Deal also embodied the continued development of the interest group politics that so clearly characterized the 1920s. Lobbying groups proved extremely influential in shaping legislation. Moreover, the legitimacy that New Deal legislation accorded to organized labor and to the representatives of the farming sector led to the emergence of "big labor" and "big agriculture" as important players in shaping public policy. The Depression thus helped to cement the role of the federal government as a broker state mediating between contending interests.

Another political innovation that marked the 1930s was the extensive use of the radio to reach citizens and potential voters. Roosevelt proved a master at it as he used his homey "fireside chats" to explain his programs and drum up support for the New Deal. Father Coughlin's impassioned radio addresses brought in even more mail than the President's and made him one of the most prominent men in the country. The radio thus became a powerful new tool that highlighted the political implications of mass culture. Just as radio illustrated the power of the media, advertising, movies, and commercial sports continued, as they had in the 1920s, to play a central role in entertaining Americans, while at the same time serving to articulate and shape their values.

These continuities between the 1920s and the 1930s serve as signposts for key developments in twentieth-century America. The themes explored in this book—the implications for personal and community autonomy in an increasingly organized and corporate-dominated society; the importance of interest group politics for shaping public policy; the tensions implicit in racial and ethnic pluralism; the social and cultural meanings of changing roles for women; the significance of mass media in helping to construct a consumer culture; the way in which the search for meaning in the modern world engaged religious leaders and intellectuals—emerged sharply in the 1920s. These issues not only set the tone for the decade but also formed central motifs that have shaped the modern American temper.

BIBLIOGRAPHIC ESSAY

The literature on the 1920s is voluminous, and I am very grateful to the scholars whose work made this book possible. The following is a selective bibliography that focuses on the material I used most extensively. Although many works were helpful in assessing a variety of topics, in the interest of conserving space few entries are cited more than once. I have noted a number of specific primary sources I consulted. In addition, the pages of popular periodicals—e.g., *The Saturday Evening Post, Good Housekeeping, The World's Work, Literary Digest, The American Magazine* —are exceptionally valuable for understanding the 1920s.

INTRODUCTION

Key sources that offer broad interpretations of the late nineteenth and early twentieth centuries include Robert Wiebe, *The Search for Order, 1877-1920* (New York, 1967); Alan Trachtenberg, *The Incorporation of America: Culture and Society in the Gilded Age* (New York, 1982); Samuel P. Hays, *The Response to Industrialism: 1885-1914* (Chicago, 1957); Nell Painter, *Standing at Armageddon: The United States, 1877-1919* (New York, 1987); Paul Boyer, *Urban Masses and Moral Order in America, 1820-1920* (Cambridge, 1978); and Lawrence W. Levine, *Highbrow/Lowbrow: The Emergence of Cultural Hierarchy in America* (Cambridge, 1988).

I. PUBLIC AND PRIVATE POWER

This chapter is indebted to the insightful analysis of the general theme of public and private power by Grant McConnell in *Private Power and Amer-*

ican Democracy (New York, 1966). On progressivism, see John C. Burnham, "Essay," in *Progressivism*, eds. John D. Buenker, John C. Burnham, and Robert M. Crunden (Cambridge, 1977), pp. 3–29; David M. Kennedy, "Overview: The Progressive Era," *The Historian* 37 (May 1975): 453–68; Daniel T. Rodgers, "In Search of Progressivism," in *The Promise of American History: Progress and Prospects*, eds. Stanley I. Kutler and Stanley N. Katz (Baltimore, 1982), pp. 113–32; and Peter G. Filene, "An Obituary for 'The Progressive Movement,'" *American Quarterly*, 22 (Spring 1970): 20–34. One of the classic, but now dated, accounts of the movement is in Richard Hofstadter, *The Age of Reform* (New York, 1955). For some of the important challenges to traditional notions of progressivism, see Wiebe, *The Search for Order*; David P. Thelen, *Robert M. La Follette and the Insurgent Spirit* (Madison, Wis., 1985); James Weinstein, *The Corporate Ideal in the Liberal State, 1900–1918* (Boston, 1968); Martin J. Sklar, *The Corporate Reconstruction of American Capitalism, 1890–1916* (Cambridge, 1988); Alan Dawley, *Struggles for Justice: Social Responsibility and the Liberal State* (Cambridge, 1991); and John D. Buenker, *Urban Liberalism and Progressive Reform* (New York, 1973). On the new urban liberalism, see Samuel Lubell, *The Future of American Politics* (Westport, Conn., 1951); John M. Allswang, *A House for All Peoples: Ethnic Politics in Chicago 1890–1936* (Lexington, Ky., 1971); and Howard Zinn, *La Guardia in Congress* (New York, 1959). Works that address progressivism and its relationship to World War I include Robert D. Cuff, *The War Industries Board: Business-Government Relations During World War I* (Baltimore, 1973); David Kennedy, *Over Here: The First World War and American Society* (New York, 1980); Allen F. Davis, "Welfare, Reform, and World War I," *American Quarterly* 19 (1967): 516–33; Charles Hirschfield, "Nationalist Progressivism and World War I," *Mid-America* 45 (July 1963): 139–56; and John F. McClymer, *War and Welfare: Social Engineering in America, 1890–1925* (Westport, Conn., 1980).

On the continuation of progressivism in the twenties, see Arthur S. Link, "What Happened to the Progressive Movement in the 1920's?" *American Historical Review* 64 (July 1959): 833–51; Clarke A. Chambers, *Seedtime of Reform: American Social Service and Social Action, 1918–1933* (Minneapolis, 1963); and J. Stanley Lemons, *The Woman Citizen: Social Feminism in the 1920s* (Urbana, 1975). John D. Hicks, *Republican Ascendancy 1921–1933* (New York, 1960), is a comprehensive account of the politics of the period, including the fate of progressivism. Other useful works include Otis L. Graham, Jr., *The Great Campaigns: Reform and War in America, 1900–1928* (Englewood Cliffs, N.J., 1971); Richard Lowitt, *George W. Norris: The Persistence of a Progressive, 1913–1933* (Urbana, 1971); J. Joseph Huthmacher, *Massachusetts People and Politics 1919–1933* (Cambridge, 1959); Robert K. Murray, *The Politics of Normalcy: Governmental Theory and Practice in the Harding-Coolidge Era* (New York, 1973);

and Paula Eldot, *Governor Alfred E. Smith: The Politician as Reformer* (New York, 1983).

Numerous studies have examined the root of Americans' antipathy to state power: Ann Shola Orloff, "The Political Origins of America's Belated Welfare State" in *The Politics of Social Policy in the United States*, eds. Margaret Weir, Ann Shola Orloff, and Theda Skocpol (Princeton, 1988), pp. 37–80; Stephen Skowronek, *Building a New American State: The Expansion of National Administrative Capacities, 1877–1920* (Cambridge and New York, 1981); Barry Karl, *The Uneasy State: The United States from 1915 to 1945* (Chicago, 1983); Paula Baker, *The Moral Frameworks of Public Life: Gender, Politics, and the State in Rural New York, 1870–1930* (New York, 1991); Walter I. Trattner, *Crusade for the Children: A History of the National Child Labor Committee and Child Labor Reform in America* (Chicago, 1970); and Christopher C. Gibbs, *The Great Silent Majority: Missouri's Resistance to World War I* (Columbia, Mo., 1988). For detailed references on 1920s antistatism, see Lynn Dumenil, " 'The Insatiable Maw of Bureaucracy': Antistatism and Education Reform in the 1920s," *Journal of American History* 77 (September 1990): 499–524.

On business ideas on service, see especially Morrell Heald, *The Social Responsibilities of Business: Company and Community, 1900–1960* (Chapel Hill, N.C., 1929); John D. Buenker, "The New Era Business Philosophy of the 1920s," *Illinois Quarterly* 38 (1976): 20–49; and James Warren Prothro, *The Dollar Decade: Business Ideas in the 1920's* (Baton Rouge, 1954). For details of the American economy, the best study is still George Soule, *Prosperity Decade: From War to Depression: 1917–1929* (New York, 1947), vol. 3 of *The Economic History of the United States*. On corporate development, see Alfred D. Chandler, *The Visible Hand: The Managerial Revolution in American Business* (Cambridge, 1977); Morton Keller, *Regulating a New Economy: Public Policy and Economic Change in America, 1900–1933* (Cambridge, 1990); and Lary May, *Screening Out the Past: The Birth of Mass Culture and the Motion Picture Industry* (Chicago, 1980).

The way in which American business expanded internationally in the interwar years with the assistance of the government is admirably analyzed by Emily Rosenberg, *Spreading the American Dream: American Economic and Cultural Expansion 1890–1945* (New York, 1982). Other useful works include Herbert Feis, *The Diplomacy of the Dollar: First Era, 1919–1932* (Baltimore, 1950); Joan Hoff Wilson, *American Business and Foreign Policy, 1921–1933* (Lexington, Ky., 1971); Joseph Brandes, *Herbert Hoover and Economic Diplomacy: Department of Commerce Policy, 1921–1928* (Pittsburgh, 1962). For the United States in Central America, see Walter LaFeber, *Inevitable Revolutions: The United States in Central America* (New York, 1983).

Any study of Hoover and the associative state must begin with Ellis Hawley, "Herbert Hoover, the Commerce Secretariat, and the Vision of an 'Associative State,' 1921–1928," *Journal of American History* 61 (June

1974): 116–40 and the anthology he has edited, *Herbert Hoover as Secretary of Commerce: Studies in New Era Thought and Practice* (Iowa City, 1981). Herbert Hoover's philosophy is accessible in *The New Day: Campaign Speeches of Herbert Hoover* (Stanford University, 1928) and *American Individualism* (New York, 1922). See also Louis Galambos, in *Competition and Cooperation: The Emergence of a National Trade Association* (Baltimore, 1966), and Richard Hume Werking, "Bureaucrats, Businessmen, and Foreign Trade: The Origins of the United States Chamber of Commerce," *Business History Review* 52 (Autumn 1978): 321–41.

Most of the material for the new lobbying is primary. E. Pendleton Herring, *Group Representation Before Congress* (Baltimore, 1929), is the most comprehensive, followed by Edward B. Logan, "Lobbying," *Annals of the American Academy of Political and Social Science*, 144 (July 1929), supplement, pp. 1–89. An important specialized study is Peter H. Odegard, *Pressure Politics: The Story of the Anti-Saloon League* (New York, 1928). The new lobbying was addressed in a number of popular books, including William Allen White, *Politics: The Citizen's Business* (New York, 1924), and Frank R. Kent, *The Great Game of Politics* (Garden City, N.Y., 1923), in addition to receiving extensive coverage in magazine literature. The power trust lobbying issue is conveniently summarized in H. S. Raushenbush, *High Power Propaganda* (New York, 1928), and in David E. Nye, *Image Worlds: Corporate Identities at General Electric, 1890–1930* (Cambridge, 1985). On farming and the AFBF, see Grant McConnell, *Agrarian Democracy* (Berkeley, 1953); Gilbert C. Fite, *George N. Peek and the Fight for Farm Parity* (Norman, Okla., 1954); and Theodore Saloutos and John D. Hicks, *Agricultural Discontent in the Middle West, 1900–1939* (Madison, Wis., 1951). On the women's lobby, see Maud Wood Park, *Front Door Lobby* (Boston, 1960), and Lemons, *The Woman Citizen*. Ellis W. Hawley in *The New Deal and the Problem of Monopoly* (Princeton, 1966) discusses the New Deal and the broker state. On interest group liberalism, see Robert A. Dahl, *Who Governs?* (New Haven, 1961); McConnell, *Private Power*; and Theodore J. Lowi, *The End of Liberalism: The Second Republic of the United States*, 2nd ed. (New York, 1979). The most recent assessment of party politics and voting participation is Michael E. McGerr, *The Decline of Popular Politics: The American North, 1865–1892* (New York, 1986). Other relevant works include Daniel T. Rodgers, *Contested Truths: Keywords in American Politics Since Independence* (New York, 1987); Samuel P. Hays, "Political Parties and the Community-Society Continuum," in *The American Party Systems: Stages of Political Development*, eds. William Nisbet Chambers and Walter Dean Burnham, 2nd ed. (New York, 1974), pp. 152–81; Richard P. McCormick, "The Discovery That Business Corrupts Politics: A Reappraisal of the Origins of Progressivism," *American Historical Review* 86 (April 1981): 247–74.

II. WORK AND CONSUMPTION

The starting point for workers in the 1920s is Irving Bernstein, *The Lean Years: A History of the American Worker, 1920–1933* (Baltimore, 1966). See also James R. Green, *The World of the Worker: Labor in Twentieth-Century America* (New York, 1980). For an oral history of laborers' lives and work, see Jacquelyn Dowd Hall et al., *Like a Family: The Making of a Southern Cotton Mill World* (Chapel Hill, 1987). For a primary account of the factory floor, see Hugh Grant Adams, *An Australian Looks at America: Are Wages Really Higher?* (Sydney, 1927).

The material on scientific management and workers is voluminous. See Dan Clawson, *Bureaucracy and the Labor Process: The Transformation of U.S. Industry, 1860–1920* (New York, 1980); David F. Noble, *America by Design: Science, Technology, and the Rise of Corporate Capitalism* (New York, 1977); Frederick W. Taylor, *The Principles of Scientific Management* (New York, 1913); Daniel Nelson, *Managers and Workers: Origins of the New Factory System in the United States 1880–1920* (Madison, Wis., 1975); Liston Pope, *Millhands and Preachers: A Study of Gastonia* (New Haven, 1942); and Stanley B. Mathewson, *Restriction of Output Among Unorganized Workers* (New York, 1931), a hostile contemporary account of workers' resistance.

On unions, see David Montgomery, *The Fall of the House of Labor: The Workplace, the State, and American Labor Activism, 1865–1925* (Cambridge, 1987); Bernstein, *The Lean Years*; David Montgomery, *Workers' Control in America: Studies in the History of Work, Technology, and Labor Struggles* (New York, 1979); Sterling D. Spero and Abram L. Harris, *The Black Worker: The Negro and the Labor Movement* (Port Washington, N.Y., 1931); Cletus E. Daniel, *Bitter Harvest: A History of California Farmworkers, 1870–1941* (Ithaca, 1981); Roger R. Keeran, "Communist Influence in the Automobile Industry, 1920–33: Paving the Way for an Industrial Union," *Labor History* 20 (Spring 1979): 189–225; and Jacquelyn Dowd Hall, "Disorderly Women: Gender and Labor Militancy in the Appalachian South," *Journal of American History* 73 (September 1986): 354–82.

Stuart D. Brandes, *American Welfare Capitalism, 1880–1940* (Chicago, 1976), is the standard account of welfare capitalism, but see also H. M. Gitelman, "Welfare Capitalism Reconsidered," *Labor History* 33 (Winter, 1992): 5–31; David Brody, "The Rise and Decline of Welfare Capitalism," in Brody, *Workers in Industrial America: Essays on the Twentieth Century Struggle* (New York, 1980), pp. 48–81; Gerald Zahavi, "Negotiated Loyalty: Welfare Capitalism and the Shoeworkers of Endicott Johnson, 1920–1940," *Journal of American History* 70 (1983): 602–20; Sanford M. Jacoby, *Employing Bureaucracy: Managers, Unions, and the Transformation of Work in American Industry, 1900–1945* (New York, 1985); and Nye, *Image Worlds*.

With the exception of studies of clerical workers, discussed in the following chapter, very few historians have examined white-collar work. Exceptions are Jurgen Köcka, *White Collar Workers in America, 1890–1940*

(London, 1980); Olivier Zunz, *Making America Corporate, 1870–1920* (Chicago, 1990); and Chandler, *The Visible Hand*. For a broad discussion of work and alienation that emphasizes the similarities between blue- and white-collar workers, see Harry Braverman, *Labor and Monopoly Capital: The Degradation of Work in the Twentieth Century* (New York, 1974).

Chain stores are discussed by Susan Strasser, *Satisfaction Guaranteed: The Making of the American Mass Market* (New York, 1989), and Boris Emmet and John E. Jeuck, *Catalogues and Counters: A History of Sears, Roebuck and Company* (Chicago, 1950). On newspapers, see Sally F. Griffith, "Mass Media Come to the Small Town: The *Emporia Gazette* in the 1920s," and John D. Stevens, "Small Town Editors and the 'Modernized' Agrarian Myth," in *Mass Media Between the Wars: Perceptions of Cultural Tension, 1918–1941*, eds. Catherine L. Covert and John D. Stevens (Syracuse, 1984), pp. 141–55.

Material on the emergence of a consumer culture is growing rapidly. The central texts are Warren I. Susman, " 'Personality' and the Making of Twentieth-Century Culture," in *Culture as History: The Transformation of American Society in the Twentieth Century* (New York, 1973), pp. 271–85; Roland Marchand, *Advertising the American Dream: Making Way for Modernity, 1920–1940* (Berkeley, 1985); May, *Screening Out the Past*; Joan Shelley Rubin, *The Making of Middlebrow Culture* (Chapel Hill, 1992); and Richard Wightman Fox and T. Jackson Lears, eds., *The Culture of Consumption* (New York, 1983). See especially Lears's article "From Salvation to Self-Realization: Advertising and the Therapeutic Roots of the Consumer Culture, 1880–1930," pp. 1–38. In "The Folklore of Industrial Society: Popular Culture and Its Audience," *American Historical Review* 97 (December 1992): 1369–99, Lawrence W. Levine addresses the role of individuals in shaping and interpreting mass culture for themselves. See also Leo Lowenthal, "The Triumph of Mass Idols," in *Literature, Popular Culture and Society* (Englewood Cliffs, N.J., 1961), pp. 145–65, and David Riesman with Nathan Glazer and Reuel Denney, *The Lonely Crowd: A Study of the Changing American Character* (New Haven, 1950).

Other works that address aspects of consumer culture include Richard Butsch, *For Fun and Profit: The Transformation of Leisure into Consumption* (Philadelphia, 1990); Lewis A. Erenberg, *Steppin' Out: New York Nightlife and the Transformation of American Culture, 1890–1930* (Westport, Conn., 1981); Daniel Horowitz, *The Morality of Spending: Attitudes Toward the Consumer Society in America, 1875–1940* (Baltimore, 1985); James J. Flink, *The Car Culture* (Boston, 1975); Vincent Vinikas, *Soft Soap, Hard Sell: American Hygiene in an Age of Advertisement* (Ames, Iowa, 1992); Stuart and Elizabeth Ewen, *Channels of Desire: Mass Images and the Shaping of American Consciousness* (New York, 1982); Robert Sklar, *Movie-Made America: A Cultural History of American Movies* (New York, 1975); and Richard Schickel, *His Picture in the Papers: A Speculation on*

Celebrity in America Based on the Life of Douglas Fairbanks, Sr. (New York, 1973).

For changing conceptions of success, see Richard Weiss, *The American Myth of Success: From Horatio Alger to Norman Vincent Peale* (New York, 1969); Donald Meyer, *The Positive Thinkers: A Study of the American Question for Health, Wealth, and Personal Power from Mary Baker Eddy to Norman Vincent Peale* (Garden City, N.Y., 1965); and Paul Carter, *Another Part of the Twenties* (New York, 1977).

Sports are covered by Elliott Gorn and Warren Goldstein, *A Brief History of American Sports* (New York, 1993); Benjamin G. Rader, *American Sports: From the Age of Folk Games to the Age of Spectators* (Englewood Cliffs, N.J., 1983); Steven A. Riess, *City Games: The Evolution of American Urban Society and the Rise of Sports* (Urbana, 1989); and Rob Ruck, *Sandlot Seasons: Sport in Black Pittsburgh* (Urbana, 1987). For the consumer culture, ethnicity, and the working class, see Roy Rosenzweig, *Eight Hours for What We Will: Workers and Leisure in an Industrial City, 1870–1920* (Harvard University, 1983); John F. Kasson, *Amusing the Millions: Coney Island at the Turn of the Century* (New York, 1978); Andrew R. Heinze, *Adapting to Abundance: Jewish Immigrants, Mass Consumption, and the Search for American Identity* (New York, 1990); Lizabeth Cohen, *Making a New Deal: Industrial Workers in Chicago, 1919–1939* (Cambridge, 1990); John Bodnar, *Workers' World: Kinship, Community, and Protest in an Industrial Society, 1900–1940* (Baltimore, 1982); Hall, *Like a Family*; Earl Lewis, *Their Own Interests: Race, Class, and Power in Twentieth-Century Norfolk, Virginia* (Berkeley, 1991); David Levering Lewis, *When Harlem Was in Vogue* (New York, 1981); Kathy J. Ogren, *The Jazz Revolution: Twenties America and the Meaning of Jazz* (New York, 1989); George M. Sánchez, *Becoming Mexican American: Ethnicity, Culture and Identity in Chicano Los Angeles, 1890–1945* (New York, 1993); Richard K. Spottswood, "Commercial Ethnic Recordings in the United States," *Ethnic Recordings in America: A Neglected Heritage* (Washington, D.C., 1982), pp. 51–66; and Frank Stricker, "Affluence for Whom? Another Look at Prosperity and the Working Classes in the 1920s," *Labor History* 24 (Winter 1983): 5–33. The concluding remarks draw upon John William Ward, "The Meaning of Lindbergh's Flight," *American Quarterly* 10 (1958): 3–26, and Elliott J. Gorn, "The Manassa Mauler and the Fighting Marine: An Interpretation of the Dempsey-Tunney Fights," *Journal of American Studies* 19 (April 1985): 27–47.

III. THE NEW WOMAN

Nancy Cott, *The Grounding of Modern Feminism* (New Haven, 1987), has been indispensable for this chapter. Other books which provide a broad analysis of the period include William H. Chafe, *The American Woman: Her Changing Social, Economic, and Political Roles, 1920–1970* (New York, 1972); Estelle B. Freedman, "The New Woman: Changing Views of

Women in the 1920s," in *Decades of Discontent: The Women's Movement, 1920–1940*, eds. Lois Scharf and Joan M. Jensen (Westport, Conn., 1983), pp. 21–42; and Dorothy M. Brown, *Setting a Course: American Women in the 1920s* (Boston, 1987).

On the history of the suffrage battle, see Eleanor Flexner, *Century of Struggle: The Woman's Rights Movement in the United States*, rev. ed. (Cambridge, 1975); Aileen S. Kraditor, *The Ideas of the Woman Suffrage Movement* (New York, 1965); and Ellen Carol DuBois, "Working Women, Class Relations, and Suffrage Militance: Harriot Stanton Blatch and the New York Woman Suffrage Movement, 1894–1909," *Journal of American History* 74 (June 1987): pp. 34–58. The continuation of the woman's movement in the 1920s is addressed in Nancy Cott, "What's in a Name? The Limits of 'Social Feminism'; or, Expanding the Vocabulary of Women's History" *Journal of American History* 76 (December 1989): 809–29; William L. O'Neill, *Feminism in America: A History*, 2nd rev. ed. (New Brunswick, 1989); Ann Firor Scott, "After Suffrage: Southern Women in the Twenties," *Journal of Southern History* 30 (August 1964): 298–318; Estelle B. Freedman, "Separatism as Strategy: Female Institution Building and American Feminism, 1870–1930," *Feminist Studies* 5 (Fall 1979): 512–29; Paula Baker, "The Domestication of Politics: Women and American Political Society, 1780–1920," *American Historical Review* 89 (June 1984): 620–47; Elaine Showalter, ed., *These Modern Women: Autobiographical Essays from the Twenties* (New York, 1978); and Lemons, *The Woman Citizen*. On African American women and reform, see Paula Giddings, *When and Where I Enter: The Impact of Black Women on Race and Sex in America* (New York, 1984), and Rosalyn Terborg-Penn, "Discontented Black Feminists: Prelude and Postscript to the Passage of the Nineteenth Amendment," in *Decades of Discontent*, pp. 261–78.

For general accounts of women and work in the 1920s, see Alice Kessler-Harris, *Out to Work: A History of Wage-Earning Women in the United States* (New York, 1982); Julie A. Matthaei, *An Economic History of Women in America: Women's Work, the Sexual Division of Labor, and the Development of Capitalism* (New York, 1982); Lynn Y. Weiner, *From Working Girl to Working Mother: The Female Labor Force in the United States, 1820–1980* (Chapel Hill, 1985); Brown, *Setting a Course*; and Winifred D. Wandersee, *Women's Work and Family Values, 1920–1940* (Cambridge, 1981). On white-collar work, see Margery W. Davies, *Woman's Place Is at the Typewriter: Office Work and Office Workers, 1870–1930* (Philadelphia, 1982); Lisa M. Fine, *The Souls of the Skyscraper: Female Clerical Workers in Chicago, 1870–1930* (Philadelphia, 1990); Sharon Strom Hartman, *Beyond the Typewriter: Gender, Class, and the Origins of Modern Office Work* (Urbana, 1992); Susan Porter Benson, *Counter Cultures: Saleswomen, Managers and Customers in American Department Stores, 1890–1940* (Urbana, 1988); and Barbara J. Harris, *Beyond Her Sphere: Women and the Professions in American History* (Greenwood, Conn., 1978).

For white working-class women, see Leslie Woodcock Tentler, *Wage-Earning Women: Industrial and Family Life in the United States, 1900–1930* (New York, 1979); Susan Estabrook Kennedy, *If All We Did Was to Weep at Home: A History of White Working-Class Women in America* (Bloomington, 1979); Susan A. Glenn, *Daughters of the Shtetl: Life and Labor in the Immigrant Generation* (Ithaca, 1990); Elizabeth Ewen, *Immigrant Women in the Land of Dollars: Life and Culture on the Lower East Side, 1890–1925* (New York, 1985); Alice Kessler-Harris, "Where Are the Organized Women Workers?" *Feminist Studies* 3 (Fall 1975): 92–110; Stephen H. Norwood, *Labor's Flaming Youth: Telephone Operators and Worker Militancy, 1878–1923* (Urbana, 1990); Ronald Edsforth, *Class Conflict and Cultural Consensus: The Making of a Mass Consumer Society in Flint, Michigan* (New Brunswick, 1987); and Hall, "Disorderly Women."

On African American women and work, see Giddings, *When and Where I Enter*; Jacqueline Jones, *Labor of Love, Labor of Sorrow: Black Women, Work and the Family, from Slavery to the Present* (New York, 1985); Darlene Clark Hines, *Black Women in White: Racial Conflict and Cooperation in the Nursing Profession, 1890–1950* (Bloomington and Indianapolis, 1989); Gerda Lerner, ed., *Black Women in White America: A Documentary History* (New York, 1973); and Elizabeth Clark-Lewis, " 'This Work Had an End': African-American Domestic Workers in Washington, D.C., 1910–1940," in *Women and Power in American History: A Reader*, vol. 2, from 1870, eds. Kathryn Kish Sklar and Thomas Dublin (Englewood Cliffs, N.J., 1991), pp. 195–208. On Mexican and Chicano women, see Rosalinda M. González, "Chicanas and Mexican Immigrant Families 1920–1940," in *Decades of Discontent*, pp. 59–84; George J. Sánchez, " 'Go After the Women': Americanization and the Mexican Immigrant Woman, 1915–1929," in *Unequal Sisters: A Multicultural Reader in Women's History*, eds. Ellen Carol DuBois and Vicki L. Ruiz (New York, 1990), pp. 250–63; Albert Camarillo, *Chicanos in a Changing Society: From Mexican Pueblos to American Barrios in Santa Barbara and Southern California, 1848–1930* (Cambridge, 1979); Sarah Deutsch, *No Separate Refuge: Culture, Class, and Gender on an Anglo-Hispanic Frontier in the American Southwest, 1880–1940* (New York, 1987); Paul S. Taylor, "Mexican Women in Los Angeles Industry," *Aztlan* 11 (Spring 1980): 99–132; and Emory S. Bogardus, *The Mexican in the United States* (Los Angeles, 1934). For Japanese women, see Evelyn Nakano Glenn, *Issei, Nisei, War Bride: Three Generations of Japanese American Women in Domestic Service* (Philadelphia, 1986), and Sucheng Chan, *Asian Americans: An Interpretive History* (Boston, 1991).

A crucial source for the changes in the private arena is Nancy Cott's chapter "Modern Times," in *The Grounding of Modern Feminism*. Other important general discussions are Sheila M. Rothman, *Woman's Proper Place: A History of Changing Ideals and Practices, 1870 to the Present* (New York, 1978), and Mary Ryan, "The Projection of a New Womanhood: The Movie Moderns in the 1920s," in *Our American Sisters: Women in Amer-*

ican Life and Thought, eds. Jean E. Friedman and William G. Shade, 3rd ed. (Lexington, Mass., 1982), pp. 500–18. For specific discussions of housework and consumption, see Glenna Matthews, *"Just a Housewife": The Rise and Fall of Domesticity in America* (New York, 1987); Susan Strasser, *Never Done: A History of American Housework* (New York, 1982); and Ruth Cowan, "Two Washes in the Morning and a Bridge Party at Night: The American Housewife Between the Wars," *Women's Studies* 2 (1976): 141–71. On the family and marriage, see Paula Fass, *The Damned and the Beautiful: American Youth in the 1920s* (New York, 1977); Elaine Tyler May, *Great Expectations: Marriage and Divorce in Post-Victorian America* (Chicago, 1980); John D'Emilio and Estelle B. Freedman, *Intimate Matters: A History of Sexuality in America* (New York, 1988); Steven Mintz and Susan Kellogg, *Domestic Revolutions: A Social History of American Family Life* (New York, 1988). On sexuality, see Caroline Ware, *Greenwich Village 1920–1930: A Comment on American Civilization in the Post-War Years* (New York, 1935); Florence Moriarty, ed., *True Confessions: Sixty Years of Sin, Suffering, and Sorrow* (New York, 1979); Kathy Peiss, *Cheap Amusements: Working Women and Leisure in Turn-of-the-Century New York* (Philadelphia, 1986); Joanne J. Meyerowitz, *Women Adrift: Independent Wage Earners in Chicago, 1880–1930* (Chicago, 1988); Beth L. Bailey, *From Front Porch to Back Seat: Courtship in Twentieth-Century America* (Baltimore, 1988); Rosalind Rosenberg, *Beyond Separate Spheres: Intellectual Roots of Modern Feminism* (New Haven, 1982); Ellen Kay Trimberger, "Feminism, Men, and Modern Love: Greenwich Village, 1900–1925," in *Powers of Desire: The Politics of Sexuality*, eds. Ann Snitown, Christine Stansell, and Sharon Tompson (New York, 1983), pp. 131–52; and Paul Robinson, *The Modernization of Sex: Havelock Ellis, Alfred Kinsey, William Masters and Virginia Johnson* (New York, 1976); Vicki L. Ruiz, " 'Star Struck': Acculturation, Adolescence, and Mexican American Women, 1920–1950," in *Small Worlds: Children and Adolescents in America, 1850–1950*, eds. Elliott West and Paula Petrik (Lawrence, Kan., 1992), pp. 61–80; Giddings, *When and Where I Enter*; Hazel V. Carby, " 'It Jus Be's Dat Way Sometime': The Sexual Politics of Women's Blues," in *Unequal Sisters*, pp. 238–49; Darlene Clark Hines, "Rape and the Inner Lives of Black Women in the Middle West: Preliminary Thoughts on the Culture of Dissemblance," in *Unequal Sisters*, pp. 292–97; and Barbara Christian, *Black Women Novelists: The Development of a Tradition, 1892–1976* (Westport, Conn., 1980). For a discussion of birth control in the twenties, see David M. Kennedy, *Birth Control in America: The Career of Margaret Sanger* (New Haven, 1970), pp. 127–217, and Linda Gordon, *Woman's Body, Woman's Right: A Social History of Birth Control in America* (New York, 1976). Homosocial bonding is discussed by Carol Smith Rosenberg, "The Female World of Love and Ritual: Relations Between Women in Nineteenth-Century America," *Signs* 1 (Autumn 1975): 1–29. For the impact of the new sexuality on bonds between women, see D'Emilio, *Intimate Matters*; Christina Simmons, "Companionate Marriage and the Lesbian Threat," in *Women and Power in American History*, vol. 2, pp. 183–94; Christina Simmons, "Modern Sexuality and the Myth of Victorian Repression," in *Passion and Power: Sexuality in History*, eds. Kathy Peiss and Christina Simmons (Philadelphia, 1989), pp. 157–77; and Lillian Faderman, *Odd Girls and Twilight Lovers: A History of Lesbian Life in Twentieth-Century America* (New York, 1991).

IV. THE ACIDS OF MODERNITY

Henry May's *The End of American Innocence: A Study of the First Years of Our Own Time, 1912–1917* (Chicago, 1964) is the most important work for understanding the prewar intellectual revolt. For the breakdown of Victorianism and its impact on intellectuals, see Stanley Coben, *Rebellion Against Victorianism: The Impetus for Cultural Change in 1920s America* (New York, 1991). Other accounts of the intellectual scene of the twenties include Roderick Nash, *The Nervous Generation: American Thought, 1917–1930* (Chicago, 1990); Paul Carter, *The Twenties in America* (New York, 1968); Casey Nelson Blake, *Beloved Community: The Cultural Criticism of Randolph Bourne, Van Wyck Brooks, Waldo Frank, and Lewis Mumford* (Chapel Hill, 1990); and Malcolm Cowley, *Exile's Return: A Literary Odyssey of the 1920s* (New York, 1969, originally published 1934). Ronald C. Tobey, in *The American Ideology of National Science, 1919–1930* (Pittsburgh, 1971), and Alan J. Friedman and Carol C. Donley, *Einstein as Myth and Muse* (Cambridge, 1985), discuss the impact of the new physics. Most general accounts discuss the influence of Freud, but see especially Frederick J. Hoffman, *Freudianism and the Literary Mind* (Baton Rouge, 1957).

On literature of the period, see Frederick J. Hoffman, *The 20s: American Writing in the Postwar Decade*, rev. ed. (New York, 1962); Alfred Kazin, *On Native Grounds: An Interpretation of Modern American Prose Literature* (New York, 1942); Dickran Tashjian, *Skyscraper Primitives: Dada and the American Avant-Garde, 1910–1925* (Middletown, Conn., 1975); and Robert M. Crunden, *From Self to Society, 1919–1941* (Englewood Cliffs, N.J., 1972). The best example of the revolt against the village is Harold E. Stearns, ed., *Civilization in the United States* (New York, 1922). For women writers, see Elaine Showalter, "Women Writers Between the Wars," in *Columbia Literary History of the United States*, ed. Emory Elliott (New York, 1988), pp. 823–41; Brown, *Setting a Course*; Elaine Showalter, ed., *Modern American Women Writers* (New York, 1991); William Drake, *The First Wave: Women Poets in America, 1915–1945* (New York, 1987); Alicia Suskin Ostriker, *Stealing the Language: The Emergence of Women's Poetry in America* (Boston, 1986); Louise Bernikow, *The World Split Open: Four Centuries of Women Poets in England and America, 1552–1950* (New York, 1974); Cheryl Walker, *Masks Outrageous and Austere: Culture, Psyche, and Person in Modern Women Poets* (Bloomington, 1991); Shari Benstock, *Women of the Left Bank: Paris, 1900–1940* (Austin, 1986); and Sandra M.

Gilbert and Susan Gubar, eds., *The Norton Anthology of Literature by Women: The Tradition in English* (New York, 1985).

Modernist artists are discussed in the art catalogue from the Whitney Museum of American Art; *Charles Demuth* by Barbara Haskell (New York, 1988); Barbara Rose, *American Art Since 1900: A Critical History* (New York, 1967); Karen Tsujimoto, *Images of America: Precisionist Painting and Modern Photography* (Seattle, 1982); and Karen Lucic, *Charles Sheeler and the Cult of the Machine* (Cambridge, 1991).

The Agrarians are best revealed in their book *I'll Take My Stand: The South and the Agrarian Tradition* by Twelve Southerners (New York, 1930). Robert M. Crunden, ed., *The Superfluous Men: Conservative Critics of American Culture, 1900–1945* (Austin, 1977), and Alexander Karanikas, *Tillers of a Myth: Southern Agrarians as Social and Literary Critics* (Madison, 1966), provide valuable insights.

Nathan Irvin Huggins, *Harlem Renaissance* (New York, 1971) is the classic account, but see also David Levering Lewis, *When Harlem Was in Vogue* (New York, 1981); Cary D. Wintz, *Black Culture and the Harlem Renaissance* (Houston, 1988); Arnold Rampersad, "Langston Hughes and Approaches to Modernism in the Harlem Renaissance," in *The Harlem Renaissance: Revaluations*, eds. Amritjit Singh, William S. Shiver, and Stanley Brodwin (New York, 1989), pp. 49–71; Arthur P. Davis, *From the Dark Tower: Afro-American Writers, 1900–1960* (Washington, D.C., 1974); and Alain Locke, ed., *The New Negro* (New York, 1968, originally published 1925). For women artists of the Renaissance, see Barbara Christian, *Black Women Novelists: The Development of a Tradition, 1892–1976* (Westport, Conn., 1980); Gloria T. Hull, *Color, Sex, and Poetry: Three Women Writers of the Harlem Renaissance* (Bloomington, 1987); and Maureen Honey, ed., *Shadowed Dreams: Women's Poetry of the Harlem Renaissance* (New Brunswick, 1989).

The major sources for Catholic intellectuals in this period are William M. Halsey, *The Survival of American Innocence: Catholicism in an Era of Disillusionment, 1920–1940* (Notre Dame, 1980) and also Robert Brooke Clements, "*The Commonweal*, 1924–1938" (Ph.D. diss., University of Notre Dame, 1972). On Jews, Henry L. Feingold, *A Time for Searching: Entering the Mainstream, 1920–1945* (Baltimore, 1992), *The Jewish People in America*, vol. 3, Feingold, gen. ed.; Deborah Dash Moore, *At Home in America: Second Generation New York Jews* (New York, 1981); and Alan M. Wald, *The New York Intellectuals: The Rise and Decline of the Anti-Stalinist Left from the 1930s to the 1980s* (Chapel Hill, 1987), are especially valuable. Kallen's major statement on cultural pluralism appeared in *Culture and Democracy in the United States: Studies in the Group Psychology of the American Peoples* (New York, 1924). For assessments, see Philip Gleason, "Pluralism and Assimilation: A Conceptual History," in *Linguistic Minorities*, ed. J. Edwards (London, 1984), pp. 221–57, and John Higham, "Ethnic Pluralism in Modern American Thought," in Higham, *Send These to Me: Jews and Other Immigrants in Urban America* (New York, 1975), pp. 198–232. On immigration and assimilation in literature and popular culture, see Werner Sollors, *Beyond Ethnicity: Consent and Descent in American Culture* (New York, 1986). Maureen Honey comments on minority women writers in " 'So Far Away from Home': Minority Woman Writers and the New Woman," *Women's Studies International Forum* 15 (1992): 473–85.

An important contribution to social science history is Dorothy Ross, *The Origins of American Social Science* (Cambridge, 1991). More specific treatments include Hamilton Cravens, *The Triumph of Evolution: American Scientists and the Heredity-Environment Controversy 1900–1941* (Philadelphia, 1978); Barbara Ballis Lal, "Black and Blue in Chicago: Robert E. Park's Perspective on Race Relations in Urban America, 1914–44," *British Journal of Sociology* 37 (1987): 547–66; Fred H. Matthews, *Quest for an American Sociology: Robert E. Park and the Chicago School* (Montreal, 1977); Richard Handler "Boasian Anthropology and the Critique of American Culture," *American Quarterly* 42 (June 1990): 252–73; Richard Wightman Fox, "Epitaph for Middletown: Robert S. Lynd and the Analysis of Consumer Culture," in *The Culture of Consumption: Critical Essays in American History, 1880–1980*, eds. Richard Wightman Fox and T. J. Jackson Lears (New York, 1983), pp. 101–42.

Sydney E. Ahlstrom, *A Religious History of the American People* (New Haven, 1972), offers a brief overview of the period's religion. Paul A. Carter, *The Decline and Revival of the Social Gospel: Social and Political Liberalism in American Protestant Churches, 1920–1940* (Ithaca, 1954); Ferenc Morton Szasz, *The Divided Mind of Protestant America, 1880–1930* (University, Ala., 1982); Robert T. Handy, "The American Religious Depression, 1925–1935," *Church History* 29 (March 1960): 3–26; and Robert Moats Miller, *American Protestantism and Social Issues, 1919–1939* (Chapel Hill, 1958), provide many insights into the religious climate. Charles H. Lippy and Peter W. Williams, eds., *The Encyclopedia of American Religious Experience*, 3 vols. (New York, 1988), is an invaluable reference. Joseph Wood Krutch, *The Modern Temper* (New York, 1956, originally published 1929); Walter Lippmann, *A Preface to Morals* (1929); Robert S. and Helen Merrell Lynd, *Middletown: A Study in Modern American Culture* (New York, 1929); Bruce Barton, *The Man Nobody Knows: A Discovery of the Real Jesus* (Indianapolis, 1924); and the chapter on religion in Report of the President's Research Committee on Social Trends, *Recent Social Trends in the United States*, vol. 2 (New York, 1933), are indispensable primary sources.

The Holiness-Pentecostal movement is analyzed in Vinson Synan, *The Holiness-Pentecostal Movement in the United States* (Grand Rapids, Mich., 1971); Charles E. Barfoot and Gerald T. Sheppard, "Prophetic vs. Priestly Religion: The Changing Role of Women Clergy in Classical Pentecostal Churches," *Review of Religious Research* 22 (September 1980): 2–17; and Cheryl Townsend Gilkes, " 'Together and in Harness': Women's Traditions in the Sanctified Church," *Signs* 10 (Summer 1985): 678–99. On McPherson, see William G. McLoughlin, "Aimee Semple McPherson: 'Your Sister in the King's Glad Service,' " *Journal of Popular Culture* 1 (Winter 1967): 193–217; Daniel Mark Epstein, *Sister Aimee: The Life of Aimee Semple McPherson* (New York, 1993); Carey McWilliams, "Aimee Semple McPherson: 'Sunlight in My Soul,' " in Isabel Leighton, ed., *The Aspirin Age, 1919–1941* (New York, 1949), pp. 50–80; and J. Harold Ellens, *Models of Religious Broadcasting* (Grand Rapids, Mich., 1974).

For an overview of African Americans and religion, see Albert J. Raboteau, "Black Christianity in North America," in Charles D. Lippy, *The Encyclopedia of American Religious Experience*, vol. 1, pp. 635–48, and E. Franklin Frazier, *The Negro Church in America* (New York, 1964). More specific discussions include Arthur E. Paris, *Black Pentecostalism: Southern Religion in an Urban World* (Amherst, 1982); Hans A. Baier and Merrill Singer, *African-American Religion in the Twentieth Century: Varieties of Protest and Accommodation* (Knoxville, 1992); Joseph R. Washington, Jr., *Black Sects and Cults* (New York, 1984); Arthur Huff Fauset, *Black Gods of the Metropolis: Negro Religious Cults in the Urban North* (Philadelphia, 1944, 1971); Jill Watts, *God, Harlem U.S.A.* (Berkeley, 1992); Howard M. Brotz, *The Black Jews of Harlem: Negro Nationalism and the Dilemmas of Negro Leadership* (New York, 1964); Gayraud S. Wilmore, *Black Religion and Black Radicalism* (Garden City, N.Y., 1972); Hans A. Baer, *The Black Spiritual Movement: A Religious Response to Racism* (Knoxville, 1984); and Randall K. Burkett, *Garveyism as a Religious Movement: The Institutionalization of a Black Religion* (Metuchen, N.J., 1978). An analysis of black urban religion is provided in a number of studies of specific cities, which are cited in the bibliography for Chapter VI. See also St. Clair Drake and Horace R. Cayton, *Black Metropolis: A Study of Negro Life in a Northern City* (New York, 1945); Allan H. Spear, *Black Chicago: The Making of a Negro Ghetto, 1890–1920* (Chicago, 1967); and Charles V. Hamilton, *Adam Clayton Powell, Jr.: The Political Biography of an American Dilemma* (New York, 1991). On the sacred/secular continuum in African American religion, see Lawrence W. Levine, *Black Culture and Black Consciousness: Afro-American Folk Thought from Slavery to Freedom* (New York, 1977), and Michael W. Harris, *The Rise of Gospel Blues: The Music of Thomas Andrew Dorsey in the Urban Church* (New York, 1992).

On fundamentalism, see George M. Marsden, *Fundamentalism and American Culture: The Shaping of Twentieth-Century Evangelicalism, 1870–1925* (New York, 1980); Lawrence W. Levine, *Defender of the Faith: William Jennings Bryan: The Last Decade 1915–1925* (New York, 1965); Norman F. Furniss, *The Fundamentalist Controversy, 1918–1931* (Hamden, Conn., 1963); Margaret Lambert Bendroth, *Fundamentalism and Gender, 1875 to the Present* (New Haven, 1993); William Vance Trollinger, Jr., *God's Empire: William Bell Riley and Midwestern Fundamentalism* (Madison, Wis., 1990); and Ray Ginger, *Six Days or Forever? Tennessee v. John Tho-*

mas Scopes (Boston, 1958). William R. Hutchison, *The Modernist Impulse in American Protestantism* (New York, 1976); Kenneth Cauthen, *The Impact of American Religious Liberalism* (New York, 1962); and Robert Moats Miller, *Harry Emerson Fosdick: Preacher, Pastor, Prophet* (New York, 1985), assess the modernists. E. Brooks Holifield, *A History of Pastoral Care in America: From Salvation to Self-Realization* (Nashville, 1983), addresses the therapeutic concerns of modernist preachers. On the Masons, see Lynn Dumenil, *Freemasonry and American Culture, 1880–1930* (Princeton, 1984).

V. CONFORMITY AND COMMUNITY

For general accounts of cultural conflict in the 1920s, see William E. Leuchtenburg, *Perils of Prosperity, 1914–32*, 2nd ed. (Chicago, 1993); Loren Baritz, ed., *The Culture of the Twenties* (Indianapolis, 1970); David Burner, *The Politics of Provincialism: The Democratic Party in Transition, 1918–1932* (Cambridge, 1986); Don S. Kirschner, *City and Country: Rural Responses to Urbanization in the 1920s* (Westport, Conn., 1970); Paul L. Murphy, "The Sources and Nature of Intolerance in the 1920s," *Journal of American History* 51 (June 1964): 60–76; and Lawrence W. Levine, "Progress and Nostalgia: The Self Image of the Nineteen Twenties," in Levine, *The Unpredictable Past: Explorations in American Cultural History* (New York, 1993), pp. 189–205.

The definitive work on nativism and immigration restriction is John Higham, *Strangers in the Land: Patterns of American Nativism, 1860–1925* (New York, 1955, 1989), but see also Roger Daniels, *The Politics of Prejudice: The Anti-Japanese Movement in California and the Struggle for Japanese Exclusion* (New York, 1962) and Stanley Coben, "The Failure of the Melting Pot," in *The Underside of American History*, ed. Thomas R. Frazier (New York, 1982), vol. 2, pp. 174–95. On anti-Mexican nativism, see Rudolpho Acuña, *Occupied America: A History of Chicanos*, 3rd. ed. (New York, 1988), and Ricardo Romo, *East Los Angeles: History of a Barrio* (Austin, 1983). On anti-Catholicism, see Higham, *Strangers in the Land*; Ray Allen Billington, *The Protestant Crusade, 1800–1860: A Study of the Origins of American Nativism* (New York, 1938); Lynn Dumenil, "The Tribal Twenties," *Journal of American Ethnic History* 11 (Fall 1991): 21–49; Allan J. Lichtman, *Prejudice and the Old Politics: The Presidential Election of 1928* (Chapel Hill, 1979); and Edward Cuddy, "The Irish Question and the Revival of Anti-Catholicism in the 1920s," *Catholic Historical Review* 67 (April 1981): 236–55. For anti-Semitism, the key sources are Leonard Dinnerstein, *Anti-Semitism in America* (New York, 1994); David A. Gerber, ed., *Anti-Semitism in American History* (Urbana, 1987); Michael Dobkowski, "American Anti-Semitism: A Reinterpretation," *American Quarterly* 29 (1977): 166–81; Leo P. Ribuffo, "Henry Ford and *The International Jew*," *American Jewish History* 69 (1980): 437–77; and *The International Jew: The World's Foremost Problem* (Dearborn, 1920–22).

The most comprehensive study of the Red Scare is Robert K. Murray, *Red Scare: A Study in National Hysteria, 1919–1920* (New York, 1955), but see also Stanley Coben, "A Study in Nativism: The American Red Scare of 1919–1920," in *The Shaping of Twentieth Century America: Interpretive Essays,* eds. Richard Abrams and Lawrence W. Levine, 2nd ed. (Boston, 1971), pp. 289–306; and William Preston, Jr., *Aliens and Dissenters: Federal Suppression of Radicals, 1903–1933* (New York, 1963).

On prohibition, see Joseph R. Gusfield, *Symbolic Crusade: Status, Politics and the American Temperance Movement* (Urbana, 1963); James H. Timberlake, *Prohibition and the Progressive Movement, 1900–1920* (Cambridge, 1963); Andrew Sinclair, *Prohibition: The Era of Excess: A Social History of the Prohibition Movement* (New York, 1962); David E. Kyvig, ed., *Law, Alcohol, and Order* (Westport, Conn., 1985); Paul Kleppner, *The Cross of Culture: A Social Analysis of Midwestern Politics* (New York, 1970); Norman Clark, *Deliver Us from Evil* (New York, 1976); K. Austin Kerr, *Organized for Prohibition: A New History of the Anti-Saloon League* (New Haven, 1985); David E. Kyvig, *Repealing National Prohibition* (Chicago, 1979); and Barbara Leslie Epstein, *The Politics of Domesticity: Women, Evangelism, and Temperance: The Quest for Power and Liberty, 1873–1900* (Philadelphia, 1980).

The standard monographs on the Klan are Kenneth T. Jackson, *The Ku Klux Klan in the City, 1915–1930* (New York, 1967); Charles C. Alexander, *The Ku Klux Klan in the Southwest* (Lexington, 1966); and David M. Chalmers, *Hooded Americanism: The First Century of the Ku Klux Klan 1865–1965* (New York, 1965). The revisionist accounts that emphasize the Klan as a reform organization include Robert Alan Goldberg, *Hooded Empire: The Ku Klux Klan in Colorado* (Urbana, 1981); Leonard J. Moore, *Citizen Klansmen: The Ku Klux Klan in Indiana, 1921–1928* (Chapel Hill, 1991); Kathleen M. Blee, *Women of the Klan: Racism and Gender in the 1920's* (Berkeley, 1990); Shawn Lay, *War, Revolution and the Ku Klux Klan: A Study of Intolerance in a Border City* (El Paso, 1985); and Shawn Lay, ed., *The Invisible Empire in the West: Toward a New Historical Appraisal of the Ku Klux Klan of the 1920's* (Urbana, 1992). See also Robert Moats Miller, "The Ku Klux Klan," in *Change and Continuity in Twentieth-Century America: The 1920s,* eds. John Braeman, Robert H. Bremner, and David Brody (Columbus, 1968), pp. 215–56.

VI. PLURALISM AND COMMUNITY

For general discussions of ethnic groups in the early twentieth century, see Ronald H. Bayor, *Neighbors in Conflict: The Irish, Germans, Jews, and Italians of New York City, 1928–1941* (Baltimore, 1978); Higham, *Send These to Me;* John Bodnar, *The Transplanted: A History of Immigrants in Urban America* (Bloomington, 1987); Thomas Kessner, *The Golden Door: Italian and Jewish Immigrant Mobility in New York City 1880–1915* (New

York, 1977); M. Sánchez, *Becoming Mexican American*; and Acuña, *Occupied America*. J. Joseph Huthmacher, *Massachusetts People and Politics*, and Allswang, *A House for All Peoples*, discuss ethnicity and politics. On the role of ethnic leaders, see John Higham, ed., *Ethnic Leadership in America* (Baltimore, 1978), and Bodnar, *The Transplanted*. On theories of assimilation and cultural pluralism, see Milton Gordon, *Assimilation in American Life: The Role of Race, Religion, and National Origins* (New York, 1964); and the references in the bibliography for Chapter IV.

A more detailed account of Catholics' response to anti-Catholicism is contained in Dumenil, "The Tribal Twenties." On Catholics and Americanization, see Philip Gleason, "Coming to Terms with American Catholic History," *Societas* 2-3 (Autumn 1973): 283-312. General treatments of Catholics include Jay Dolan, *The American Catholic Experience* (Notre Dame, 1985); Robert D. Cross, *The Emergence of Liberal Catholicism in America* (Cambridge, 1958); and Aaron I. Abell, *American Catholicism and Social Action: A Search for Social Justice, 1865-1950* (New York, 1960). Ethnic groups within Catholicism are analyzed by Charles Shanabruch, *Chicago's Catholics: The Evolution of an American Identity* (Notre Dame, 1981); Joseph John Parot, *Polish Catholics in Chicago, 1850-1920* (De Kalb, Ill., 1981); Robert A. Orsi, *The Madonna of 115th Street: Faith and Community in Italian Harlem* (New Haven, 1985); and Humbert S. Nelli, *Italians in Chicago, 1880-1930* (New York, 1970). For accounts of the National Catholic Welfare Council, see Elizabeth McKeown, "War and Welfare: A Study of American Catholic Leadership" (Ph.D. diss., University of Chicago, 1972); Joseph M. McShane, *"Sufficiently Radical": Catholicism, Progressivism, and the Bishops' Program of 1919* (Washington, D.C., 1986); and Mary T. Hanna, *Catholics and American Politics* (Cambridge, 1979). On the Knights of Columbus, see Christopher J. Kauffman, *Faith and Fraternalism: The History of the Knights of Columbus, 1882-1982* (New York, 1982).

For general overviews of Jews in America, see Arthur Hertzberg, *The Jews in America: Four Centuries of an Uneasy Encounter: A History* (New York, 1989); Abraham J. Karp, *Haven and Home: A History of the Jews in America* (New York, 1985); and Stanley Feldstein, *The Land That I Show You: Three Centuries of Jewish Life in America* (New York, 1978). On the German/Eastern European Jewish conflict, see Ronald Sanders, *The Downtown Jews: Portrait of an Immigrant Generation* (New York, 1969), and Arthur A. Goren, *New York Jews and the Quest for Community: The Kehillah Experiment, 1908-1922* (New York, 1970). On discrimination, see Marcia Graham Synott, *The Half-Opened Door: Discrimination and Admissions at Harvard, Yale, and Princeton, 1900-1970* (Westport, Conn., 1970).

Henry L. Feingold, *A Time for Searching*, and Deborah Dash Moore, *At Home in America*, are especially valuable accounts of the second generation. On Zionism, see Melvin Urofsky, *American Zionism from Herzl to* the Holocaust (New York, 1975), and Naomi Cohen, American Jews and the Zionist Idea (New York, 1975). Studies of the leading Jewish organizations include Naomi Cohen, Not Free to Desist: The American Jewish Committee 1906–1966, and Deborah Dash Moore, B'nai B'rith and the Challenge of Ethnic Leadership (Albany, N.Y., 1981). Important biographies are Morton Rosenstock, Louis Marshall, Defender of Jewish Rights (Detroit, 1965), and Melvin Urofsky, A Voice That Spoke for Justice: The Life and Times of Stephen S. Wise (Albany, N.Y., 1982), which also provides an account of the American Jewish Congress.

For general accounts of Asian Americans or Japanese Americans, see Roger Daniels, Asian America: Chinese and Japanese in the United States Since 1850 (Seattle, 1988); Chan, Asian Americans; and Ronald Takaki, Strangers from a Different Shore (Boston, 1989). On the Issei, see Yuji Ichioka, The Issei: The World of the First Generation Japanese Immigrants, 1885–1924 (New York, 1988). For the second generation, see William C. Smith, The Second Generation Oriental in America (Honolulu, 1927); Bill Hosokawa, Nisei: The Quiet Americans (New York, 1969); and Hosokawa, Japanese American Citizens League: JACL: In Quest of Justice (New York, 1982). Glenn's Issei, Nisei, War Bride provides an analysis of women's experiences, as well as offering background for the Japanese community. An invaluable primary source is the Survey of Race Relations (Stanford University, 1924).

August Meier and Elliott M. Rudwick, From Plantation to Ghetto: An Interpretive History of American Negroes (New York, 1966), offer a general survey of African American history. On the migration and its impact, see James R. Grossman, Land of Hope: Chicago, Black Southerners, and the Great Migration (Chicago, 1989); Carole Marks, Farewell—We're Good and Gone: The Great Black Migration (Bloomington, 1989); Joe William Trotter, Jr., Black Milwaukee: The Making of an Industrial Proletariat, 1915–1945 (Urbana, 1985); Kenneth Kusmer, A Ghetto Takes Shape: Black Cleveland, 1870–1930 (Urbana, 1976); James Weldon Johnson, Black Manhattan (New York, 1930); and Chicago Commission on Race Relations, The Negro in Chicago: A Study of Race Relations and a Race Riot (Chicago, 1922). Two studies which examine the South in this period are Lester C. Lamon, Black Tennesseans, 1900–1930 (Knoxville, 1977); and I. A. Newby, Black Carolinians: A History of Blacks in South Carolina from 1895 to 1968 (Columbia, S.C., 1973). See also Jones, Labor of Love, and Giddings, When and Where I Enter. For specific treatment of the riots, see William M. Tuttle, Jr., Race Riot: Chicago in the Red Summer of 1919 (New York, 1970), and Arthur I. Waskow, From Race Riot to Sit-in, 1919 and the 1960s (Garden City, N.Y., 1966). Herbert Shapiro, White Violence and Black Response: From Reconstruction to Montgomery (Amherst, 1988), goes beyond riots to discuss a variety of forms of violence and African American response. An excellent primary source for the "New Negro" is Robert T. Kerlin, The Voice of the Negro: 1919 (New York, 1920). On students, see Raymond Wolters, The

New Negro on Campus: Black College Rebellions of the 1920s (Princeton, 1975). Eliott M. Rudwick, *W. E. B. Du Bois: Propagandist of the Negro Protest* (New York, 1969); Nancy Weiss, *The National Urban League, 1910–1940* (New York, 1974); and Charles Kellogg, *NAACP: A History of the National Association for the Advancement of Colored People,* vol. 1 (Baltimore, 1967), are valuable institutional studies. On A. Philip Randolph, see Theodore Kornweibel, Jr., *No Crystal Stair: Black Life and The Messenger, 1917–1928* (Westport, Conn., 1975), and William H. Harris, *Keeping the Faith: A Philip Randolph, Milton P. Webster, and the Brotherhood of Sleeping Car Porters, 1925–1937* (Urbana, 1991).

Much has been written on Garvey. The most useful are Emory J. Tolbert, *The UNIA and Black Los Angeles* (Los Angeles, 1980); Judith Stein, *The World of Marcus Garvey: Race and Class in Modern Society* (Baton Rouge, 1986); Lawrence W. Levine, "Marcus Garvey and the Politics of Revitalization," in *Black Leaders of the Twentieth Century,* eds. John Hope Franklin and August Meier (Urbana, 1982), pp. 105–38; Tony Martin, *Race First: The Ideological and Organizational Struggles of Marcus Garvey and the Universal Negro Improvement Association* (Westport, Conn., 1976); E. David Cronon, *Black Moses: The Story of Marcus Garvey and the Universal Negro Improvement Association* (Madison, Wis., 1955); and Robert A. Hill, "General Introduction," *The Marcus Garvey and Universal Negro Improvement Association Papers,* vol. 1 (Berkeley, 1983), pp. xxxv–xc.

EPILOGUE

Roger M. Olien and Diana Davids Olien, *Oil Promoters and Investors in the Jazz Age* (Chapel Hill, 1990), offer valuable insights into the speculative mania. Popular historian Frederick Lewis Allen, *Only Yesterday: An Informal History of the Nineteen-twenties* (New York, 1931), provides a lively account of the Florida boom. See also Michael E. Parrish, *Anxious Decades: America in Prosperity and Depression, 1920–1941* (New York, 1992). The most comprehensive discussion of the stock market boom and bust is Robert T. Patterson, *The Great Boom and Panic 1921–1929* (Chicago, 1965). John Kenneth Galbraith's *The Great Crash 1929,* 3rd ed. (Boston, 1972), places the crash in the context of broader weaknesses in the U.S. economy. For important analyses of the thirties, see Alan Brinkley, *Voices of Protest: Huey Long, Father Coughlin, and the Great Depression* (New York, 1982); Lizabeth Cohen, *Making a New Deal: Industrial Workers in Chicago, 1919–1939* (Cambridge, 1990); and essays on the Depression in Levine, *The Unpredictable Past.*

INDEX